ITALIAN
VOCABULARY

FOR ENGLISH SPEAKERS

ENGLISH-
ITALIAN

The most useful words
To expand your lexicon and sharpen
your language skills

7000 words

Italian vocabulary for English speakers - 7000 words

By Andrey Taranov

T&P Books vocabularies are intended for helping you learn, memorize and review foreign words. The dictionary is divided into themes, covering all major spheres of everyday activities, business, science, culture, etc.

The process of learning words using T&P Books' theme-based dictionaries gives you the following advantages:

- Correctly grouped source information predetermines success at subsequent stages of word memorization
- Availability of words derived from the same root allowing memorization of word units (rather than separate words)
- Small units of words facilitate the process of establishing associative links needed for consolidation of vocabulary
- Level of language knowledge can be estimated by the number of learned words

T&P Books Publishing
www.tpbooks.com

ISBN: 978-1-78071-297-0

This book is also available in E-book formats.
Please visit www.tpbooks.com or the major online bookstores.

ITALIAN VOCABULARY
for English speakers

T&P Books vocabularies are intended to help you learn, memorize, and review foreign words. The vocabulary contains over 7000 commonly used words arranged thematically.

- Vocabulary contains the most commonly used words
- Recommended as an addition to any language course
- Meets the needs of beginners and advanced learners of foreign languages
- Convenient for daily use, revision sessions, and self-testing activities
- Allows you to assess your vocabulary

Special features of the vocabulary

- Words are organized according to their meaning, not alphabetically
- Words are presented in three columns to facilitate the reviewing and self-testing processes
- Words in groups are divided into small blocks to facilitate the learning process
- The vocabulary offers a convenient and simple transcription of each foreign word

The vocabulary has 198 topics including:

Basic Concepts, Numbers, Colors, Months, Seasons, Units of Measurement, Clothing & Accessories, Food & Nutrition, Restaurant, Family Members, Relatives, Character, Feelings, Emotions, Diseases, City, Town, Sightseeing, Shopping, Money, House, Home, Office, Working in the Office, Import & Export, Marketing, Job Search, Sports, Education, Computer, Internet, Tools, Nature, Countries, Nationalities and more ...

T&P BOOKS' THEME-BASED DICTIONARIES

The Correct System for Memorizing Foreign Words

Acquiring vocabulary is one of the most important elements of learning a foreign language, because words allow us to express our thoughts, ask questions, and provide answers. An inadequate vocabulary can impede communication with a foreigner and make it difficult to understand a book or movie well.

The pace of activity in all spheres of modern life, including the learning of modern languages, has increased. Today, we need to memorize large amounts of information (grammar rules, foreign words, etc.) within a short period. However, this does not need to be difficult. All you need to do is to choose the right training materials, learn a few special techniques, and develop your individual training system.

Having a system is critical to the process of language learning. Many people fail to succeed in this regard; they cannot master a foreign language because they fail to follow a system comprised of selecting materials, organizing lessons, arranging new words to be learned, and so on. The lack of a system causes confusion and eventually, lowers self-confidence.

T&P Books' theme-based dictionaries can be included in the list of elements needed for creating an effective system for learning foreign words. These dictionaries were specially developed for learning purposes and are meant to help students effectively memorize words and expand their vocabulary.

Generally speaking, the process of learning words consists of three main elements:

- Reception (creation or acquisition) of a training material, such as a word list
- Work aimed at memorizing new words
- Work aimed at reviewing the learned words, such as self-testing

All three elements are equally important since they determine the quality of work and the final result. All three processes require certain skills and a well-thought-out approach.

New words are often encountered quite randomly when learning a foreign language and it may be difficult to include them all in a unified list. As a result, these words remain written on scraps of paper, in book margins, textbooks, and so on. In order to systematize such words, we have to create and continually update a "book of new words." A paper notebook, a netbook, or a tablet PC can be used for these purposes.

This "book of new words" will be your personal, unique list of words. However, it will only contain the words that you came across during the learning process. For example, you might have written down the words "Sunday," "Tuesday," and "Friday." However, there are additional words for days of the week, for example, "Saturday," that are missing, and your list of words would be incomplete. Using a theme dictionary, in addition to the "book of new words," is a reasonable solution to this problem.

The theme-based dictionary may serve as the basis for expanding your vocabulary.

It will be your big "book of new words" containing the most frequently used words of a foreign language already included. There are quite a few theme-based dictionaries available, and you should ensure that you make the right choice in order to get the maximum benefit from your purchase.

Therefore, we suggest using theme-based dictionaries from T&P Books Publishing as an aid to learning foreign words. Our books are specially developed for effective use in the sphere of vocabulary systematization, expansion and review.

Theme-based dictionaries are not a magical solution to learning new words. However, they can serve as your main database to aid foreign-language acquisition. Apart from theme dictionaries, you can have copybooks for writing down new words, flash cards, glossaries for various texts, as well as other resources; however, a good theme dictionary will always remain your primary collection of words.

T&P Books' theme-based dictionaries are specialty books that contain the most frequently used words in a language.

The main characteristic of such dictionaries is the division of words into themes. For example, the *City* theme contains the words "street," "crossroads," "square," "fountain," and so on. The *Talking* theme might contain words like "to talk," "to ask," "question," and "answer".

All the words in a theme are divided into smaller units, each comprising 3–5 words. Such an arrangement improves the perception of words and makes the learning process less tiresome. Each unit contains a selection of words with similar meanings or identical roots. This allows you to learn words in small groups and establish other associative links that have a positive effect on memorization.

The words on each page are placed in three columns: a word in your native language, its translation, and its transcription. Such positioning allows for the use of techniques for effective memorization. After closing the translation column, you can flip through and review foreign words, and vice versa. "This is an easy and convenient method of review – one that we recommend you do often."

Our theme-based dictionaries contain transcriptions for all the foreign words. Unfortunately, none of the existing transcriptions are able to convey the exact nuances of foreign pronunciation. That is why we recommend using the transcriptions only as a supplementary learning aid. Correct pronunciation can only be acquired with the help of sound. Therefore our collection includes audio theme-based dictionaries.

The process of learning words using T&P Books' theme-based dictionaries gives you the following advantages:

- You have correctly grouped source information, which predetermines your success at subsequent stages of word memorization
- Availability of words derived from the same root (lazy, lazily, lazybones), allowing you to memorize word units instead of separate words
- Small units of words facilitate the process of establishing associative links needed for consolidation of vocabulary
- You can estimate the number of learned words and hence your level of language knowledge
- The dictionary allows for the creation of an effective and high-quality revision process
- You can revise certain themes several times, modifying the revision methods and techniques
- Audio versions of the dictionaries help you to work out the pronunciation of words and develop your skills of auditory word perception

The T&P Books' theme-based dictionaries are offered in several variants differing in the number of words: 1.500, 3.000, 5.000, 7.000, and 9.000 words. There are also dictionaries containing 15,000 words for some language combinations. Your choice of dictionary will depend on your knowledge level and goals.

We sincerely believe that our dictionaries will become your trusty assistant in learning foreign languages and will allow you to easily acquire the necessary vocabulary.

TABLE OF CONTENTS

REGIONAL GEOGRAPHY 197
Countries. Nationalities 197

MISCELLANEOUS 205

PRONUNCIATION GUIDE

T&P phonetic alphabet	Italian example	English example
[a]	casco ['kasko]	shorter than in ask
[e]	sfera ['sfera]	elm, medal
[i]	filo ['filo]	shorter than in feet
[o]	dolce ['doltʃe]	pod, John
[u]	siluro [si'luro]	book
[y]	würstel ['vyrstel]	fuel, tuna
[b]	busta ['busta]	baby, book
[d]	andare [an'dare]	day, doctor
[ʣ]	zinco ['ʣinko]	beads, kids
[ʤ]	Norvegia [nor'veʤa]	joke, general
[ʒ]	garage [ga'raʒ]	forge, pleasure
[f]	ferrovia [ferro'via]	face, food
[g]	ago ['ago]	game, gold
[k]	cocktail ['koktejl]	clock, kiss
[j]	piazza ['pjattsa]	yes, New York
[l]	olive [o'live]	lace, people
[ʎ]	figlio ['fiʎʎo]	daily, million
[m]	mosaico [mo'zaiko]	magic, milk
[n]	treno ['treno]	name, normal
[ŋ]	granchio ['graŋkio]	English, ring
[ɲ]	magnete [ma'ɲete]	canyon, new
[p]	pallone [pal'lone]	pencil, private
[r]	futuro [fu'turo]	rice, radio
[s]	triste ['triste]	city, boss
[ʃ]	piscina [pi'ʃina]	machine, shark
[t]	estintore [estin'tore]	tourist, trip
[ts]	spezie ['spetsie]	cats, tsetse fly
[tʃ]	lancia ['lantʃa]	church, French
[v]	volo ['volo]	very, river
[w]	whisky ['wiski]	vase, winter
[z]	deserto [de'zerto]	zebra, please

ABBREVIATIONS
used in the vocabulary

English abbreviations

ab.	-	about
adj	-	adjective
adv	-	adverb
anim.	-	animate
as adj	-	attributive noun used as adjective
e.g.	-	for example
etc.	-	et cetera
fam.	-	familiar
fem.	-	feminine
form.	-	formal
inanim.	-	inanimate
masc.	-	masculine
math	-	mathematics
mil.	-	military
n	-	noun
pl	-	plural
pron.	-	pronoun
sb	-	somebody
sing.	-	singular
sth	-	something
v aux	-	auxiliary verb
vi	-	intransitive verb
vi, vt	-	intransitive, transitive verb
vt	-	transitive verb

Italian abbreviations

agg	-	adjective
f	-	feminine noun
f pl	-	feminine plural
m	-	masculine noun
m pl	-	masculine plural
m, f	-	masculine, feminine
pl	-	plural

v aus	-	auxiliary verb
vi	-	intransitive verb
vi, vt	-	intransitive, transitive verb
vr	-	reflexive verb
vt	-	transitive verb

BASIC CONCEPTS

Basic concepts. Part 1

1. Pronouns

I, me	**io**	['io]
you	**tu**	['tu]
he	**lui**	['luj]
she	**lei**	['lej]
we	**noi**	['noj]
you (to a group)	**voi**	['voi]
they	**loro, essi**	['loro], ['essi]

2. Greetings. Salutations. Farewells

Hello! (fam.)	**Buongiorno!**	[buon'dʒorno]
Hello! (form.)	**Salve!**	['salve]
Good morning!	**Buongiorno!**	[buon'dʒorno]
Good afternoon!	**Buon pomeriggio!**	[bu'on pome'ridʒo]
Good evening!	**Buonasera!**	[buona'sera]
to say hello	**salutare** (vt)	[salu'tare]
Hi! (hello)	**Ciao! Salve!**	['tʃao], ['salve]
greeting (n)	**saluto** (m)	[sa'luto]
to greet (vt)	**salutare** (vt)	[salu'tare]
How are you?	**Come va?**	['kome 'va]
What's new?	**Che c'è di nuovo?**	[ke tʃe di nu'ovo]
Bye-Bye! Goodbye!	**Arrivederci!**	[arrive'dertʃi]
See you soon!	**A presto!**	[a 'presto]
Farewell!	**Addio!**	[ad'dio]
to say goodbye	**congedarsi** (vr)	[kondʒe'darsi]
So long!	**Ciao!**	['tʃao]
Thank you!	**Grazie!**	['gratsie]
Thank you very much!	**Grazie mille!**	['gratsie 'mille]
You're welcome	**Prego**	['prego]
Don't mention it!	**Non c'è di che!**	[non tʃe di 'ke]
It was nothing	**Di niente**	[di 'njente]
Excuse me! (fam.)	**Scusa!**	['skuza]

| Excuse me! (form.) | Scusi! | ['skuzi] |
| to excuse (forgive) | scusare (vt) | [sku'zare] |

to apologize (vi)	scusarsi (vr)	[sku'zarsi]
My apologies	Chiedo scusa	['kjedo 'skuza]
I'm sorry!	Mi perdoni!	[mi per'doni]
to forgive (vt)	perdonare (vt)	[perdo'nare]
It's okay! (that's all right)	Non fa niente	[non fa 'njente]
please (adv)	per favore	[per fa'vore]

Don't forget!	Non dimentichi!	[non di'mentiki]
Certainly!	Certamente!	[tʃerta'mente]
Of course not!	Certamente no!	[tʃerta'mente no]
Okay! (I agree)	D'accordo!	[dak'kordo]
That's enough!	Basta!	['basta]

3. Cardinal numbers. Part 1

0 zero	zero (m)	['dzero]
1 one	uno	['uno]
2 two	due	['due]
3 three	tre	['tre]
4 four	quattro	['kwattro]

5 five	cinque	['tʃinkwe]
6 six	sei	['sej]
7 seven	sette	['sette]
8 eight	otto	['otto]
9 nine	nove	['nove]

10 ten	dieci	['djetʃi]
11 eleven	undici	['unditʃi]
12 twelve	dodici	['doditʃi]
13 thirteen	tredici	['treditʃi]
14 fourteen	quattordici	[kwat'torditʃi]

15 fifteen	quindici	['kwinditʃi]
16 sixteen	sedici	['seditʃi]
17 seventeen	diciassette	[ditʃas'sette]
18 eighteen	diciotto	[di'tʃotto]
19 nineteen	diciannove	[ditʃan'nove]

20 twenty	venti	['venti]
21 twenty-one	ventuno	[ven'tuno]
22 twenty-two	ventidue	['venti 'due]
23 twenty-three	ventitre	['venti 'tre]

30 thirty	trenta	['trenta]
31 thirty-one	trentuno	[tren'tuno]
32 thirty-two	trentadue	[trenta 'due]

33 thirty-three	**trentatre**	[trenta 'tre]
40 forty	**quaranta**	[kwa'ranta]
41 forty-one	**quarantuno**	[kwa'rant'uno]
42 forty-two	**quarantadue**	[kwa'ranta 'due]
43 forty-three	**quarantatre**	[kwa'ranta 'tre]
50 fifty	**cinquanta**	[tʃin'kwanta]
51 fifty-one	**cinquantuno**	[tʃin'kwant'uno]
52 fifty-two	**cinquantadue**	[tʃin'kwanta 'due]
53 fifty-three	**cinquantatre**	[tʃin'kwanta 'tre]
60 sixty	**sessanta**	[ses'santa]
61 sixty-one	**sessantuno**	[sessan'tuno]
62 sixty-two	**sessantadue**	[ses'santa 'due]
63 sixty-three	**sessantatre**	[ses'santa 'tre]
70 seventy	**settanta**	[set'tanta]
71 seventy-one	**settantuno**	[settan'tuno]
72 seventy-two	**settantadue**	[set'tanta 'due]
73 seventy-three	**settantatre**	[set'tanta 'tre]
80 eighty	**ottanta**	[ot'tanta]
81 eighty-one	**ottantuno**	[ottan'tuno]
82 eighty-two	**ottantadue**	[ot'tanta 'due]
83 eighty-three	**ottantatre**	[ot'tanta 'tre]
90 ninety	**novanta**	[no'vanta]
91 ninety-one	**novantuno**	[novan'tuno]
92 ninety-two	**novantadue**	[no'vanta 'due]
93 ninety-three	**novantatre**	[no'vanta 'tre]

4. Cardinal numbers. Part 2

100 one hundred	**cento**	['tʃento]
200 two hundred	**duecento**	[due'tʃento]
300 three hundred	**trecento**	[tre'tʃento]
400 four hundred	**quattrocento**	[kwattro'tʃento]
500 five hundred	**cinquecento**	[tʃinkwe'tʃento]
600 six hundred	**seicento**	[sej'tʃento]
700 seven hundred	**settecento**	[sette'tʃento]
800 eight hundred	**ottocento**	[otto'tʃento]
900 nine hundred	**novecento**	[nove'tʃento]
1000 one thousand	**mille**	['mille]
2000 two thousand	**duemila**	[due'mila]
3000 three thousand	**tremila**	[tre'mila]
10000 ten thousand	**diecimila**	['djetʃi 'mila]
one hundred thousand	**centomila**	[tʃento'mila]
million	**milione** (m)	[mi'ljone]
billion	**miliardo** (m)	[mi'ljardo]

5. Numbers. Fractions

fraction	**frazione** (f)	[fra'tsjone]
one half	**un mezzo**	[un 'meddzo]
one third	**un terzo**	[un 'tertso]
one quarter	**un quarto**	[un 'kwarto]
one eighth	**un ottavo**	[un ot'tavo]
one tenth	**un decimo**	[un 'detʃimo]
two thirds	**due terzi**	['due 'tertsi]
three quarters	**tre quarti**	[tre 'kwarti]

6. Numbers. Basic operations

subtraction	**sottrazione** (f)	[sottra'tsjone]
to subtract (vi, vt)	**sottrarre** (vt)	[sot'trarre]
division	**divisione** (f)	[divi'zjone]
to divide (vt)	**dividere** (vt)	[di'videre]
addition	**addizione** (f)	[addi'tsjone]
to add up (vt)	**addizionare** (vt)	[additsjo'nare]
to add (vi, vt)	**addizionare** (vt)	[additsjo'nare]
multiplication	**moltiplicazione** (f)	[moltiplika'tsjone]
to multiply (vt)	**moltiplicare** (vt)	[moltipli'kare]

7. Numbers. Miscellaneous

digit, figure	**cifra** (f)	['tʃifra]
number	**numero** (m)	['numero]
numeral	**numerale** (m)	[nume'rale]
minus sign	**meno** (m)	['meno]
plus sign	**più** (m)	['pju]
formula	**formula** (f)	['formula]
calculation	**calcolo** (m)	['kalkolo]
to count (vi, vt)	**contare** (vt)	[kon'tare]
to count up	**calcolare** (vt)	[kalko'lare]
to compare (vt)	**comparare** (vt)	[kompa'rare]
How much?	**Quanto?**	['kwanto]
How many?	**Quanti?**	['kwanti]
sum, total	**somma** (f)	['somma]
result	**risultato** (m)	[rizul'tato]
remainder	**resto** (m)	['resto]
a few (e.g., ~ years ago)	**qualche ...**	['kwalke]
little (I had ~ time)	**un po'di ...**	[un po di]

the rest	resto (m)	['resto]
one and a half	uno e mezzo	['uno e 'meddzo]
dozen	dozzina (f)	[dod'dzina]

in half (adv)	in due	[in 'due]
equally (evenly)	in parti uguali	[in 'parti u'gwali]
half	metà (f), mezzo (m)	[me'ta], ['meddzo]
time (three ~s)	volta (f)	['volta]

8. The most important verbs. Part 1

to advise (vt)	consigliare (vt)	[konsiʎ'ʎare]
to agree (say yes)	essere d'accordo	['essere dak'kordo]
to answer (vi, vt)	rispondere (vi, vt)	[ris'pondere]
to apologize (vi)	scusarsi (vr)	[sku'zarsi]
to arrive (vi)	arrivare (vi)	[arri'vare]

to ask (~ oneself)	chiedere, domandare	['kjedere], [doman'dare]
to ask (~ sb to do sth)	chiedere, domandare	['kjedere], [doman'dare]
to be (vi)	essere (vi)	['essere]

to be afraid	avere paura	[a'vere pa'ura]
to be hungry	avere fame	[a'vere 'fame]
to be interested in …	interessarsi di …	[interes'sarsi di]
to be needed	occorrere	[ok'korrere]
to be surprised	stupirsi (vr)	[stu'pirsi]

to be thirsty	avere sete	[a'vere 'sete]
to begin (vt)	cominciare (vt)	[komin'tʃare]
to belong to …	appartenere (vi)	[apparte'nere]
to boast (vi)	vantarsi (vr)	[van'tarsi]
to break (split into pieces)	rompere (vt)	['rompere]

to call (~ for help)	chiamare (vt)	[kja'mare]
can (v aux)	potere (v aus)	[po'tere]
to catch (vt)	afferrare (vt)	[affer'rare]
to change (vt)	cambiare (vt)	[kam'bjare]
to choose (select)	scegliere (vt)	['ʃeʎʎere]

to come down (the stairs)	scendere (vi)	['ʃendere]
to compare (vt)	comparare (vt)	[kompa'rare]
to complain (vi, vt)	lamentarsi (vr)	[lamen'tarsi]
to confuse (mix up)	confondere (vt)	[kon'fondere]
to continue (vt)	continuare (vt)	[kontinu'are]
to control (vt)	controllare (vt)	[kontrol'lare]

to cook (dinner)	cucinare (vi)	[kutʃi'nare]
to cost (vt)	costare (vt)	[ko'stare]
to count (add up)	contare (vt)	[kon'tare]
to count on …	contare su …	[kon'tare su]

| to create (vt) | creare (vt) | [kre'are] |
| to cry (weep) | piangere (vi) | ['pjandʒere] |

9. The most important verbs. Part 2

to deceive (vi, vt)	ingannare (vt)	[ingan'nare]
to decorate (tree, street)	decorare (vt)	[deko'rare]
to defend (a country, etc.)	difendere (vt)	[di'fendere]
to demand (request firmly)	esigere (vt)	[e'zidʒere]
to dig (vt)	scavare (vt)	[ska'vare]

to discuss (vt)	discutere (vt)	[di'skutere]
to do (vt)	fare (vt)	['fare]
to doubt (have doubts)	dubitare (vi)	[dubi'tare]
to drop (let fall)	lasciar cadere	[la'ʃar ka'dere]
to enter (room, house, etc.)	entrare (vi)	[en'trare]

to excuse (forgive)	battaglia (f)	[bat'taʎʎa]
to exist (vi)	esistere (vi)	[e'zistere]
to expect (foresee)	prevedere (vt)	[preve'dere]
to explain (vt)	spiegare (vt)	[spje'gare]
to fall (vi)	cadere (vi)	[ka'dere]

to find (vt)	trovare (vt)	[tro'vare]
to finish (vt)	finire (vt)	[fi'nire]
to fly (vi)	volare (vi)	[vo'lare]
to follow ... (come after)	seguire (vt)	[se'gwire]
to forget (vi, vt)	dimenticare (vt)	[dimenti'kare]

to forgive (vt)	perdonare (vt)	[perdo'nare]
to give (vt)	dare (vt)	['dare]
to give a hint	dare un suggerimento	[dare un sudʒeri'mento]
to go (on foot)	andare (vi)	[an'dare]

to go for a swim	fare il bagno	['fare il 'baɲo]
to go out (for dinner, etc.)	uscire (vi)	[u'ʃire]
to guess (the answer)	indovinare (vt)	[indovi'nare]

to have (vt)	avere (vt)	[a'vere]
to have breakfast	fare colazione	['fare kola'tsjone]
to have dinner	cenare (vi)	[tʃe'nare]
to have lunch	pranzare (vi)	[pran'tsare]
to hear (vt)	sentire (vt)	[sen'tire]

to help (vt)	aiutare (vt)	[aju'tare]
to hide (vt)	nascondere (vt)	[na'skondere]
to hope (vi, vt)	sperare (vi, vt)	[spe'rare]
to hunt (vi, vt)	cacciare (vt)	[ka'tʃare]
to hurry (vi)	avere fretta	[a'vere 'fretta]

10. The most important verbs. Part 3

to inform (vt)	informare (vt)	[infor'mare]
to insist (vi, vt)	insistere (vi)	[in'sistere]
to insult (vt)	insultare (vt)	[insul'tare]
to invite (vt)	invitare (vt)	[invi'tare]
to joke (vi)	scherzare (vi)	[sker'tsare]
to keep (vt)	conservare (vt)	[konser'vare]
to keep silent, to hush	tacere (vi)	[ta't∫ere]
to kill (vt)	uccidere (vt)	[u't∫idere]
to know (sb)	conoscere	[ko'noʃere]
to know (sth)	sapere (vt)	[sa'pere]
to laugh (vi)	ridere (vi)	['ridere]
to liberate (city, etc.)	liberare (vt)	[libe'rare]
to like (I like …)	piacere (vi)	[pja't∫ere]
to look for … (search)	cercare (vt)	[t∫er'kare]
to love (sb)	amare qn	[a'mare]
to make a mistake	sbagliare (vi)	[zbaʎ'ʎare]
to manage, to run	dirigere (vt)	[di'ridʒere]
to mean (signify)	significare (vt)	[siɲifi'kare]
to mention (talk about)	menzionare (vt)	[mentsjo'nare]
to miss (school, etc.)	mancare le lezioni	[man'kare le le'tsjoni]
to notice (see)	accorgersi (vr)	[ak'kordʒersi]
to object (vi, vt)	obiettare (vt)	[objet'tare]
to observe (see)	osservare (vt)	[osser'vare]
to open (vt)	aprire (vt)	[a'prire]
to order (meal, etc.)	ordinare (vt)	[ordi'nare]
to order (mil.)	ordinare (vt)	[ordi'nare]
to own (possess)	possedere (vt)	[posse'dere]
to participate (vi)	partecipare (vi)	[partet∫i'pare]
to pay (vi, vt)	pagare (vi, vt)	[pa'gare]
to permit (vt)	permettere (vt)	[per'mettere]
to plan (vt)	pianificare (vt)	[pjanifi'kare]
to play (children)	giocare (vi)	[dʒo'kare]
to pray (vi, vt)	pregare (vi, vt)	[pre'gare]
to prefer (vt)	preferire (vt)	[prefe'rire]
to promise (vt)	promettere (vt)	[pro'mettere]
to pronounce (vt)	pronunciare (vt)	[pronun't∫are]
to propose (vt)	proporre (vt)	[pro'porre]
to punish (vt)	punire (vt)	[pu'nire]

11. The most important verbs. Part 4

to read (vi, vt)	leggere (vi, vt)	['ledʒere]
to recommend (vt)	raccomandare (vt)	[rakkoman'dare]

to refuse (vi, vt)	**rifiutarsi** (vr)	[rifju'tarsi]
to regret (be sorry)	**rincrescere** (vi)	[rin'kreʃere]
to rent (sth from sb)	**affittare** (vt)	[affit'tare]
to repeat (say again)	**ripetere** (vt)	[ri'petere]
to reserve, to book	**riservare** (vt)	[rizer'vare]
to run (vi)	**correre** (vi)	['korrere]
to save (rescue)	**salvare** (vt)	[sal'vare]
to say (~ thank you)	**dire** (vt)	['dire]
to scold (vt)	**sgridare** (vt)	[zgri'dare]
to see (vt)	**vedere** (vt)	[ve'dere]
to sell (vt)	**vendere** (vt)	['vendere]
to send (vt)	**mandare** (vt)	[man'dare]
to shoot (vi)	**sparare** (vi)	[spa'rare]
to shout (vi)	**gridare** (vi)	[gri'dare]
to show (vt)	**mostrare** (vt)	[mo'strare]
to sign (document)	**firmare** (vt)	[fir'mare]
to sit down (vi)	**sedersi** (vr)	[se'dersi]
to smile (vi)	**sorridere** (vi)	[sor'ridere]
to speak (vi, vt)	**parlare** (vi, vt)	[par'lare]
to steal (money, etc.)	**rubare** (vt)	[ru'bare]
to stop (for pause, etc.)	**fermarsi** (vr)	[fer'marsi]
to stop (please ~ calling me)	**cessare** (vt)	[tʃes'sare]
to study (vt)	**studiare** (vt)	[stu'djare]
to swim (vi)	**nuotare** (vi)	[nuo'tare]
to take (vt)	**prendere** (vt)	['prendere]
to think (vi, vt)	**pensare** (vi, vt)	[pen'sare]
to threaten (vt)	**minacciare** (vt)	[mina'tʃare]
to touch (with hands)	**toccare** (vt)	[tok'kare]
to translate (vt)	**tradurre** (vt)	[tra'durre]
to trust (vt)	**fidarsi** (vr)	[fi'darsi]
to try (attempt)	**tentare** (vt)	[ten'tare]
to turn (e.g., ~ left)	**girare** (vi)	[dʒi'rare]
to underestimate (vt)	**sottovalutare** (vt)	[sottovalu'tare]
to understand (vt)	**capire** (vt)	[ka'pire]
to unite (vt)	**unire** (vt)	[u'nire]
to wait (vt)	**aspettare** (vt)	[aspet'tare]
to want (wish, desire)	**volere** (vt)	[vo'lere]
to warn (vt)	**avvertire** (vt)	[avver'tire]
to work (vi)	**lavorare** (vi)	[lavo'rare]
to write (vt)	**scrivere** (vt)	['skrivere]
to write down	**annotare** (vt)	[anno'tare]

12. Colors

color	colore (m)	[ko'lore]
shade (tint)	sfumatura (f)	[sfuma'tura]
hue	tono (m)	['tono]
rainbow	arcobaleno (m)	[arkoba'leno]

white (adj)	bianco	['bjanko]
black (adj)	nero	['nero]
gray (adj)	grigio	['gridʒo]

green (adj)	verde	['verde]
yellow (adj)	giallo	['dʒallo]
red (adj)	rosso	['rosso]

blue (adj)	blu	['blu]
light blue (adj)	azzurro	[ad'dzurro]
pink (adj)	rosa	['roza]
orange (adj)	arancione	[aran'tʃone]
violet (adj)	violetto	[vio'letto]
brown (adj)	marrone	[mar'rone]

golden (adj)	d'oro	['doro]
silvery (adj)	argenteo	[ar'dʒenteo]

beige (adj)	beige	[beʒ]
cream (adj)	color crema	[ko'lor 'krema]
turquoise (adj)	turchese	[tur'keze]
cherry red (adj)	rosso ciliegia (f)	['rosso tʃi'ljedʒa]
lilac (adj)	lilla	['lilla]
crimson (adj)	rosso lampone	['rosso lam'pone]

light (adj)	chiaro	['kjaro]
dark (adj)	scuro	['skuro]
bright, vivid (adj)	vivo, vivido	['vivo], ['vivido]

colored (pencils)	colorato	[kolo'rato]
color (e.g., ~ film)	a colori	[a ko'lori]
black-and-white (adj)	bianco e nero	['bjanko e 'nero]
plain (one-colored)	in tinta unita	[in 'tinta u'nita]
multicolored (adj)	multicolore	[multiko'lore]

13. Questions

Who?	Chi?	[ki]
What?	Che cosa?	[ke 'koza]
Where? (at, in)	Dove?	['dove]
Where (to)?	Dove?	['dove]
From where?	Di dove?, Da dove?	[di 'dove], [da 'dove]

When?	Quando?	['kwando]
Why? (What for?)	Perché?	[per'ke]
Why? (~ are you crying?)	Perché?	[per'ke]

What for?	Per che cosa?	[per ke 'koza]
How? (in what way)	Come?	['kome]
What? (What kind of ...?)	Che?	[ke]
Which?	Quale?	['kwale]

To whom?	A chi?	[a 'ki]
About whom?	Di chi?	[di 'ki]
About what?	Di che cosa?	[di ke 'koza]
With whom?	Con chi?	[kon 'ki]

How many?	Quanti?	['kwanti]
How much?	Quanto?	['kwanto]
Whose?	Di chi?	[di 'ki]

14. Function words. Adverbs. Part 1

Where? (at, in)	Dove?	['dove]
here (adv)	qui	[kwi]
there (adv)	lì	[li]

| somewhere (to be) | da qualche parte | [da 'kwalke 'parte] |
| nowhere (not in any place) | da nessuna parte | [da nes'suna 'parte] |

| by (near, beside) | vicino a ... | [vi'tʃino a] |
| by the window | vicino alla finestra | [vi'tʃino 'alla fi'nestra] |

Where (to)?	Dove?	['dove]
here (e.g., come ~!)	di qui	[di kwi]
there (e.g., to go ~)	ci	[tʃi]
from here (adv)	da qui	[da kwi]
from there (adv)	da lì	[da 'li]

| close (adv) | vicino, accanto | [vi'tʃino], [a'kanto] |
| far (adv) | lontano | [lon'tano] |

near (e.g., ~ Paris)	vicino a ...	[vi'tʃino a]
nearby (adv)	vicino	[vi'tʃino]
not far (adv)	non lontano	[non lon'tano]

left (adj)	sinistro	[si'nistro]
on the left	a sinistra	[a si'nistra]
to the left	a sinistra	[a si'nistra]

right (adj)	destro	['destro]
on the right	a destra	[a 'destra]
to the right	a destra	[a 'destra]

in front (adv)	davanti	[da'vanti]
front (as adj)	anteriore	[ante'rjore]
ahead (the kids ran ~)	avanti	[a'vanti]

behind (adv)	dietro	['djetro]
from behind	da dietro	[da 'djetro]
back (towards the rear)	indietro	[in'djetro]

| middle | mezzo (m), centro (m) | ['meddzo], ['tʃentro] |
| in the middle | in mezzo, al centro | [in 'meddzo], [al 'tʃentro] |

at the side	di fianco	[di 'fjanko]
everywhere (adv)	dappertutto	[dapper'tutto]
around (in all directions)	attorno	[at'torno]

from inside	da dentro	[da 'dentro]
somewhere (to go)	da qualche parte	[da 'kwalke 'parte]
straight (directly)	dritto	['dritto]
back (e.g., come ~)	indietro	[in'djetro]

| from anywhere | da qualsiasi parte | [da kwal'siazi 'parte] |
| from somewhere | da qualche posto | [da 'kwalke 'posto] |

firstly (adv)	in primo luogo	[in 'primo lu'ogo]
secondly (adv)	in secondo luogo	[in se'kondo lu'ogo]
thirdly (adv)	in terzo luogo	[in 'tertso lu'ogo]

suddenly (adv)	all'improvviso	[all improv'vizo]
at first (in the beginning)	all'inizio	[all i'nitsio]
for the first time	per la prima volta	[per la 'prima 'volta]
long before ...	molto tempo prima di ...	['molto 'tempo 'prima dl]
anew (over again)	di nuovo	[di nu'ovo]
for good (adv)	per sempre	[per 'sempre]

never (adv)	mai	[maj]
again (adv)	ancora	[an'kora]
now (at present)	adesso	[a'desso]
often (adv)	spesso	['spesso]
then (adv)	allora	[al'lora]
urgently (quickly)	urgentemente	[urdʒente'mente]
usually (adv)	di solito	[di 'solito]

by the way, ...	a proposito, ...	[a pro'pozito]
possibly	è possibile	[e pos'sibile]
probably (adv)	probabilmente	[probabil'mente]
maybe (adv)	forse	['forse]
besides ...	inoltre ...	[i'noltre]
that's why ...	ecco perché ...	['ekko per'ke]
in spite of ...	nonostante	[nono'stante]
thanks to ...	grazie a ...	['gratsie a]
what (pron.)	che cosa	[ke 'koza]
that (conj.)	che	[ke]

something	qualcosa	[kwal'koza]
anything (something)	qualcosa	[kwal'koza]
nothing	niente	['njente]

who (pron.)	chi	[ki]
someone	qualcuno	[kwal'kuno]
somebody	qualcuno	[kwal'kuno]

nobody	nessuno	[nes'suno]
nowhere (a voyage to ~)	da nessuna parte	[da nes'suna 'parte]
nobody's	di nessuno	[di nes'suno]
somebody's	di qualcuno	[di kwal'kuno]

so (I'm ~ glad)	così	[ko'zi]
also (as well)	anche	['aŋke]
too (as well)	anche, pure	['aŋke], ['pure]

15. Function words. Adverbs. Part 2

Why?	Perché?	[per'ke]
for some reason	per qualche ragione	[per 'kwalke ra'dʒone]
because …	perché …	[per'ke]
for some purpose	per qualche motivo	[per 'kwalke mo'tivo]

and	e	[e]
or	o …	[o]
but	ma	[ma]
for (e.g., ~ me)	per	[per]

too (~ many people)	troppo	['troppo]
only (exclusively)	solo	['solo]
exactly (adv)	esattamente	[ezatta'mente]
about (more or less)	circa	['tʃirka]

approximately (adv)	approssimativamente	[approsimativa'mente]
approximate (adj)	approssimativo	[approssima'tivo]
almost (adv)	quasi	['kwazi]
the rest	resto (m)	['resto]

each (adj)	ogni	['oɲi]
any (no matter which)	qualsiasi	[kwal'siazi]
many (adj)	molti	['molti]
much (adv)	molto	['molto]
many people	molta gente	['molta 'dʒente]
all (everyone)	tutto, tutti	['tutto], ['tutti]

in return for …	in cambio di …	[in 'kambio di]
in exchange (adv)	in cambio	[in 'kambio]
by hand (made)	a mano	[a 'mano]
hardly (negative opinion)	poco probabile	['poko pro'babile]

probably (adv)	**probabilmente**	[probabil'mente]
— on purpose (intentionally)	**apposta**	[ap'posta]
— by accident (adv)	**per caso**	[per 'kazo]
very (adv)	**molto**	['molto]
for example (adv)	**per esempio**	[per e'zempjo]
between	**fra**	[fra]
among	**fra**	[fra]
so much (such a lot)	**tanto**	['tanto]
especially (adv)	**soprattutto**	[sopra'tutto]

Basic concepts. Part 2

16. Weekdays

Monday	**lunedì** (m)	[lune'di]
Tuesday	**martedì** (m)	[marte'di]
Wednesday	**mercoledì** (m)	[merkole'di]
Thursday	**giovedì** (m)	[dʒove'di]
Friday	**venerdì** (m)	[vener'di]
Saturday	**sabato** (m)	['sabato]
Sunday	**domenica** (f)	[do'menika]
today (adv)	**oggi**	['odʒi]
tomorrow (adv)	**domani**	[do'mani]
the day after tomorrow	**dopodomani**	[dopodo'mani]
yesterday (adv)	**ieri**	['jeri]
the day before yesterday	**l'altro ieri**	['laltro 'jeri]
day	**giorno** (m)	['dʒorno]
working day	**giorno** (m) **lavorativo**	['dʒorno lavora'tivo]
public holiday	**giorno** (m) **festivo**	['dʒorno fes'tivo]
day off	**giorno** (m) **di riposo**	['dʒorno di ri'pozo]
weekend	**fine** (m) **settimana**	['fine setti'mana]
all day long	**tutto il giorno**	['tutto il 'dʒorno]
the next day (adv)	**l'indomani**	[lindo'mani]
two days ago	**due giorni fa**	['due 'dʒorni fa]
the day before	**il giorno prima**	[il 'dʒorno 'prima]
daily (adj)	**quotidiano**	[kwoti'djano]
every day (adv)	**ogni giorno**	['oɲi 'dʒorno]
week	**settimana** (f)	[setti'mana]
last week (adv)	**la settimana scorsa**	[la setti'mana 'skorsa]
next week (adv)	**la settimana prossima**	[la setti'mana 'prossima]
weekly (adj)	**settimanale**	[settima'nale]
every week (adv)	**ogni settimana**	['oɲi setti'mana]
twice a week	**due volte alla settimana**	['due 'volte 'alla setti'mana]
every Tuesday	**ogni martedì**	['oɲi marte'di]

17. Hours. Day and night

morning	**mattina** (f)	[mat'tina]
in the morning	**di mattina**	[di mat'tina]

| noon, midday | mezzogiorno (m) | [meddzo'dʒorno] |
| in the afternoon | nel pomeriggio | [nel pome'ridʒo] |

evening	sera (f)	['sera]
in the evening	di sera	[di 'sera]
night	notte (f)	['notte]
at night	di notte	[di 'notte]
midnight	mezzanotte (f)	[meddza'notte]

second	secondo (m)	[se'kondo]
minute	minuto (m)	[mi'nuto]
hour	ora (f)	['ora]
half an hour	mezzora (f)	[med'dzora]
a quarter-hour	un quarto d'ora	[un 'kwarto 'dora]
fifteen minutes	quindici minuti	['kwinditʃi mi'nuti]
24 hours	ventiquattro ore	[venti'kwattro 'ore]

sunrise	levata (f) del sole	[le'vata del 'sole]
dawn	alba (f)	['alba]
early morning	mattutino (m)	[mattu'tino]
sunset	tramonto (m)	[tra'monto]

early in the morning	di buon mattino	[di bu'on mat'tino]
this morning	stamattina	[stamat'tina]
tomorrow morning	domattina	[domat'tina]

this afternoon	oggi pomeriggio	['odʒi pome'ridʒo]
in the afternoon	nel pomeriggio	[nel pome'ridʒo]
tomorrow afternoon	domani pomeriggio	[do'mani pome'ridʒo]

| tonight (this evening) | stasera | [sta'sera] |
| tomorrow night | domani sera | [do'mani 'sera] |

at 3 o'clock sharp	alle tre precise	['alle tre pre'tʃize]
about 4 o'clock	verso le quattro	['verso le 'kwattro]
by 12 o'clock	per le dodici	[per le 'doditʃi]

in 20 minutes	fra venti minuti	[fra 'venti mi'nuti]
in an hour	fra un'ora	[fra un 'ora]
on time (adv)	puntualmente	[puntual'mente]

a quarter to ...	un quarto di ...	[un 'kwarto di]
within an hour	entro un'ora	['entro un 'ora]
every 15 minutes	ogni quindici minuti	['oɲi 'kwinditʃi mi'nuti]
round the clock	giorno e notte	['dʒorno e 'notte]

18. Months. Seasons

| January | gennaio (m) | [dʒen'najo] |
| February | febbraio (m) | [feb'brajo] |

March	**marzo** (m)	['martso]
April	**aprile** (m)	[a'prile]
May	**maggio** (m)	['madʒo]
June	**giugno** (m)	['dʒuɲo]

July	**luglio** (m)	['luʎʎo]
August	**agosto** (m)	[a'gosto]
September	**settembre** (m)	[set'tembre]
October	**ottobre** (m)	[ot'tobre]
November	**novembre** (m)	[no'vembre]
December	**dicembre** (m)	[di'tʃembre]

spring	**primavera** (f)	[prima'vera]
in spring	**in primavera**	[in prima'vera]
spring (as adj)	**primaverile**	[primave'rile]

summer	**estate** (f)	[e'state]
in summer	**in estate**	[in e'state]
summer (as adj)	**estivo**	[e'stivo]

fall	**autunno** (m)	[au'tunno]
in fall	**in autunno**	[in au'tunno]
fall (as adj)	**autunnale**	[autun'nale]

winter	**inverno** (m)	[in'verno]
in winter	**in inverno**	[in in'verno]
winter (as adj)	**invernale**	[inver'nale]

month	**mese** (m)	['meze]
this month	**questo mese**	['kwesto 'meze]
next month	**il mese prossimo**	[il 'meze 'prossimo]
last month	**il mese scorso**	[il 'meze 'skorso]

a month ago	**un mese fa**	[un 'meze fa]
in a month (a month later)	**fra un mese**	[fra un 'meze]
in 2 months (2 months later)	**fra due mesi**	[fra 'due 'mezi]
the whole month	**un mese intero**	[un 'meze in'tero]
all month long	**per tutto il mese**	[per 'tutto il 'meze]

monthly (~ magazine)	**mensile**	[men'sile]
monthly (adv)	**mensilmente**	[mensil'mente]
every month	**ogni mese**	['oɲi 'meze]
twice a month	**due volte al mese**	['due 'volte al 'meze]

year	**anno** (m)	['anno]
this year	**quest'anno**	[kwest'anno]
next year	**l'anno prossimo**	['lanno 'prossimo]
last year	**l'anno scorso**	['lanno 'skorso]

| a year ago | **un anno fa** | [un 'anno fa] |
| in a year | **fra un anno** | [fra un 'anno] |

in two years	fra due anni	[fra 'due 'anni]
the whole year	un anno intero	[un 'anno in'tero]
all year long	per tutto l'anno	[per 'tutto 'lanno]

every year	ogni anno	['oɲi 'anno]
annual (adj)	annuale	[annu'ale]
annually (adv)	annualmente	[annual'mente]
4 times a year	quattro volte all'anno	['kwattro 'volte all 'anno]

date (e.g., today's ~)	data (f)	['data]
date (e.g., ~ of birth)	data (f)	['data]
calendar	calendario (m)	[kalen'dario]

half a year	mezz'anno (m)	[med'dzanno]
six months	semestre (m)	[se'mestre]
season (summer, etc.)	stagione (f)	[sta'dʒone]
century	secolo (m)	['sekolo]

19. Time. Miscellaneous

time	tempo (m)	['tempo]
moment	istante (m)	[i'stante]
instant (n)	momento (m)	[mo'mento]
instant (adj)	istantaneo	[istan'taneo]
lapse (of time)	periodo (m)	[pe'riodo]
life	vita (f)	['vita]
eternity	eternità (f)	[eterni'ta]

epoch	epoca (f)	['epoka]
era	era (f)	['era]
cycle	ciclo (m)	['tʃiklo]
period	periodo (m)	[pe'riodo]
term (short-~)	scadenza (f)	[ska'dentsa]

the future	futuro (m)	[fu'turo]
future (as adj)	futuro	[fu'turo]
next time	la prossima volta	[la 'prossima 'volta]
the past	passato (m)	[pas'sato]
past (recent)	scorso	['skorso]
last time	la volta scorsa	[la 'volta 'skorsa]

later (adv)	più tardi	[pju 'tardi]
after (prep.)	dopo	['dopo]
nowadays (adv)	oggigiorno	[odʒi'dʒorno]
now (at this moment)	adesso, ora	[a'desso], [ora]
immediately (adv)	subito	['subito]
soon (adv)	fra poco, presto	[fra 'poko], ['presto]
in advance (beforehand)	in anticipo	[in an'titʃipo]
a long time ago	tanto tempo fa	['tanto 'tempo fa]
recently (adv)	di recente	[di re'tʃente]

destiny	**destino** (m)	[de'stino]
memories (childhood ~)	**ricordi** (m pl)	[ri'kordi]
archives	**archivio** (m)	[ar'kiwio]
during …	**durante** …	[du'rante]
long, a long time (adv)	**a lungo**	[a 'lungo]
not long (adv)	**per poco tempo**	[per 'poko 'tempo]
early (in the morning)	**presto**	['presto]
late (not early)	**tardi**	['tardi]
forever (for good)	**per sempre**	[per 'sempre]
to start (begin)	**cominciare** (vt)	[komin'tʃare]
to postpone (vt)	**posticipare** (vt)	[postitʃi'pare]
at the same time	**simultaneamente**	[simultanea'mento]
permanently (adv)	**tutto il tempo**	['tutto il 'tempo]
constant (noise, pain)	**costante**	[ko'stante]
temporary (adj)	**temporaneo**	[tempo'raneo]
sometimes (adv)	**a volte**	[a 'volte]
rarely (adv)	**raramente**	[rara'mente]
often (adv)	**spesso**	['spesso]

20. Opposites

rich (adj)	**ricco**	['rikko]
poor (adj)	**povero**	['povero]
ill, sick (adj)	**malato**	[ma'lato]
well (not sick)	**sano**	['sano]
big (adj)	**grande**	['grande]
small (adj)	**piccolo**	['pikkolo]
quickly (adv)	**rapidamente**	[rapida'mente]
slowly (adv)	**lentamente**	[lenta'mente]
fast (adj)	**veloce**	[ve'lotʃe]
slow (adj)	**lento**	['lento]
glad (adj)	**allegro**	[al'legro]
sad (adj)	**triste**	['triste]
together (adv)	**insieme**	[in'sjeme]
separately (adv)	**separatamente**	[separata'mente]
aloud (to read)	**ad alta voce**	[ad 'alta 'votʃe]
silently (to oneself)	**in silenzio**	[in si'lentsio]
tall (adj)	**alto**	['alto]
low (adj)	**basso**	['basso]

deep (adj)	**profondo**	[pro'fondo]
shallow (adj)	**basso**	['basso]
yes	**sì**	[si]
no	**no**	[no]
distant (in space)	**lontano**	[lon'tano]
nearby (adj)	**vicino**	[vi'tʃino]
far (adv)	**lontano**	[lon'tano]
nearby (adv)	**vicino**	[vi'tʃino]
long (adj)	**lungo**	['lungo]
short (adj)	**corto**	['korto]
good (kindhearted)	**buono**	[bu'ono]
evil (adj)	**cattivo**	[kat'tivo]
married (adj)	**sposato**	[spo'zato]
single (adj)	**celibe**	['tʃelibe]
to forbid (vt)	**vietare** (vt)	[vje'tare]
to permit (vt)	**permettere** (vt)	[per'mettere]
end	**fine** (f)	['fine]
beginning	**inizio** (m)	[i'nitsio]
left (adj)	**sinistro**	[si'nistro]
right (adj)	**destro**	['destro]
first (adj)	**primo**	['primo]
last (adj)	**ultimo**	['ultimo]
crime	**delitto** (m)	[de'litto]
punishment	**punizione** (f)	[puni'tsjone]
to order (vt)	**ordinare** (vt)	[ordi'nare]
to obey (vi, vt)	**obbedire** (vi)	[obbe'dire]
straight (adj)	**dritto**	['dritto]
curved (adj)	**curvo**	['kurvo]
paradise	**paradiso** (m)	[para'dizo]
hell	**inferno** (m)	[in'ferno]
to be born	**nascere** (vi)	['naʃere]
to die (vi)	**morire** (vi)	[mo'rire]
strong (adj)	**forte**	['forte]
weak (adj)	**debole**	['debole]
old (adj)	**vecchio**	['vekkio]
young (adj)	**giovane**	['dʒovane]

old (adj)	vecchio	['vekkio]
new (adj)	nuovo	[nu'ovo]
hard (adj)	duro	['duro]
soft (adj)	morbido	['morbido]
warm (tepid)	caldo	['kaldo]
cold (adj)	freddo	['freddo]
fat (adj)	grasso	['grasso]
thin (adj)	magro	['magro]
narrow (adj)	stretto	['stretto]
wide (adj)	largo	['largo]
good (adj)	buono	[bu'ono]
bad (adj)	cattivo	[kat'tivo]
brave (adj)	valoroso	[valo'rozo]
cowardly (adj)	codardo	[ko'dardo]

21. Lines and shapes

square	quadrato (m)	[kwa'drato]
square (as adj)	quadrato	[kwa'drato]
circle	cerchio (m)	['tʃerkio]
round (adj)	rotondo	[ro'tondo]
triangle	triangolo (m)	[tri'angolo]
triangular (adj)	triangolare	[triango'lare]
oval	ovale (m)	[o'vale]
oval (as adj)	ovale	[o'vale]
rectangle	rettangolo (m)	[ret'tangolo]
rectangular (adj)	rettangolare	[rettango'lare]
pyramid	piramide (f)	[pi'ramide]
rhombus	rombo (m)	['rombo]
trapezoid	trapezio (m)	[tra'petsio]
cube	cubo (m)	['kubo]
prism	prisma (m)	['prizma]
circumference	circonferenza (f)	[tʃirkonfe'rentsa]
sphere	sfera (f)	['sfera]
ball (solid sphere)	palla (f)	['palla]
diameter	diametro (m)	[di'ametro]
radius	raggio (m)	['radʒo]
perimeter (circle's ~)	perimetro (m)	[pe'rimetro]
center	centro (m)	['tʃentro]
horizontal (adj)	orizzontale	[oriddzon'tale]
vertical (adj)	verticale	[verti'kale]

| parallel (n) | parallela (f) | [paral'lela] |
| parallel (as adj) | parallelo | [paral'lelo] |

line	linea (f)	['linea]
stroke	tratto (m)	['tratto]
straight line	linea (f) retta	['linea 'retta]
curve (curved line)	linea (f) curva	['linea 'kurva]
thin (line, etc.)	sottile	[sot'tile]
contour (outline)	contorno (m)	[kon'torno]

intersection	intersezione (f)	[interse'tsjone]
right angle	angolo (m) retto	['angolo 'retto]
segment	segmento	[seg'mento]
sector (circular ~)	settore (m)	[set'tore]
side (of triangle)	lato (m)	['lato]
angle	angolo (m)	['angolo]

22. Units of measurement

weight	peso (m)	['pezo]
length	lunghezza (f)	[lun'gettsa]
width	larghezza (f)	[lar'gettsa]
height	altezza (f)	[al'tettsa]
depth	profondità (f)	[profondi'ta]
volume	volume (m)	[vo'lume]
area	area (f)	['area]

gram	grammo (m)	['grammo]
milligram	milligrammo (m)	[milli'grammo]
kilogram	chilogrammo (m)	[kilo'grammo]
ton	tonnellata (f)	[tonnel'lata]
pound	libbra (f)	['libbra]
ounce	oncia (f)	['ontʃa]

meter	metro (m)	['metro]
millimeter	millimetro (m)	[mil'limetro]
centimeter	centimetro (m)	[tʃen'timetro]
kilometer	chilometro (m)	[ki'lometro]
mile	miglio (m)	['miʎʎo]

inch	pollice (m)	['pollitʃe]
foot	piede (f)	['pjede]
yard	iarda (f)	[jarda]

| square meter | metro (m) quadro | ['metro 'kwadro] |
| hectare | ettaro (m) | ['ettaro] |

liter	litro (m)	['litro]
degree	grado (m)	['grado]
volt	volt (m)	[volt]

ampere	**ampere** (m)	[am'pere]
horsepower	**cavallo vapore** (m)	[ka'vallo va'pore]
quantity	**quantità** (f)	[kwanti'ta]
a little bit of ...	**un po'di** ...	[un po di]
half	**metà** (f)	[me'ta]
dozen	**dozzina** (f)	[dod'dzina]
piece (item)	**pezzo** (m)	['pettso]
size	**dimensione** (f)	[dimen'sjone]
scale (map ~)	**scala** (f)	['skala]
minimal (adj)	**minimo**	['minimo]
the smallest (adj)	**minore**	[mi'nore]
medium (adj)	**medio**	['medio]
maximal (adj)	**massimo**	['massimo]
the largest (adj)	**maggiore**	[ma'dʒore]

23. Containers

canning jar (glass ~)	**barattolo** (m) **di vetro**	[ba'rattolo di 'vetro]
can	**latta** (f), **lattina** (f)	['latta], [lat'tina]
bucket	**secchio** (m)	['sekkio]
barrel	**barile** (m), **botte** (f)	[ba'rile], ['botte]
wash basin (e.g., plastic ~)	**catino** (m)	[ka'tino]
tank (100L water ~)	**serbatoio** (m)	[serba'tojo]
hip flask	**fiaschetta** (f)	[fias'ketta]
jerrycan	**tanica** (f)	['tanika]
tank (e.g., tank car)	**cisterna** (f)	[tʃi'sterna]
mug	**tazza** (f)	['tattsa]
cup (of coffee, etc.)	**tazzina** (f)	[tat'tsina]
saucer	**piattino** (m)	[pjat'tino]
glass (tumbler)	**bicchiere** (m)	[bik'kjere]
wine glass	**calice** (m)	['kalitʃe]
stock pot (soup pot)	**casseruola** (f)	[kasseru'ola]
bottle (~ of wine)	**bottiglia** (f)	[bot'tiʎʎa]
neck (of the bottle, etc.)	**collo** (m)	['kollo]
carafe (decanter)	**caraffa** (f)	[ka'raffa]
pitcher	**brocca** (f)	['brokka]
vessel (container)	**recipiente** (m)	[retʃi'pjente]
pot (crock, stoneware ~)	**vaso** (m) **di coccio**	['vazo di 'kotʃo]
vase	**vaso** (m)	['vazo]
flacon, bottle (perfume ~)	**boccetta** (f)	[bo'tʃetta]
vial, small bottle	**fiala** (f)	[fi'ala]

tube (of toothpaste)	tubetto (m)	[tu'betto]
sack (bag)	sacco (m)	['sakko]
bag (paper ~, plastic ~)	sacchetto (m)	[sak'ketto]
pack (of cigarettes, etc.)	pacchetto (m)	[pak'ketto]
box (e.g., shoebox)	scatola (f)	['skatola]
crate	cassa (f)	['kassa]
basket	cesta (f)	['tʃesta]

24. Materials

material	materiale (m)	[mate'rjale]
wood (n)	legno (m)	['leɲo]
wood-, wooden (adj)	di legno	[di 'leɲo]
glass (n)	vetro (m)	['vetro]
glass (as adj)	di vetro	[di 'vetro]
stone (n)	pietra (f)	['pjetra]
stone (as adj)	di pietra	[di 'pjetra]
plastic (n)	plastica (f)	['plastika]
plastic (as adj)	di plastica	[di 'plastika]
rubber (n)	gomma (f)	['gomma]
rubber (as adj)	di gomma	[di 'gomma]
cloth, fabric (n)	stoffa (f)	['stoffa]
fabric (as adj)	di stoffa	[di 'stoffa]
paper (n)	carta (f)	['karta]
paper (as adj)	di carta	[di 'karta]
cardboard (n)	cartone (m)	[kar'tone]
cardboard (as adj)	di cartone	[di kar'tone]
polyethylene	polietilene (m)	[polieti'lene]
cellophane	cellofan (m)	['tʃellofan]
linoleum	linoleum (m)	[li'noleum]
plywood	legno (m) compensato	['leɲo kompen'sato]
porcelain (n)	porcellana (f)	[portʃel'lana]
porcelain (as adj)	di porcellana	[di portʃel'lana]
clay (n)	argilla (f)	[ar'dʒilla]
clay (as adj)	d'argilla	[dar'dʒilla]
ceramic (n)	ceramica (f)	[tʃe'ramika]
ceramic (as adj)	ceramico	[tʃe'ramiko]

25. Metals

metal (n)	**metallo** (m)	[me'tallo]
metal (as adj)	**metallico**	[me'talliko]
alloy (n)	**lega** (f)	['lega]
gold (n)	**oro** (m)	['oro]
gold, golden (adj)	**d'oro**	['doro]
silver (n)	**argento** (m)	[ar'dʒento]
silver (as adj)	**d'argento**	[dar'dʒento]
iron (n)	**ferro** (m)	['ferro]
iron-, made of iron (adj)	**di ferro**	[di 'ferro]
steel (n)	**acciaio** (m)	[a'tʃajo]
steel (as adj)	**d'acciaio**	[da'tʃajo]
copper (n)	**rame** (m)	['rame]
copper (as adj)	**di rame**	[di 'rame]
aluminum (n)	**alluminio** (m)	[allu'minio]
aluminum (as adj)	**di alluminio**	[allu'minio]
bronze (n)	**bronzo** (m)	['brondzo]
bronze (as adj)	**di bronzo**	[di 'brondzo]
brass	**ottone** (m)	[ot'tone]
nickel	**nichel** (m)	['nikel]
platinum	**platino** (m)	['platino]
mercury	**mercurio** (m)	[mer'kurio]
tin	**stagno** (m)	['staɲo]
lead	**piombo** (m)	['pjombo]
zinc	**zinco** (m)	['dzinko]

HUMAN BEING

Human being. The body

26. Humans. Basic concepts

human being	uomo (m), essere umano (m)	[u'omo], ['essere u'mano]
man (adult male)	uomo (m)	[u'omo]
woman	donna (f)	['donna]
child	bambino (m)	[bam'bino]
girl	bambina (f)	[bam'bina]
boy	bambino (m)	[bam'bino]
teenager	adolescente (m, f)	[adole'ʃente]
old man	vecchio (m)	['vekkio]
old woman	vecchia (f)	['vekkia]

27. Human anatomy

organism (body)	organismo (m)	[orga'nizmo]
heart	cuore (m)	[ku'ore]
blood	sangue (m)	['sangue]
artery	arteria (f)	[ar'teria]
vein	vena (f)	['vena]
brain	cervello (m)	[tʃer'vello]
nerve	nervo (m)	['nervo]
nerves	nervi (m pl)	['nervi]
vertebra	vertebra (f)	['vertebra]
spine (backbone)	colonna (f) vertebrale	[ko'lonna verte'brale]
stomach (organ)	stomaco (m)	['stomako]
intestines, bowels	intestini (m pl)	[inte'stini]
intestine (e.g., large ~)	intestino (m)	[inte'stino]
liver	fegato (m)	['fegato]
kidney	rene (m)	['rene]
bone	osso (m)	['osso]
skeleton	scheletro (m)	['skeletro]
rib	costola (f)	['kostola]
skull	cranio (m)	['kranio]
muscle	muscolo (m)	['muskolo]

biceps	**bicipite** (m)	[bit͡ʃi'pite]
triceps	**tricipite** (m)	[trit͡ʃi'pite]
tendon	**tendine** (m)	['tendine]
joint	**articolazione** (f)	[artikola'tsjone]
lungs	**polmoni** (m pl)	[pol'moni]
genitals	**genitali** (m pl)	[dʒeni'tali]
skin	**pelle** (f)	['pelle]

28. Head

head	**testa** (f)	['testa]
face	**viso** (m)	['vizo]
nose	**naso** (m)	['nazo]
mouth	**bocca** (f)	['bokka]
eye	**occhio** (m)	['okkio]
eyes	**occhi** (m pl)	['okki]
pupil	**pupilla** (f)	[pu'pilla]
eyebrow	**sopracciglio** (m)	[sopra't͡ʃiʎʎo]
eyelash	**ciglio** (m)	['t͡ʃiʎʎo]
eyelid	**palpebra** (f)	['palpebra]
tongue	**lingua** (f)	['lingua]
tooth	**dente** (m)	['dente]
lips	**labbra** (f pl)	['labbra]
cheekbones	**zigomi** (m pl)	['dzigomi]
gum	**gengiva** (f)	[dʒen'dʒiva]
palate	**palato** (m)	[pa'lato]
nostrils	**narici** (f pl)	[na'rit͡ʃi]
chin	**mento** (m)	['mento]
jaw	**mascella** (f)	[ma'ʃella]
cheek	**guancia** (f)	['gwant͡ʃa]
forehead	**fronte** (f)	['fronte]
temple	**tempia** (f)	['tempia]
ear	**orecchio** (m)	[o'rekkio]
back of the head	**nuca** (f)	['nuka]
neck	**collo** (m)	['kollo]
throat	**gola** (f)	['gola]
hair	**capelli** (m pl)	[ka'pelli]
hairstyle	**pettinatura** (f)	[pettina'tura]
haircut	**taglio** (m)	['taʎʎo]
wig	**parrucca** (f)	['parrukka]
mustache	**baffi** (m pl)	['baffi]
beard	**barba** (f)	['barba]
to have (a beard, etc.)	**portare** (vt)	[por'tare]

| braid | **treccia** (f) | ['tretʃa] |
| sideburns | **basette** (f pl) | [ba'zette] |

red-haired (adj)	**rosso**	['rosso]
~ gray (hair)	**brizzolato**	[brittso'lato]
bald (adj)	**calvo**	['kalvo]
bald patch	**calvizie** (f)	[kal'vitsie]

| ponytail | **coda** (f) **di cavallo** | ['koda di ka'vallo] |
| bangs | **frangetta** (f) | [fran'dʒetta] |

29. Human body

| hand | **mano** (f) | ['mano] |
| arm | **braccio** (m) | ['bratʃo] |

finger	**dito** (m)	['dito]
~ toe	**dito** (m) **del piede**	['dito del 'pjede]
thumb	**pollice** (m)	['pollitʃe]
~ little finger	**mignolo** (m)	[mi'ɲolo]
nail	**unghia** (f)	['ungia]

fist	**pugno** (m)	['puɲo]
palm	**palmo** (m)	['palmo]
wrist	**polso** (m)	['polso]
forearm	**avambraccio** (m)	[avam'bratʃo]
elbow	**gomito** (m)	['gomito]
shoulder	**spalla** (f)	['spalla]

leg	**gamba** (f)	['gamba]
foot	**pianta** (f) **del piede**	['pjanta del 'pjede]
knee	**ginocchio** (m)	[dʒi'nokkio]
~ calf (part of leg)	**polpaccio** (m)	[pol'patʃo]
~ hip	**anca** (f)	['anka]
~ heel	**tallone** (m)	[tal'lone]

body	**corpo** (m)	['korpo]
stomach	**pancia** (f)	['pantʃa]
chest	**petto** (m)	['petto]
breast	**seno** (m)	['seno]
flank	**fianco** (m)	['fjanko]
back	**schiena** (f)	['skjena]
~ lower back	**zona** (f) **lombare**	['dzona lom'bare]
~ waist	**vita** (f)	['vita]
~ navel (belly button)	**ombelico** (m)	[ombe'liko]
~ buttocks	**natiche** (f pl)	['natike]
~ bottom	**sedere** (m)	[se'dere]
~ beauty mark	**neo** (m)	['neo]
~ birthmark (café au lait spot)	**voglia** (f)	['voʎʎa]

| tattoo | **tatuaggio** (m) | [tatu'adʒo] |
| scar | **cicatrice** (f) | [tʃika'tritʃe] |

Clothing & Accessories

30. Outerwear. Coats

clothes	vestiti (m pl)	[ve'stiti]
outerwear	soprabito (m)	[so'prabito]
winter clothing	abiti (m pl) invernali	['abiti inver'nali]
coat (overcoat)	cappotto (m)	[kap'potto]
fur coat	pelliccia (f)	[pel'litʃa]
fur jacket	pellicciotto (m)	[pelli'tʃotto]
down coat	piumino (m)	[pju'mino]
jacket (e.g., leather ~)	giubbotto (m), giaccha (f)	[dʒub'botto], ['dʒakka]
raincoat (trenchcoat, etc.)	impermeabile (m)	[imperme'abile]
waterproof (adj)	impermeabile	[imperme'abile]

31. Men's & women's clothing

shirt (button shirt)	camicia (f)	[ka'mitʃa]
pants	pantaloni (m pl)	[panta'loni]
jeans	jeans (m pl)	['dʒins]
suit jacket	giacca (f)	['dʒakka]
suit	abito (m) da uomo	['abito da u'omo]
dress (frock)	abito (m)	['abito]
skirt	gonna (f)	['gonna]
blouse	camicetta (f)	[kami'tʃetta]
knitted jacket (cardigan, etc.)	giacca (f) a maglia	['dʒakka a 'maʎʎa]
jacket (of woman's suit)	giacca (f) tailleur	['dʒakka ta'jer]
T-shirt	maglietta (f)	[maʎ'ʎetta]
shorts (short trousers)	pantaloni (m pl) corti	[panta'loni 'korti]
tracksuit	tuta (f) sportiva	['tuta spor'tiva]
bathrobe	accappatoio (m)	[akkappa'tojo]
pajamas	pigiama (m)	[pi'dʒama]
sweater	maglione (m)	[maʎ'ʎone]
pullover	pullover (m)	[pul'lover]
vest	gilè (m)	[dʒi'le]
tailcoat	frac (m)	[frak]
tuxedo	smoking (m)	['zmoking]

uniform	**uniforme** (f)	[uni'forme]
workwear	**tuta** (f) **da lavoro**	['tuta da la'voro]
overalls	**salopette** (f)	[salo'pett]
coat (e.g., doctor's smock)	**camice** (m)	[ka'mitʃe]

32. Clothing. Underwear

underwear	**intimo** (m)	['intimo]
boxers, briefs	**boxer briefs** (m)	['bokser brifs]
panties	**mutandina** (f)	[mutan'dina]
undershirt (A-shirt)	**maglietta** (f) **intima**	[maʎ'ʎetta 'intima]
socks	**calzini** (m pl)	[kal'tsini]
nightdress	**camicia** (f) **da notte**	[ka'mitʃa da 'notte]
bra	**reggiseno** (m)	[redʒi'seno]
knee highs (knee-high socks)	**calzini** (m pl) **alti**	[kal'tsini 'alti]
pantyhose	**collant** (m)	[kol'lant]
stockings (thigh highs)	**calze** (f pl)	['kaltse]
bathing suit	**costume** (m) **da bagno**	[ko'stume da 'baɲo]

33. Headwear

hat	**cappello** (m)	[kap'pello]
fedora	**cappello** (m) **di feltro**	[kap'pello di feltro]
baseball cap	**cappello** (m) **da baseball**	[kap'pello da 'bejzbol]
flatcap	**coppola** (f)	['koppola]
beret	**basco** (m)	['basko]
hood	**cappuccio** (m)	[kap'putʃo]
panama hat	**panama** (m)	['panama]
knit cap (knitted hat)	**berretto** (m) **a maglia**	[ber'retto a 'maʎʎa]
headscarf	**fazzoletto** (m) **da capo**	[fattso'letto da 'kapo]
women's hat	**cappellino** (m) **donna**	[kappel'lino 'donna]
hard hat	**casco** (m)	['kasko]
garrison cap	**bustina** (f)	[bu'stina]
helmet	**casco** (m)	['kasko]
derby	**bombetta** (f)	[bom'betta]
top hat	**cilindro** (m)	[tʃi'lindro]

34. Footwear

footwear	**calzature** (f pl)	[kaltsa'ture]
shoes (men's shoes)	**stivaletti** (m pl)	[stiva'letti]

shoes (women's shoes)	**scarpe** (f pl)	['skarpe]
boots (e.g., cowboy ~)	**stivali** (m pl)	[sti'vali]
slippers	**pantofole** (f pl)	[pan'tofole]
tennis shoes (e.g., Nike ~)	**scarpe** (f pl) **da tennis**	['skarpe da 'tennis]
sneakers (e.g., Converse ~)	**scarpe** (f pl) **da ginnastica**	['skarpe da dʒin'nastika]
sandals	**sandali** (m pl)	['sandali]
cobbler (shoe repairer)	**calzolaio** (m)	[kaltso'lajo]
heel	**tacco** (m)	['takko]
pair (of shoes)	**paio** (m)	['pajo]
shoestring	**laccio** (m)	['latʃo]
to lace (vt)	**allacciare** (vt)	[ala'tʃare]
shoehorn	**calzascarpe** (m)	[kaltsa'skarpe]
shoe polish	**lucido** (m) **per le scarpe**	['lutʃido per le 'skarpe]

35. Textile. Fabrics

cotton (n)	**cotone** (m)	[ko'tone]
cotton (as adj)	**di cotone**	[di ko'tone]
flax (n)	**lino** (m)	['lino]
flax (as adj)	**di lino**	[di 'lino]
silk (n)	**seta** (f)	['seta]
silk (as adj)	**di seta**	[di 'seta]
wool (n)	**lana** (f)	['lana]
wool (as adj)	**di lana**	[di 'lana]
velvet	**velluto** (m)	[vel'luto]
suede	**camoscio** (m)	[ka'moʃo]
corduroy	**velluto** (m) **a coste**	[vel'luto a 'koste]
nylon (n)	**nylon** (m)	['najlon]
nylon (as adj)	**di nylon**	[di 'najlon]
polyester (n)	**poliestere** (m)	[poli'estere]
polyester (as adj)	**di poliestere**	[di poli'estere]
leather (n)	**pelle** (f)	['pelle]
leather (as adj)	**di pelle**	[di 'pelle]
fur (n)	**pelliccia** (f)	[pel'litʃa]
fur (e.g., ~ coat)	**di pelliccia**	[di pel'litʃa]

36. Personal accessories

gloves	**guanti** (m pl)	['gwanti]
mittens	**manopole** (f pl)	[ma'nopole]

scarf (muffler)	sciarpa (f)	['ʃarpa]
glasses (eyeglasses)	occhiali (m pl)	[ok'kjali]
frame (eyeglass ~)	montatura (f)	[monta'tura]
umbrella	ombrello (m)	[om'brello]
walking stick	bastone (m)	[ba'stone]
hairbrush	spazzola (f) per capelli	['spattsola per ka'pelli]
fan	ventaglio (m)	[ven'taʎʎo]

tie (necktie)	cravatta (f)	[kra'vatta]
bow tie	cravatta (f) a farfalla	[kra'vatta a far'falla]
suspenders	bretelle (f pl)	[bre'telle]
handkerchief	fazzoletto (m)	[fattso'letto]

comb	pettine (m)	['pettine]
barrette	fermaglio (m)	[fer'maʎʎo]
hairpin	forcina (f)	[for'tʃina]
buckle	fibbia (f)	['fibbia]

| belt | cintura (f) | [tʃin'tura] |
| shoulder strap | spallina (f) | [spal'lina] |

bag (handbag)	borsa (f)	['borsa]
purse	borsetta (f)	[bor'setta]
backpack	zaino (m)	['dzajno]

37. Clothing. Miscellaneous

fashion	moda (f)	['moda]
in vogue (adj)	di moda	[di 'moda]
fashion designer	stilista (m)	[sti'lista]

collar	collo (m)	['kollo]
pocket	tasca (f)	['taska]
pocket (as adj)	tascabile	[ta'skabile]
sleeve	manica (f)	['manika]
hanging loop	asola (f) per appendere	['azola per ap'pendere]
fly (on trousers)	patta (f)	['patta]

zipper (fastener)	cerniera (f) lampo	[tʃer'njera 'lampo]
fastener	chiusura (f)	[kju'zura]
button	bottone (m)	[bot'tone]
buttonhole	occhiello (m)	[ok'kjello]
to come off (ab. button)	staccarsi (vr)	[stak'karsi]

to sew (vi, vt)	cucire (vi, vt)	[ku'tʃire]
to embroider (vi, vt)	ricamare (vi, vt)	[rika'mare]
embroidery	ricamo (m)	[ri'kamo]
sewing needle	ago (m)	['ago]
thread	filo (m)	['filo]
seam	cucitura (f)	[kutʃi'tura]

to get dirty (vi)	sporcarsi (vr)	[spor'karsi]
stain (mark, spot)	macchia (f)	['makkia]
to crease, crumple (vt)	sgualcirsi (vr)	[zgwal'tʃirsi]
to tear, to rip (vt)	strappare (vt)	[strap'pare]
clothes moth	tarma (f)	['tarma]

38. Personal care. Cosmetics

toothpaste	dentifricio (m)	[denti'fritʃo]
toothbrush	spazzolino (m) da denti	[spatso'lino da 'denti]
to brush one's teeth	lavarsi i denti	[la'varsi i 'denti]

razor	rasoio (m)	[ra'zojo]
shaving cream	crema (f) da barba	['krema da 'barba]
to shave (vi)	rasarsi (vr)	[ra'zarsi]

| soap | sapone (m) | [sa'pone] |
| shampoo | shampoo (m) | ['ʃampo] |

scissors	forbici (f pl)	['forbitʃi]
nail file	limetta (f)	[li'metta]
nail clippers	tagliaunghie (m)	[taʎʎa'ungje]
tweezers	pinzette (f pl)	[pin'tsette]

cosmetics	cosmetica (f)	[ko'zmetika]
face mask	maschera (f) di bellezza	['maskera di bel'lettsa]
manicure	manicure (m)	[mani'kure]
to have a manicure	fare la manicure	['fare la mani'kure]
pedicure	pedicure (m)	[pedi'kure]

make-up bag	borsa (f) del trucco	['borsa del 'trukko]
face powder	cipria (f)	['tʃipria]
powder compact	portacipria (m)	[porta·'tʃipria]
blusher	fard (m)	[far]

perfume (bottled)	profumo (m)	[pro'fumo]
toilet water (lotion)	acqua (f) da toeletta	['akwa da toe'letta]
lotion	lozione (f)	[lo'tsjone]
cologne	acqua (f) di Colonia	['akwa di ko'lonia]

eyeshadow	ombretto (m)	[om'bretto]
eyeliner	eyeliner (m)	[aj'lajner]
mascara	mascara (m)	[ma'skara]

lipstick	rossetto (m)	[ros'setto]
nail polish, enamel	smalto (m)	['zmalto]
hair spray	lacca (f) per capelli	['lakka per ka'pelli]
deodorant	deodorante (m)	[deodo'rante]
cream	crema (f)	['krema]
face cream	crema (f) per il viso	['krema per il 'vizo]

hand cream	**crema** (f) **per le mani**	['krema per le 'mani]
anti-wrinkle cream	**crema** (f) **antirughe**	['krema anti'ruge]
day cream	**crema** (f) **da giorno**	['krema da 'dʒorno]
night cream	**crema** (f) **da notte**	['krema da 'notte]
day (as adj)	**da giorno**	[da 'dʒorno]
night (as adj)	**da notte**	[da 'notte]
tampon	**tampone** (m)	[tam'pone]
− toilet paper (toilet roll)	**carta** (f) **igienica**	['karta i'dʒenika]
⁻ hair dryer	**fon** (m)	[fon]

39. Jewelry

jewelry, jewels	**gioielli** (m pl)	[dʒo'jelli]
precious (e.g., ~ stone)	**prezioso**	[pre'tsjozo]
hallmark stamp	**marchio** (m)	['markio]
ring	**anello** (m)	[a'nello]
⁻ wedding ring	**anello** (m) **nuziale**	[a'nello nu'tsjale]
⁻ bracelet	**braccialetto** (m)	[bratʃa'letto]
earrings	**orecchini** (m pl)	[orek'kini]
⁻ necklace (~ of pearls)	**collana** (f)	[kol'lana]
crown	**corona** (f)	[ko'rona]
bead necklace	**perline** (f pl)	[per'line]
diamond	**diamante** (m)	[dia'mante]
emerald	**smeraldo** (m)	[zme'raldo]
⁻ ruby	**rubino** (m)	[ru'bino]
sapphire	**zaffiro** (m)	[dzaf'firo]
⁻ pearl le	**perle** (f pl)	['perle]
amber	**ambra** (f)	['ambra]

40. Watches. Clocks

˪ watch (wristwatch)	**orologio** (m)	[oro'lodʒo]
˷ dial	**quadrante** (m)	[kwa'drante]
˷ hand (of clock, watch)	**lancetta** (f)	[lan'tʃetta]
metal watch band	**braccialetto** (m)	[bratʃa'letto]
˷ watch strap	**cinturino** (m)	[tʃintu'rino]
battery	**pila** (f)	['pila]
to be dead (battery)	**essere scarico**	['essere 'skariko]
to change a battery	**cambiare la pila**	[kam'bjare la 'pila]
to run fast	**andare avanti**	[an'dare a'vanti]
to run slow	**andare indietro**	[an'dare in'djetro]
− wall clock	**orologio** (m) **da muro**	[oro'lodʒo da 'muro]
˷ hourglass	**clessidra** (f)	['klessidra]

sundial	orologio (m) solare	[oro'lodʒo so'lare]
alarm clock	sveglia (f)	['zveʎʎa]
watchmaker	orologiaio (m)	[orolo'dʒajo]
to repair (vt)	riparare (vt)	[ripa'rare]

Food. Nutricion

41. Food

meat	**carne** (f)	['karne]
chicken	**pollo** (m)	['pollo]
Rock Cornish hen (poussin)	**pollo** (m) **novello**	['pollo no'vello]
duck	**anatra** (f)	['anatra]
goose	**oca** (f)	['oka]
game	**cacciagione** (f)	[katʃa'dʒone]
turkey	**tacchino** (m)	[tak'kino]
pork	**maiale** (m)	[ma'jale]
veal	**vitello** (m)	[vi'tello]
lamb	**agnello** (m)	[a'ɲello]
beef	**manzo** (m)	['mandzo]
rabbit	**coniglio** (m)	[ko'niʎʎo]
sausage (bologna, etc.)	**salame** (m)	[sa'lame]
vienna sausage (frankfurter)	**würstel** (m)	['vyrstel]
bacon	**pancetta** (f)	[pan'tʃetta]
ham	**prosciutto** (m)	[pro'ʃutto]
gammon	**prosciutto** (m) **affumicato**	[pro'ʃutto affumi'kato]
pâté	**pâté** (m)	[pa'te]
liver	**fegato** (m)	['fegato]
hamburger (ground beef)	**carne** (f) **trita**	['karne 'trita]
tongue	**lingua** (f)	['lingua]
egg	**uovo** (m)	[u'ovo]
eggs	**uova** (f pl)	[u'ova]
egg white	**albume** (m)	[al'bume]
egg yolk	**tuorlo** (m)	[tu'orlo]
fish	**pesce** (m)	['peʃe]
seafood	**frutti** (m pl) **di mare**	['frutti di 'mare]
crustaceans	**crostacei** (m pl)	[kro'statʃei]
caviar	**caviale** (m)	[ka'vjale]
crab	**granchio** (m)	['graŋkio]
shrimp	**gamberetto** (m)	[gambe'retto]
oyster	**ostrica** (f)	['ostrika]
spiny lobster	**aragosta** (f)	[ara'gosta]
octopus	**polpo** (m)	['polpo]

squid	calamaro (m)	[kala'maro]
sturgeon	storione (m)	[sto'rjone]
salmon	salmone (m)	[sal'mone]
halibut	ippoglosso (m)	[ippo'glosso]

cod	merluzzo (m)	[mer'luttso]
mackerel	scombro (m)	['skombro]
tuna	tonno (m)	['tonno]
eel	anguilla (f)	[an'gwilla]

trout	trota (f)	['trota]
sardine	sardina (f)	[sar'dina]
pike	luccio (m)	['lutʃo]
herring	aringa (f)	[a'ringa]

| bread | pane (m) | ['pane] |
| cheese | formaggio (m) | [for'madʒo] |

| sugar | zucchero (m) | ['dzukkero] |
| salt | sale (m) | ['sale] |

rice	riso (m)	['rizo]
pasta (macaroni)	pasta (f)	['pasta]
noodles	tagliatelle (f pl)	[taʎʎa'telle]

| butter | burro (m) | ['burro] |
| vegetable oil | olio (m) vegetale | ['oljo vedʒe'tale] |

| sunflower oil | olio (m) di girasole | ['oljo di dʒira'sole] |
| margarine | margarina (f) | [marga'rina] |

| olives | olive (f pl) | [o'live] |
| olive oil | olio (m) d'oliva | ['oljo do'liva] |

milk	latte (m)	['latte]
condensed milk	latte (m) condensato	['latte konden'sato]
yogurt	yogurt (m)	['jogurt]

| sour cream | panna (f) acida | ['panna 'atʃida] |
| cream (of milk) | panna (f) | ['panna] |

| mayonnaise | maionese (m) | [majo'neze] |
| buttercream | crema (f) | ['krema] |

groats (barley ~, etc.)	cereali (m pl)	[tʃere'ali]
flour	farina (f)	[fa'rina]
canned food	cibi (m pl) in scatola	['tʃibi in 'skatola]

cornflakes	fiocchi (m pl) di mais	['fjokki di 'mais]
honey	miele (m)	['mjele]
jam	marmellata (f)	[marmel'lata]
chewing gum	gomma (f) da masticare	['gomma da masti'kare]

42. Drinks

water	**acqua** (f)	['akwa]
drinking water	**acqua** (f) **potabile**	['akwa po'tabile]
mineral water	**acqua** (f) **minerale**	['akwa mine'rale]
still (adj)	**liscia, non gassata**	['liʃa], [non gas'sata]
carbonated (adj)	**gassata**	[gas'sata]
sparkling (adj)	**frizzante**	[frid'dzante]
ice	**ghiaccio** (m)	['gjatʃo]
with ice	**con ghiaccio**	[kon 'gjatʃo]
non-alcoholic (adj)	**analcolico**	[anal'koliko]
soft drink	**bevanda** (f) **analcolica**	[be'vanda anal'kolika]
refreshing drink	**bibita** (f)	['bibita]
lemonade	**limonata** (f)	[limo'nata]
liquors	**bevande** (f pl) **alcoliche**	[be'vande al'kolike]
wine	**vino** (m)	['vino]
white wine	**vino** (m) **bianco**	['vino 'bjanko]
red wine	**vino** (m) **rosso**	['vino 'rosso]
liqueur	**liquore** (m)	[li'kwore]
champagne	**champagne** (m)	[ʃam'paɲ]
vermouth	**vermouth** (m)	['vermut]
whiskey	**whisky**	['wiski]
vodka	**vodka** (f)	['vodka]
gin	**gin** (m)	[dʒin]
cognac	**cognac** (m)	['koɲak]
rum	**rum** (m)	[rum]
coffee	**caffè** (m)	[kaf'fe]
black coffee	**caffè** (m) **nero**	[kaf'fe 'nero]
coffee with milk	**caffè latte** (m)	[kaf'fe 'latte]
cappuccino	**cappuccino** (m)	[kappu'tʃino]
instant coffee	**caffè** (m) **solubile**	[kaf'fe so'lubile]
milk	**latte** (m)	['latte]
cocktail	**cocktail** (m)	['koktejl]
milkshake	**frullato** (m)	[frul'lato]
juice	**succo** (m)	['sukko]
tomato juice	**succo** (m) **di pomodoro**	['sukko di pomo'doro]
orange juice	**succo** (m) **d'arancia**	['sukko da'rantʃa]
freshly squeezed juice	**spremuta** (f)	[spre'muta]
beer	**birra** (f)	['birra]
light beer	**birra** (f) **chiara**	['birra 'kjara]
dark beer	**birra** (f) **scura**	['birra 'skura]
tea	**tè** (m)	[te]

| black tea | tè (m) nero | [te 'nero] |
| green tea | tè (m) verde | [te 'verde] |

43. Vegetables

| ~ vegetables | ortaggi (m pl) | [or'tadʒi] |
| ~ greens | verdura (f) | [ver'dura] |

tomato	pomodoro (m)	[pomo'doro]
~ cucumber	cetriolo (m)	[tʃetri'olo]
carrot	carota (f)	[ka'rota]
potato	patata (f)	[pa'tata]
onion	cipolla (f)	[tʃi'polla]
garlic	aglio (m)	['aʎʎo]

~ cabbage	cavolo (m)	['kavolo]
cauliflower	cavolfiore (m)	[kavol'fjore]
Brussels sprouts	cavoletti (m pl) di Bruxelles	[kavo'letti di bruk'sel]
broccoli	broccolo (m)	['brokkolo]

~ beet	barbabietola (f)	[barba'bjetola]
eggplant	melanzana (f)	[melan'tsana]
zucchini	zucchina (f)	[dzuk'kina]
~ pumpkin	zucca (f)	['dzukka]
~ turnip	rapa (f)	['rapa]

~ parsley	prezzemolo (m)	[pret'tsemolo]
~ dill	aneto (m)	[a'neto]
~ lettuce	lattuga (f)	[lat'tuga]
~ celery	sedano (m)	['sedano]
asparagus	asparago (m)	[a'sparago]
spinach	spinaci (m pl)	[spi'natʃi]

pea	pisello (m)	[pi'zello]
beans	fave (f pl)	['fave]
corn (maize)	mais (m)	['mais]
~ kidney bean	fagiolo (m)	[fa'dʒolo]

bell pepper	peperone (m)	[pepe'rone]
~ radish	ravanello (m)	[rava'nello]
artichoke	carciofo (m)	[kar'tʃofo]

44. Fruits. Nuts

fruit	frutto (m)	['frutto]
apple	mela (f)	['mela]
pear	pera (f)	['pera]

lemon	**limone** (m)	[li'mone]
orange	**arancia** (f)	[a'rantʃa]
strawberry (garden ~)	**fragola** (f)	['fragola]
mandarin	**mandarino** (m)	[manda'rino]
plum	**prugna** (f)	['pruɲa]
peach	**pesca** (f)	['peska]
apricot	**albicocca** (f)	[albi'kokka]
raspberry	**lampone** (m)	[lam'pone]
pineapple	**ananas** (m)	[ana'nas]
banana	**banana** (f)	[ba'nana]
watermelon	**anguria** (f)	[an'guria]
grape	**uva** (f)	['uva]
sour cherry	**amarena** (f)	[ama'rena]
sweet cherry	**ciliegia** (f)	[tʃi'ljedʒa]
melon	**melone** (m)	[me'lone]
grapefruit	**pompelmo** (m)	[pom'pelmo]
avocado	**avocado** (m)	[avo'kado]
papaya	**papaia** (f)	[pa'paja]
mango	**mango** (m)	['mango]
pomegranate	**melagrana** (f)	[mela'grana]
redcurrant	**ribes** (m) **rosso**	['ribes 'rosso]
blackcurrant	**ribes** (m) **nero**	['ribes 'nero]
gooseberry	**uva** (f) **spina**	['uva 'spina]
bilberry	**mirtillo** (m)	[mir'tillo]
blackberry	**mora** (f)	['mora]
raisin	**uvetta** (f)	[u'vetta]
fig	**fico** (m)	['fiko]
date	**dattero** (m)	['dattero]
peanut	**arachide** (f)	[a'rakide]
almond	**mandorla** (f)	['mandorla]
walnut	**noce** (f)	['notʃe]
hazelnut	**nocciola** (f)	[no'tʃola]
coconut	**noce** (f) **di cocco**	['notʃe di 'kokko]
pistachios	**pistacchi** (m pl)	[pi'stakki]

45. Bread. Candy

bakers' confectionery (pastry)	**pasticceria** (f)	[pastitʃe'ria]
bread	**pane** (m)	['pane]
cookies	**biscotti** (m pl)	[bi'skotti]
chocolate (n)	**cioccolato** (m)	[tʃokko'lato]
chocolate (as adj)	**al cioccolato**	[al tʃokko'lato]

candy (wrapped)	caramella (f)	[kara'mella]
cake (e.g., cupcake)	tortina (f)	[tor'tina]
cake (e.g., birthday ~)	torta (f)	['torta]

| pie (e.g., apple ~) | crostata (f) | [kro'stata] |
| filling (for cake, pie) | ripieno (m) | [ri'pjeno] |

jam (whole fruit jam)	marmellata (f)	[marmel'lata]
marmalade	marmellata (f) di agrumi	[marmel'lata di a'grumi]
wafers	wafer (m)	['vafer]
ice-cream	gelato (m)	[dʒe'lato]
pudding	budino (m)	[bu'dino]

46. Cooked dishes

course, dish	piatto (m)	['pjatto]
cuisine	cucina (f)	[ku'tʃina]
recipe	ricetta (f)	[ri'tʃetta]
portion	porzione (f)	[por'tsjone]

| salad | insalata (f) | [insa'lata] |
| soup | minestra (f) | [mi'nestra] |

clear soup (broth)	brodo (m)	['brodo]
sandwich (bread)	panino (m)	[pa'nino]
fried eggs	uova (f pl) al tegamino	[u'ova al tega'mino]

| hamburger (beefburger) | hamburger (m) | [am'burger] |
| beefsteak | bistecca (f) | [bi'stekka] |

side dish	contorno (m)	[kon'torno]
spaghetti	spaghetti (m pl)	[spa'getti]
mashed potatoes	purè (m) di patate	[pu're di pa'tate]
pizza	pizza (f)	['pittsa]
porridge (oatmeal, etc.)	porridge (m)	[por'ridʒe]
omelet	frittata (f)	[frit'tata]

boiled (e.g., ~ beef)	bollito	[bol'lito]
smoked (adj)	affumicato	[affumi'kato]
fried (adj)	fritto	['fritto]
dried (adj)	secco	['sekko]
frozen (adj)	congelato	[kondʒe'lato]
pickled (adj)	sottoaceto	[sottoa'tʃeto]

sweet (sugary)	dolce	['doltʃe]
salty (adj)	salato	[sa'lato]
cold (adj)	freddo	['freddo]
hot (adj)	caldo	['kaldo]
bitter (adj)	amaro	[a'maro]
tasty (adj)	buono, gustoso	[bu'ono], [gu'stozo]

to cook in boiling water	cuocere, preparare (vt)	[ku'otʃere], [prepa'rare]
to cook (dinner)	cucinare (vi)	[kutʃi'nare]
to fry (vt)	friggere (vt)	['fridʒere]
to heat up (food)	riscaldare (vt)	[riskal'dare]
to salt (vt)	salare (vt)	[sa'lare]
to pepper (vt)	pepare (vt)	[pe'pare]
− to grate (vt)	grattugiare (vt)	[grattu'dʒare]
⤙ peel (n)	buccia (f)	['butʃa]
− to peel (vt)	sbucciare (vt)	[zbu'tʃare]

47. Spices

salt	sale (m)	['sale]
salty (adj)	salato	[sa'lato]
to salt (vt)	salare (vt)	[sa'lare]
black pepper	pepe (m) nero	['pepe 'nero]
red pepper (milled ~)	peperoncino (m)	[peperon'tʃino]
− mustard	senape (f)	[se'nape]
− horseradish	cren (m)	['kren]
⤙ condiment	condimento (m)	[kondi'mento]
− spice	spezie (f pl)	['spetsie]
sauce	salsa (f)	['salsa]
vinegar	aceto (m)	[a'tʃeto]
anise	anice (m)	['anitʃe]
basil	basilico (m)	[ba'ziliko]
cloves	chiodi (m pl) di garofano	['kjodi di ga'rofano]
ginger	zenzero (m)	['dzendzero]
coriander	coriandolo (m)	[kori'andolo]
cinnamon	cannella (f)	[kan'nella]
sesame	sesamo (m)	[sezamo]
⤙ bay leaf	alloro (m)	[al'loro]
paprika	paprica (f)	['paprika]
caraway	cumino, comino (m)	[ku'mino], [ko'mino]
saffron	zafferano (m)	[dzaffe'rano]

48. Meals

food	cibo (m)	['tʃibo]
to eat (vi, vt)	mangiare (vi, vt)	[man'dʒare]
breakfast	colazione (f)	[kola'tsjone]
to have breakfast	fare colazione	['fare kola'tsjone]
lunch	pranzo (m)	['prantso]

to have lunch	pranzare (vi)	[pran'tsare]
dinner	cena (f)	['tʃena]
to have dinner	cenare (vi)	[tʃe'nare]

| appetite | appetito (m) | [appe'tito] |
| Enjoy your meal! | Buon appetito! | [bu'on appe'tito] |

to open (~ a bottle)	aprire (vt)	[a'prire]
- to spill (liquid)	rovesciare (vt)	[rove'ʃare]
to spill out (vi)	rovesciarsi (vi)	[rove'ʃarsi]

to boil (vi)	bollire (vi)	[bol'lire]
to boil (vt)	far bollire	[far bol'lire]
boiled (~ water)	bollito	[bol'lito]

| to chill, cool down (vt) | raffreddare (vt) | [raffred'dare] |
| to chill (vi) | raffreddarsi (vr) | [raffred'darsi] |

| taste, flavor | gusto (m) | ['gusto] |
| - aftertaste | retrogusto (m) | [retro'gusto] |

to slim down (lose weight)	essere a dieta	['essere a di'eta]
diet	dieta (f)	[di'eta]
vitamin	vitamina (f)	[vita'mina]
calorie	caloria (f)	[kalo'ria]

| vegetarian (n) | vegetariano (m) | [vedʒeta'rjano] |
| vegetarian (adj) | vegetariano | [vedʒeta'rjano] |

fats (nutrient)	grassi (m pl)	['grassi]
proteins	proteine (f pl)	[prote'ine]
carbohydrates	carboidrati (m pl)	[karboi'drati]

slice (of lemon, ham)	fetta (f), fettina (f)	['fetta], [fet'tina]
piece (of cake, pie)	pezzo (m)	['pettso]
- crumb	briciola (f)	['britʃola]
(of bread, cake, etc.)		

49. Table setting

spoon	cucchiaio (m)	[kuk'kjajo]
knife	coltello (m)	[kol'tello]
fork	forchetta (f)	[for'ketta]

| cup (e.g., coffee ~) | tazza (f) | ['tattsa] |
| plate (dinner ~) | piatto (m) | ['pjatto] |

saucer	piattino (m)	[pjat'tino]
- napkin (on table)	tovagliolo (m)	[tovaʎ'ʎolo]
- toothpick	stuzzicadenti (m)	[stuttsika'denti]

50. Restaurant

restaurant	**ristorante** (m)	[risto'rante]
coffee house	**caffè** (m)	[kaf'fe]
pub, bar	**pub** (m), **bar** (m)	[pab], [bar]
tearoom	**sala** (f) **da tè**	['sala da 'te]
waiter	**cameriere** (m)	[kame'rjere]
waitress	**cameriera** (f)	[kame'rjera]
bartender	**barista** (m)	[ba'rista]
menu	**menù** (m)	[me'nu]
wine list	**lista** (f) **dei vini**	['lista 'dei 'vini]
to book a table	**prenotare un tavolo**	[preno'tare un 'tavolo]
course, dish	**piatto** (m)	['pjatto]
to order (meal)	**ordinare** (vt)	[ordi'nare]
— to make an order	**fare un'ordinazione**	['fare unordina'tsjone]
aperitif	**aperitivo** (m)	[aperi'tivo]
appetizer	**antipasto** (m)	[anti'pasto]
dessert	**dolce** (m)	['doltʃe]
check	**conto** (m)	['konto]
to pay the check	**pagare il conto**	[pa'gare il 'konto]
— to give change	**dare il resto**	['dare il 'resto]
— tip	**mancia** (f)	['mantʃa]

Family, relatives and friends

51. Personal information. Forms

name (first name)	nome (m)	['nome]
surname (last name)	cognome (m)	[ko'ɲome]
date of birth	data (f) di nascita	['data di 'naʃita]
place of birth	luogo (m) di nascita	[lu'ogo di 'naʃita]
nationality	nazionalità (f)	[natsjonali'ta]
place of residence	domicilio (m)	[domi'tʃilio]
country	paese (m)	[pa'eze]
profession (occupation)	professione (f)	[profes'sjone]
gender, sex	sesso (m)	['sesso]
height	statura (f)	[sta'tura]
weight	peso (m)	['pezo]

52. Family members. Relatives

mother	madre (f)	['madre]
father	padre (m)	['padre]
son	figlio (m)	['fiʎʎo]
daughter	figlia (f)	['fiʎʎa]
younger daughter	figlia (f) minore	['fiʎʎa mi'nore]
younger son	figlio (m) minore	['fiʎʎo mi'nore]
eldest daughter	figlia (f) maggiore	['fiʎʎa ma'dʒore]
eldest son	figlio (m) maggiore	['fiʎʎo ma'dʒore]
brother	fratello (m)	[fra'tello]
sister	sorella (f)	[so'rella]
cousin (masc.)	cugino (m)	[ku'dʒino]
cousin (fem.)	cugina (f)	[ku'dʒina]
mom, mommy	mamma (f)	['mamma]
dad, daddy	papà (m)	[pa'pa]
parents	genitori (m pl)	[dʒeni'tori]
child	bambino (m)	[bam'bino]
children	bambini (m pl)	[bam'bini]
grandmother	nonna (f)	['nonna]
grandfather	nonno (m)	['nonno]
grandson	nipote (m)	[ni'pote]

granddaughter	nipote (f)	[ni'pote]
grandchildren	nipoti (pl)	[ni'poti]
uncle	zio (m)	['tsio]
aunt	zia (f)	['tsia]
nephew	nipote (m)	[ni'pote]
niece	nipote (f)	[ni'pote]
— mother-in-law (wife's mother)	suocera (f)	[su'otʃera]
— father-in-law (husband's father)	suocero (m)	[su'otʃero]
— son-in-law (daughter's husband)	genero (m)	['dʒenero]
— stepmother	matrigna (f)	[ma'triɲa]
— stepfather	patrigno (m)	[pa'triɲo]
— infant	neonato (m)	[neo'nato]
baby (infant)	infante (m)	[in'fante]
little boy, kid	bimbo (m)	['bimbo]
wife	moglie (f)	['moʎʎe]
husband	marito (m)	[ma'rito]
spouse (husband)	coniuge (m)	['konjudʒe]
spouse (wife)	coniuge (f)	['konjudʒe]
married (masc.)	sposato	[spo'zato]
married (fem.)	sposata	[spo'zata]
single (unmarried)	celibe	['tʃelibe]
— bachelor	scapolo (m)	['skapolo]
divorced (masc.)	divorziato	[divortsi'ato]
widow	vedova (f)	['vedova]
widower	vedovo (m)	['vedovo]
— relative	parente (m)	[pa'rente]
close relative	parente (m) stretto	[pa'rente 'stretto]
distant relative	parente (m) lontano	[pa'rente lon'tano]
relatives	parenti (m pl)	[pa'renti]
orphan (boy)	orfano (m)	['orfano]
orphan (girl)	orfana (f)	['orfana]
guardian (of a minor)	tutore (m)	[tu'tore]
to adopt (a boy)	adottare (vt)	[adot'tare]
to adopt (a girl)	adottare (vt)	[adot'tare]

53. Friends. Coworkers

friend (masc.)	amico (m)	[a'miko]
friend (fem.)	amica (f)	[a'mika]
friendship	amicizia (f)	[ami'tʃitsia]

to be friends	essere amici	['essere a'mitʃi]
buddy (masc.)	amico (m)	[a'miko]
buddy (fem.)	amica (f)	[a'mika]
partner	partner (m)	['partner]
chief (boss)	capo (m)	['kapo]
superior (n)	capo (m), superiore (m)	['kapo], [supe'rjore]
subordinate (n)	subordinato (m)	[subordi'nato]
colleague	collega (m)	[kol'lega]
acquaintance (person)	conoscente (m)	[kono'ʃente]
fellow traveler	compagno (m) di viaggio	[kom'paɲo di 'vjadʒo]
classmate	compagno (m) di classe	[kom'paɲo di 'klasse]
neighbor (masc.)	vicino (m)	[vi'tʃino]
neighbor (fem.)	vicina (f)	[vi'tʃina]
neighbors	vicini (m pl)	[vi'tʃini]

54. Man. Woman

woman	donna (f)	['donna]
girl (young woman)	ragazza (f)	[ra'gattsa]
bride	sposa (f)	['spoza]
beautiful (adj)	bella	['bella]
tall (adj)	alta	['alta]
slender (adj)	snella	['znella]
short (adj)	bassa	['bassa]
blonde (n)	bionda (f)	['bjonda]
brunette (n)	bruna (f)	['bruna]
ladies' (adj)	da donna	[da 'donna]
virgin (girl)	vergine (f)	['verdʒine]
pregnant (adj)	incinta	[in'tʃinta]
man (adult male)	uomo (m)	[u'omo]
blond (n)	biondo (m)	['bjondo]
brunet (n)	bruno (m)	['bruno]
tall (adj)	alto	['alto]
short (adj)	basso	['basso]
rude (rough)	sgarbato	[sgar'bato]
stocky (adj)	tozzo	['tottso]
robust (adj)	robusto	[ro'busto]
strong (adj)	forte	['forte]
strength	forza (f)	['fortsa]
stout, fat (adj)	grasso	['grasso]
swarthy (adj)	bruno	['bruno]

| slender (well-built) | snello | ['znello] |
| elegant (adj) | elegante | [ele'gante] |

55. Age

age	età (f)	[e'ta]
youth (young age)	giovinezza (f)	[dʒovi'nettsa]
young (adj)	giovane	['dʒovane]

| younger (adj) | più giovane | [pju 'dʒovane] |
| older (adj) | più vecchio | [pju 'vekkio] |

young man	giovane (m)	['dʒovane]
teenager	adolescente (m, f)	[adole'ʃente]
guy, fellow	ragazzo (m)	[ra'gattso]

| old man | vecchio (m) | ['vekkio] |
| old woman | vecchia (f) | ['vekkia] |

adult (adj)	adulto (m)	[a'dulto]
~ middle-aged (adj)	di mezza età	[di 'meddza e'ta]
~ elderly (adj)	anziano	[an'tsjano]
old (adj)	vecchio	['vekkio]

retirement	pensionamento (m)	[pensjona'mento]
~ to retire (from job)	andare in pensione	[an'dare in pen'sjone]
retiree	pensionato (m)	[pensjo'nato]

56. Children

child	bambino (m)	[bam'bino]
children	bambini (m pl)	[bam'bini]
twins	gemelli (m pl)	[dʒe'melli]

~ cradle	culla (f)	['kulla]
~ rattle	sonaglio (m)	[so'naʎʎo]
~ diaper	pannolino (m)	[panno'lino]

~ pacifier	tettarella (f)	[tetta'rella]
~ baby carriage	carrozzina (f)	[karrot'tsina]
~ kindergarten	scuola (f) materna	['skwola ma'terna]
_ babysitter	baby-sitter (f)	[bebi'siter]

childhood	infanzia (f)	[in'fantsia]
doll	bambola (f)	['bambola]
~ toy	giocattolo (m)	[dʒo'kattolo]
construction set (toy)	gioco (m) di costruzione	['dʒoko di konstru'tsjone]
well-bred (adj)	educato	[edu'kato]

| ill-bred (adj) | maleducato | [maledu'kato] |
| spoiled (adj) | viziato | [vitsi'ato] |

to be naughty	essere disubbidiente	['essere dizubi'djente]
mischievous (adj)	birichino	[biri'kino]
mischievousness	birichinata (f)	[biriki'nata]
mischievous child	monello (m)	[mo'nello]

| obedient (adj) | ubbidiente | [ubidi'ente] |
| disobedient (adj) | disubbidiente | [dizubi'djente] |

docile (adj)	docile	['dotʃile]
clever (smart)	intelligente	[intelli'dʒente]
child prodigy	bambino (m) prodigio	[bam'bino pro'didʒo]

57. Married couples. Family life

to kiss (vt)	baciare (vt)	[ba'tʃare]
to kiss (vi)	baciarsi (vr)	[ba'tʃarsi]
family (n)	famiglia (f)	[fa'miʎʎa]
family (as adj)	familiare	[fami'ljare]
couple	coppia (f)	['koppia]
marriage (state)	matrimonio (m)	[matri'monio]
hearth (home)	focolare (m) domestico	[foko'lare do'mestiko]
dynasty	dinastia (f)	[dina'stia]

| date | appuntamento (m) | [appunta'mento] |
| kiss | bacio (m) | ['batʃo] |

love (for sb)	amore (m)	[a'more]
to love (sb)	amare	[a'mare]
beloved	amato	[a'mato]

tenderness	tenerezza (f)	[tene'rettsa]
tender (affectionate)	dolce, tenero	['doltʃe], ['tenero]
faithfulness	fedeltà (f)	[fedel'ta]
faithful (adj)	fedele	[fe'dele]
care (attention)	premura (f)	[pre'mura]
caring (~ father)	premuroso	[premu'rozo]

newlyweds	sposi (m pl) novelli	['spozi no'velli]
honeymoon	luna (f) di miele	['luna di 'mjele]
to get married (ab. woman)	sposarsi (vr)	[spo'zarsi]
to get married (ab. man)	sposarsi (vr)	[spo'zarsi]

wedding	nozze (f pl)	['nottse]
golden wedding	nozze (f pl) d'oro	['nottse 'doro]
anniversary	anniversario (m)	[anniver'sario]
lover (masc.)	amante (m)	[a'mante]

mistress (lover)	amante (f)	[a'mante]
adultery	adulterio (m)	[adul'terio]
to cheat on ... (commit adultery)	tradire	[tra'dire]
jealous (adj)	geloso	[dʒe'lozo]
to be jealous	essere geloso	['essere dʒe'lozo]
divorce	divorzio (m)	[di'vortsio]
to divorce (vi)	divorziare (vi)	[divor'tsjare]
to quarrel (vi)	litigare (vi)	[liti'gare]
to be reconciled (after an argument)	fare pace	['fare 'patʃe]
together (adv)	insieme	[in'sjeme]
sex	sesso (m)	['sesso]
happiness	felicità (f)	[felitʃi'ta]
happy (adj)	felice	[fe'litʃe]
misfortune (accident)	disgrazia (f)	[dis'gratsia]
unhappy (adj)	infelice	[infe'litʃe]

Character. Feelings. Emotions

58. Feelings. Emotions

feeling (emotion)	sentimento (m)	[senti'mento]
feelings	sentimenti (m pl)	[senti'menti]
to feel (vt)	sentire (vt)	[sen'tire]
hunger	fame (f)	['fame]
to be hungry	avere fame	[a'vere 'fame]
thirst	sete (f)	['sete]
to be thirsty	avere sete	[a'vere 'sete]
sleepiness	sonnolenza (f)	[sonno'lentsa]
to feel sleepy	avere sonno	[a'vere 'sonno]
tiredness	stanchezza (f)	[staŋ'kettsa]
tired (adj)	stanco	['stanko]
to get tired	stancarsi (vr)	[stan'karsi]
mood (humor)	umore (m)	[u'more]
boredom	noia (f)	['noja]
to be bored	annoiarsi (vr)	[anno'jarsi]
seclusion	isolamento (f)	[izola'mento]
to seclude oneself	isolarsi (vr)	[izo'larsi]
to worry (make anxious)	preoccupare (vt)	[preokku'pare]
to be worried	essere preoccupato	['essere preokku'pato]
worrying (n)	agitazione (f)	[adʒita'tsjone]
anxiety	preoccupazione (f)	[preokkupa'tsjone]
preoccupied (adj)	preoccupato	[preokku'pato]
to be nervous	essere nervoso	['essere ner'vozo]
to panic (vi)	andare in panico	[an'dare in 'paniko]
hope	speranza (f)	[spe'rantsa]
to hope (vi, vt)	sperare (vi, vt)	[spe'rare]
certainty	certezza (f)	[tʃer'tettsa]
certain, sure (adj)	sicuro	[si'kuro]
uncertainty	incertezza (f)	[intʃer'tettsa]
uncertain (adj)	incerto	[in'tʃerto]
drunk (adj)	ubriaco	[ubri'ako]
sober (adj)	sobrio	['sobrio]
weak (adj)	debole	['debole]
happy (adj)	fortunato	[fortu'nato]
to scare (vt)	spaventare (vt)	[spaven'tare]

| fury (madness) | rabbia (f) | ['rabbia] |
| rage (fury) | rabbia (f) | ['rabbia] |

depression	depressione (f)	[depres'sjone]
discomfort (unease)	disagio (m)	[di'zadʒo]
comfort	conforto (m)	[kon'forto]
to regret (be sorry)	rincrescere (vi)	[rin'kreʃere]
regret	rincrescimento (m)	[rinkreʃi'mento]
bad luck	sfortuna (f)	[sfor'tuna]
sadness	tristezza (f)	[tri'stettsa]

shame (remorse)	vergogna (f)	[ver'goɲa]
gladness	allegria (f)	[alle'gria]
enthusiasm, zeal	entusiasmo (m)	[entu'zjazmo]
enthusiast	entusiasta (m)	[entu'zjasta]
to show enthusiasm	mostrare entusiasmo	[mo'strare entu'zjazmo]

59. Character. Personality

character	carattere (m)	[ka'rattere]
character flaw	difetto (m)	[di'fetto]
mind	mente (f)	['mente]
reason	intelletto (m)	[intel'letto]

conscience	coscienza (f)	[ko'ʃentsa]
habit (custom)	abitudine (f)	[abi'tudine]
ability (talent)	capacità (f)	[kapatʃi'ta]
can (e.g., ~ swim)	sapere (vt)	[sa'pere]

patient (adj)	paziente	[pa'tsjente]
impatient (adj)	impaziente	[impa'tsjente]
curious (inquisitive)	curioso	[ku'rjozo]
curiosity	curiosità (f)	[kuriozi'ta]

modesty	modestia (f)	[mo'destia]
modest (adj)	modesto	[mo'desto]
immodest (adj)	immodesto	[immo'desto]

laziness	pigrizia (f)	[pi'gritsia]
lazy (adj)	pigro	['pigro]
lazy person (masc.)	poltrone (m)	[pol'trone]

cunning (n)	furberia (f)	[furbe'ria]
cunning (as adj)	furbo	['furbo]
distrust	diffidenza (f)	[diffi'dentsa]
distrustful (adj)	diffidente	[diffi'dente]

generosity	generosità (f)	[dʒenerozi'ta]
generous (adj)	generoso	[dʒene'rozo]
talented (adj)	di talento	[di ta'lento]

talent	talento (m)	[ta'lento]
courageous (adj)	coraggioso	[kora'dʒozo]
courage	coraggio (m)	[ko'radʒo]
honest (adj)	onesto	[o'nesto]
honesty	onestà (f)	[one'sta]

careful (cautious)	prudente	[pru'dente]
brave (courageous)	valoroso	[valo'rozo]
serious (adj)	serio	['serio]
strict (severe, stern)	severo	[se'vero]

decisive (adj)	deciso	[de'tʃizo]
indecisive (adj)	indeciso	[inde'tʃizo]
shy, timid (adj)	timido	['timido]
shyness, timidity	timidezza (f)	[timi'dettsa]

confidence (trust)	fiducia (f)	[fi'dutʃa]
to believe (trust)	fidarsi (vr)	[fi'darsi]
trusting (credulous)	fiducioso	[fidu'tʃozo]

sincerely (adv)	sinceramente	[sintʃera'mente]
sincere (adj)	sincero	[sin'tʃero]
sincerity	sincerità (f)	[sintʃeri'ta]
open (person)	aperto	[a'perto]

calm (adj)	tranquillo	[tran'kwillo]
frank (sincere)	sincero	[sin'tʃero]
naïve (adj)	ingenuo	[in'dʒenuo]
absent-minded (adj)	distratto	[di'stratto]
funny (odd)	buffo	['buffo]

greed, stinginess	avidità (f)	[avidi'ta]
greedy, stingy (adj)	avido	['avido]
stingy (adj)	avaro	[a'varo]
evil (adj)	cattivo	[kat'tivo]
stubborn (adj)	testardo	[te'stardo]
unpleasant (adj)	antipatico	[anti'patiko]

selfish person (masc.)	egoista (m)	[ego'ista]
selfish (adj)	egoistico	[ego'istiko]
coward	codardo (m)	[ko'dardo]
cowardly (adj)	codardo	[ko'dardo]

60. Sleep. Dreams

to sleep (vi)	dormire (vi)	[dor'mire]
sleep, sleeping	sonno (m)	['sonno]
dream	sogno (m)	['soɲo]
to dream (in sleep)	sognare (vi)	[so'ɲare]
sleepy (adj)	sonnolento	[sonno'lento]

bed	letto (m)	['letto]
mattress	materasso (m)	[mate'rasso]
blanket (comforter)	coperta (f)	[ko'perta]
pillow	cuscino (m)	[ku'ʃino]
sheet	lenzuolo (m)	[lentsu'olo]

insomnia	insonnia (f)	[in'sonnia]
sleepless (adj)	insonne	[in'sonne]
sleeping pill	sonnifero (m)	[son'nifero]
to take a sleeping pill	prendere il sonnifero	['prendere il son'nifero]

to feel sleepy	avere sonno	[a'vere 'sonno]
to yawn (vi)	sbadigliare (vi)	[zbadiʎ'ʎare]
to go to bed	andare a letto	[an'dare a 'letto]
to make up the bed	fare il letto	['fare il 'letto]
to fall asleep	addormentarsi (vr)	[addormen'tarsi]

nightmare	incubo (m)	['inkubo]
snore, snoring	russare (m)	[rus'sare]
to snore (vi)	russare (vi)	[rus'sare]

alarm clock	sveglia (f)	['zveʎʎa]
to wake (vt)	svegliare (vt)	[zveʎ'ʎare]
to wake up	svegliarsi (vr)	[zveʎ'ʎarsi]
to get up (vi)	alzarsi (vr)	[al'tsarsi]
to wash up (wash face)	lavarsi (vr)	[la'varsi]

61. Humour. Laughter. Gladness

humor (wit, fun)	umorismo (m)	[umo'rizmo]
sense of humor	senso (m) dello humour	['senso 'dello u'mur]
to enjoy oneself	divertirsi (vr)	[diver'tirsi]
cheerful (merry)	allegro	[al'legro]
merriment (gaiety)	allegria (f)	[alle'gria]

smile	sorriso (m)	[sor'rizo]
to smile (vi)	sorridere (vi)	[sor'ridere]
to start laughing	mettersi a ridere	['mettersi a 'ridere]
to laugh (vi)	ridere (vi)	['ridere]
laugh, laughter	riso (m)	['rizo]

anecdote	aneddoto (m)	[a'neddoto]
funny (anecdote, etc.)	divertente	[diver'tente]
funny (odd)	ridicolo	[ri'dikolo]

to joke (vi)	scherzare (vi)	[sker'tsare]
joke (verbal)	scherzo (m)	['skertso]
joy (emotion)	gioia (f)	['dʒoja]
to rejoice (vi)	rallegrarsi (vr)	[ralle'grarsi]
joyful (adj)	allegro	[al'legro]

62. Discussion, conversation. Part 1

| communication | comunicazione (f) | [komunika'tsjone] |
| to communicate | comunicare (vi) | [komuni'kare] |

conversation	conversazione (f)	[konversa'tsjone]
dialog	dialogo (m)	[di'alogo]
discussion (discourse)	discussione (f)	[diskus'sjone]
dispute (debate)	dibattito (m)	[di'battito]
to dispute	discutere (vi)	[di'skutere]

interlocutor	interlocutore (m)	[interloku'tore]
topic (theme)	tema (m)	['tema]
point of view	punto (m) di vista	['punto di 'vista]
opinion (point of view)	opinione (f)	[opi'njone]
speech (talk)	discorso (m)	[di'skorso]

discussion (of report, etc.)	discussione (f)	[diskus'sjone]
to discuss (vt)	discutere (vt)	[di'skutere]
talk (conversation)	conversazione (f)	[konversa'tsjone]
to talk (to chat)	conversare (vi)	[konver'sare]
meeting (encounter)	incontro (m)	[in'kontro]
to meet (vi, vt)	incontrarsi (vr)	[inkon'trarsi]

proverb	proverbio (m)	[pro'verbio]
saying	detto (m)	['detto]
riddle (poser)	indovinello (m)	[indovi'nello]
to pose a riddle	fare un indovinello	['fare un indovi'nello]
password	parola (f) d'ordine	[pa'rola 'dordine]
secret	segreto (m)	[se'greto]

oath (vow)	giuramento (m)	[dʒura'mento]
to swear (an oath)	giurare (vi)	[dʒu'rare]
promise	promessa (f)	[pro'messa]
to promise (vt)	promettere (vt)	[pro'mettere]

advice (counsel)	consiglio (m)	[kon'siʎʎo]
to advise (vt)	consigliare (vt)	[konsiʎ'ʎare]
to listen to ... (obey)	ubbidire (vi)	[ubi'dire]

news	notizia (f)	[no'titsia]
sensation (news)	sensazione (f)	[sensa'tsjone]
information (report)	informazioni (f pl)	[informa'tsjoni]
conclusion (decision)	conclusione (f)	[konklu'zjone]
voice	voce (f)	['votʃe]
compliment	complimento (m)	[kompli'mento]
kind (nice)	gentile	[dʒen'tile]

word	parola (f)	[pa'rola]
phrase	frase (f)	['fraze]
answer	risposta (f)	[ris'posta]

truth	verità (f)	[veri'ta]
lie	menzogna (f) *bugia*	[men'tsoɲa]
thought	pensiero (m)	[pen'sjero]
idea (inspiration)	idea (f), pensiero (m)	[i'dea], [pen'sjero]
fantasy	fantasia (f)	[fanta'zia]

63. Discussion, conversation. Part 2

respected (adj)	rispettato	[rispet'tato]
to respect (vt)	rispettare (vt)	[rispet'tare]
respect	rispetto (m)	[ris'petto]
Dear ... (letter)	Egregio ...	[e'gredʒo]
to introduce (sb to sb)	presentare (vt)	[prezen'tare]
intention	intenzione (f)	[inten'tsjone]
to intend (have in mind)	avere intenzione	[a'vere inten'tsjone]
wish	augurio (m)	[au'gurio]
to wish (~ good luck)	augurare (vt)	[augu'rare]
surprise (astonishment)	sorpresa (f)	[sor'preza]
to surprise (amaze)	sorprendere (vt)	[sor'prendere]
to be surprised	stupirsi (vr)	[stu'pirsi]
to give (vt)	dare (vt)	['dare]
to take (get hold of)	prendere (vt)	['prendere]
to give back	rendere (vt)	['rendere]
to return (give back)	restituire (vt)	[restitu'ire]
to apologize (vi)	scusarsi (vr)	[sku'zarsi]
apology	scusa (f)	['skuza]
to forgive (vt)	perdonare (vt)	[perdo'nare]
to talk (speak)	parlare (vi, vt)	[par'lare]
to listen (vi)	ascoltare (vi)	[askol'tare]
to hear out	ascoltare fino in fondo	[askol'tare 'fino in 'fondo]
to understand (vt)	capire (vt)	[ka'pire]
to show (to display)	mostrare (vt)	[mo'strare]
to look at ...	guardare (vt)	[gwar'dare]
to call (yell for sb)	chiamare (vt)	[kja'mare]
to disturb (vt)	disturbare (vt)	[distur'bare]
to pass (to hand sth)	consegnare (vt)	[konse'ɲare]
demand (request)	richiesta (f)	[ri'kjesta]
to request (ask)	chiedere (vt)	['kjedere]
demand (firm request)	esigenza (f)	[ezi'dʒentsa]
to demand (request firmly)	esigere (vt)	[e'zidʒere]
to tease (call names)	stuzzicare (vt)	[stuttsi'kare]
to mock (make fun of)	canzonare (vt)	[kantso'nare]

| mockery, derision | burla (f), beffa (f) | ['burla], ['beffa] |
| nickname | soprannome (m) | [sopran'nome] |

insinuation	allusione (f)	[allu'zjone]
to insinuate (imply)	alludere (vi)	[al'ludere]
to mean (vt)	intendere (vt)	[in'tendere]

description	descrizione (f)	[deskri'tsjone]
to describe (vt)	descrivere (vt)	[de'skrivere]
praise (compliments)	lode (f)	['lode]
to praise (vt)	lodare (vt)	[lo'dare]

disappointment	delusione (f)	[delu'zjone]
to disappoint (vt)	deludere (vt)	[de'ludere]
to be disappointed	rimanere deluso	[rima'nere de'luzo]

supposition	supposizione (f)	[suppozi'tsjone]
to suppose (assume)	supporre (vt)	[sup'porre]
warning (caution)	avvertimento (m)	[avverti'mento]
to warn (vt)	avvertire (vt)	[avver'tire]

64. Discussion, conversation. Part 3

| to talk into (convince) | persuadere (vt) | [persua'dere] |
| to calm down (vt) | tranquillizzare (vt) | [trankwillid'dzare] |

silence (~ is golden)	silenzio (m)	[si'lentsio]
to be silent (not speaking)	tacere (vi)	[ta'tʃere]
to whisper (vi, vt)	sussurrare (vt)	[sussur'rare]
whisper	sussurro (m)	[sus'surro]

| frankly, sincerely (adv) | francamente | [franka'mente] |
| in my opinion ... | secondo me ... | [se'kondo me] |

detail (of the story)	dettaglio (m)	[det'taʎʎo]
detailed (adj)	dettagliato	[dettaʎ'ʎato]
in detail (adv)	dettagliatamente	[dettaʎʎata'mente]

| hint, clue | suggerimento (m) | [sudʒeri'mento] |
| to give a hint | suggerire (vt) | [sudʒe'rire] |

look (glance)	sguardo (m)	['zgwardo]
to have a look	gettare uno sguardo	[dʒet'tare 'uno 'zgwardo]
fixed (look)	fisso	['fisso]
to blink (vi)	battere le palpebre	['battere le 'palpebre]
to wink (vi)	ammiccare (vi)	[ammik'kare]
to nod (in assent)	accennare col capo	[atʃen'nare kol 'kapo]

| sigh | sospiro (m) | [sos'piro] |
| to sigh (vi) | sospirare (vi) | [sospi'rare] |

to shudder (vi)	sussultare (vi)	[sussul'tare]
gesture	gesto (m)	['dʒesto]
to touch (one's arm, etc.)	toccare (vt)	[tok'kare]
to seize	afferrare (vt)	[affer'rare]
(e.g., ~ by the arm)		
to tap (on the shoulder)	picchiettare (vt)	[pikjet'tare]

Look out!	Attenzione!	[atten'tsjone]
Really?	Davvero?	[dav'vero]
Are you sure?	Sei sicuro?	[sej si'kuro]
Good luck!	Buona fortuna!	[bu'ona for'tuna]
I see!	Capito!	[ka'pito]
What a pity!	Peccato!	[pek'kato]

65. Agreement. Refusal

consent	accordo (m)	[ak'kordo]
to consent (vi)	essere d'accordo	['essere dak'kordo]
approval	approvazione (f)	[approva'tsjone]
to approve (vt)	approvare (vt)	[appro'vare]
refusal	rifiuto (m)	[ri'fjuto]
to refuse (vi, vt)	rifiutarsi (vr)	[rifju'tarsi]

Great!	Perfetto!	[per'fetto]
All right!	Va bene!	[va 'bene]
Okay! (I agree)	D'accordo!	[dak'kordo]

| forbidden (adj) | vietato, proibito | [vje'tato], [proi'bito] |
| it's forbidden | è proibito | [e proi'bito] |

| it's impossible | è impossibile | [e impos'sibile] |
| incorrect (adj) | sbagliato | [zbaʎ'ʎato] |

to reject (~ a demand)	respingere (vt)	[re'spindʒere]
to support (cause, idea)	sostenere (vt)	[soste'nere]
to accept (~ an apology)	accettare (vt)	[atʃet'tare]

to confirm (vt)	confermare (vt)	[konfer'mare]
confirmation	conferma (f)	[kon'ferma]
permission	permesso (m)	[per'messo]
to permit (vt)	permettere (vt)	[per'mettere]

decision	decisione (f)	[detʃi'zjone]
to say nothing	non dire niente	[non 'dire 'njente]
(hold one's tongue)		

condition (term)	condizione (f)	[kondi'tsjone]
excuse (pretext)	pretesto (m)	[pre'testo]
praise (compliments)	lode (f)	['lode]
to praise (vt)	lodare (vt)	[lo'dare]

66. Success. Good luck. Failure

success	successo (m)	[su'tʃesso]
successfully (adv)	con successo	[kon su'tʃesso]
successful (adj)	ben riuscito	[ben riu'ʃito]
luck (good luck)	fortuna (f)	[for'tuna]
Good luck!	Buona fortuna!	[bu'ona for'tuna]
lucky (e.g., ~ day)	felice, fortunato	[fe'litʃe], [fortu'nato]
lucky (fortunate)	fortunato	[fortu'nato]
failure	fiasco (m)	[fi'asko]
misfortune	disdetta (f)	[diz'detta]
bad luck	sfortuna (f)	[sfor'tuna]
unsuccessful (adj)	fallito	[fal'lito]
catastrophe	disastro (m)	[di'zastro]
pride	orgoglio (m)	[or'goʎʎo]
proud (adj)	orgoglioso	[orgoʎ'ʎozo]
to be proud	essere fiero di ...	['essere 'fjero di]
winner	vincitore (m)	[vintʃi'tore]
to win (vi)	vincere (vi)	['vintʃere]
to lose (not win)	perdere (vi)	['perdere]
try	tentativo (m)	[tenta'tivo]
to try (vi)	tentare (vi)	[ten'tare]
chance (opportunity)	chance (f)	[ʃans]

67. Quarrels. Negative emotions

shout (scream)	grido (m)	['grido]
to shout (vi)	gridare (vi)	[gri'dare]
to start to cry out	mettersi a gridare	['mettersi a gri'dare]
quarrel	litigio (m)	[li'tidʒo]
to quarrel (vi)	litigare (vi)	[liti'gare]
fight (squabble)	lite (f)	['lite]
to make a scene	litigare (vi)	[liti'gare]
conflict	conflitto (m)	[kon'flitto]
misunderstanding	fraintendimento (m)	[fraintendi'mento]
insult	insulto (m)	[in'sulto]
to insult (vt)	insultare (vt)	[insul'tare]
insulted (adj)	offeso	[of'fezo]
resentment	offesa (f)	[of'feza]
to offend (vt)	offendere (vt)	[of'fendere]
to take offense	offendersi (vr)	[of'fendersi]
indignation	indignazione (f)	[indiɲa'tsjone]
to be indignant	indignarsi (vr)	[indi'ɲarsi]

complaint	lamentela (f)	[lamen'tela]
to complain (vi, vt)	lamentarsi (vr)	[lamen'tarsi]
apology	scusa (f)	['skuza]
to apologize (vi)	scusarsi (vr)	[sku'zarsi]
to beg pardon	chiedere scusa	['kjedere 'skuza]
criticism	critica (f)	['kritika]
to criticize (vt)	criticare (vt)	[kriti'kare]
accusation (charge)	accusa (f)	[ak'kuza]
to accuse (vt)	accusare (vt)	[akku'zare]
revenge	vendetta (f)	[ven'detta]
to avenge (get revenge)	vendicare (vt)	[vendi'kare]
to pay back	vendicarsi (vr)	[vendi'karsi]
disdain	disprezzo (m)	[dis'prettso]
to despise (vt)	disprezzare (vt)	[dispret'tsare]
hatred, hate	odio (m)	['odio]
to hate (vt)	odiare (vt)	[odi'are]
nervous (adj)	nervoso	[ner'vozo]
to be nervous	essere nervoso	['essere ner'vozo]
angry (mad)	arrabbiato	[arrab'bjato]
to make angry	fare arrabbiare	['fare arrab'bjare]
humiliation	umiliazione (f)	[umilja'tsjone]
to humiliate (vt)	umiliare (vt)	[umi'ljare]
to humiliate oneself	umiliarsi (vr)	[umi'ljarsi]
shock	shock (m)	[ʃok]
to shock (vt)	scandalizzare (vt)	[skandalid'dzare]
trouble (e.g., serious ~)	problema (m)	[pro'blema]
unpleasant (adj)	spiacevole	[spja'tʃevole]
fear (dread)	spavento (m), paura (f)	[spa'vento], [pa'ura]
terrible (storm, heat)	terribile	[ter'ribile]
scary (e.g., ~ story)	spaventoso	[spaven'tozo]
horror	orrore (m)	[or'rore]
awful (crime, news)	orrendo	[orrendo]
to begin to tremble	cominciare a tremare	[komin'tʃare a tre'mare]
to cry (weep)	piangere (vi)	['pjandʒere]
to start crying	mettersi a piangere	['mettersi a 'pjandʒere]
tear	lacrima (f)	['lakrima]
fault	colpa (f)	['kolpa]
guilt (feeling)	senso (m) di colpa	['senso di 'kolpa]
dishonor (disgrace)	vergogna (f)	[ver'goɲa]
protest	protesta (f)	[pro'testa]
stress	stress (m)	['stress]

to disturb (vt)	**disturbare** (vt)	[distur'bare]
to be furious	**essere arrabbiato**	['essere arrab'bjato]
mad, angry (adj)	**arrabbiato**	[arrab'bjato]
to end (~ a relationship)	**porre fine a ...**	['porre 'fine a]
to swear (at sb)	**rimproverare** (vt)	[rimprove'rare]
to scare (become afraid)	**spaventarsi** (vr)	[spaven'tarsi]
to hit (strike with hand)	**colpire** (vt)	[kol'pire]
to fight (street fight, etc.)	**picchiarsi** (vr)	[pik'kjarsi]
to settle (a conflict)	**regolare** (vt)	[rego'lare]
discontented (adj)	**scontento**	[skon'tento]
furious (adj)	**furioso**	[fu'rjozo]
It's not good!	**Non sta bene!**	[non sta 'bene]
It's bad!	**Fa male!**	[fa 'male]

Medicine

68. Diseases

sickness	**malattia** (f)	[malat'tia]
to be sick	**essere malato**	['essere ma'lato]
health	**salute** (f)	[sa'lute]
runny nose (coryza)	**raffreddore** (m)	[raffred'dore]
tonsillitis	**tonsillite** (f)	[tonsil'lite]
cold (illness)	**raffreddore** (m)	[raffred'dore]
— to catch a cold	**raffreddarsi** (vr)	[raffred'darsi]
bronchitis	**bronchite** (f)	[bron'kite]
pneumonia	**polmonite** (f)	[polmo'nite]
flu, influenza	**influenza** (f)	[influ'entsa]
nearsighted (adj)	**miope**	['miope]
farsighted (adj)	**presbite**	['prezbite]
strabismus (crossed eyes)	**strabismo** (m)	[stra'bizmo]
cross-eyed (adj)	**strabico**	['strabiko]
cataract	**cateratta** (f)	[kate'ratta]
glaucoma	**glaucoma** (m)	[glau'koma]
— stroke	**ictus** (m) **cerebrale**	['iktus tʃere'brale]
— heart attack	**attacco** (m) **di cuore**	[at'tako di ku'ore]
myocardial infarction	**infarto** (m) **miocardico**	[in'farto miokar'diko]
paralysis	**paralisi** (f)	[pa'ralizi]
to paralyze (vt)	**paralizzare** (vt)	[paralid'dzare]
— allergy	**allergia** (f)	[aller'dʒia]
asthma	**asma** (f)	['azma]
diabetes	**diabete** (m)	[dia'bete]
toothache	**mal** (m) **di denti**	[mal di 'denti]
caries	**carie** (f)	['karie]
diarrhea	**diarrea** (f)	[diar'rea]
constipation	**stitichezza** (f)	[stiti'kettsa]
stomach upset	**disturbo** (m) **gastrico**	[di'sturbo 'gastriko]
food poisoning	**intossicazione** (f) **alimentare**	[intossika'tsjone alimen'tare]
to get food poisoning	**intossicarsi** (vr)	[intossi'karsi]
arthritis	**artrite** (f)	[ar'trite]
rickets	**rachitide** (f)	[ra'kitide]

| rheumatism | reumatismo (m) | [reuma'tizmo] |
| atherosclerosis | aterosclerosi (f) | [ateroskle'rozi] |

gastritis	gastrite (f)	[ga'strite]
appendicitis	appendicite (f)	[appendi'tʃite]
cholecystitis	colecistite (f)	[koletʃi'stite]
ulcer	ulcera (f)	['ultʃera]

measles	morbillo (m)	[mor'billo]
rubella (German measles)	rosolia (f)	[rozo'lia]
jaundice	itterizia (f)	[itte'ritsia]
hepatitis	epatite (f)	[epa'tite]

schizophrenia	schizofrenia (f)	[skidzofre'nia]
rabies (hydrophobia)	rabbia (f)	['rabbia]
neurosis	nevrosi (f)	[ne'vrozi]
concussion	commozione (f) cerebrale	[kommo'tsjone tʃere'brale]

cancer	cancro (m)	['kankro]
sclerosis	sclerosi (f)	[skle'rozi]
multiple sclerosis	sclerosi (f) multipla	[skle'rozi 'multipla]

alcoholism	alcolismo (m)	[alko'lizmo]
alcoholic (n)	alcolizzato (m)	[alkolid'dzato]
syphilis	sifilide (f)	[si'filide]
AIDS	AIDS (m)	['aids]

tumor	tumore (m)	[tu'more]
malignant (adj)	maligno	[ma'liɲo]
benign (adj)	benigno	[be'niɲo]
fever	febbre (f)	['febbre]
malaria	malaria (f)	[ma'laria]
gangrene	cancrena (f)	[kan'krena]
seasickness	mal (m) di mare	[mal di 'mare]
epilepsy	epilessia (f)	[epiles'sia]

epidemic	epidemia (f)	[epide'mia]
typhus	tifo (m)	['tifo]
tuberculosis	tubercolosi (f)	[tuberko'lozi]
cholera	colera (m)	[ko'lera]
plague (bubonic ~)	peste (f)	['peste]

69. Symptoms. Treatments. Part 1

symptom	sintomo (m)	['sintomo]
temperature	temperatura (f)	[tempera'tura]
high temperature (fever)	febbre (f) alta	['febbre 'alta]
pulse (heartbeat)	polso (m)	['polso]
dizziness (vertigo)	capogiro (m)	[kapo'dʒiro]
hot (adj)	caldo	['kaldo]

shivering	**brivido** (m)	['brivido]
pale (e.g., ~ face)	**pallido**	['pallido]
cough	**tosse** (f)	['tosse]
to cough (vi)	**tossire** (vi)	[tos'sire]
to sneeze (vi)	**starnutire** (vi)	[starnu'tire]
faint	**svenimento** (m)	[zveni'mento]
to faint (vi)	**svenire** (vi)	[zve'nire]
bruise (hématome)	**livido** (m)	['livido]
bump (lump)	**bernoccolo** (m)	[ber'nokkolo]
to bang (bump)	**farsi un livido**	['farsi un 'livido]
contusion (bruise)	**contusione** (f)	[kontu'zjone]
to get a bruise	**farsi male**	['farsi 'male]
to limp (vi)	**zoppicare** (vi)	[dzoppi'kare]
dislocation	**slogatura** (f)	[zloga'tura]
to dislocate (vt)	**slogarsi** (vr)	[zlo'garsi]
fracture	**frattura** (f)	[frat'tura]
to have a fracture	**fratturarsi** (vr)	[frattu'rarsi]
cut (e.g., paper ~)	**taglio** (m)	['taʎʎo]
to cut oneself	**tagliarsi** (vr)	[taʎ'ʎarsi]
bleeding	**emorragia** (f)	[emorra'dʒia]
burn (injury)	**scottatura** (f)	[skotta'tura]
to get burned	**scottarsi** (vr)	[skot'tarsi]
to prick (vt)	**pungere** (vt)	['pundʒere]
to prick oneself	**pungersi** (vr)	['pundʒersi]
to injure (vt)	**ferire** (vt)	[fe'rire]
injury	**ferita** (f)	[fe'rita]
wound	**lesione** (f)	[le'zjone]
trauma	**trauma** (m)	['trauma]
to be delirious	**delirare** (vi)	[deli'rare]
to stutter (vi)	**tartagliare** (vi)	[tartaʎ'ʎare]
sunstroke	**colpo** (m) **di sole**	['kolpo di 'sole]

70. Symptoms. Treatments. Part 2

pain, ache	**dolore** (m), **male** (m)	[do'lore], ['male]
splinter (in foot, etc.)	**scheggia** (f)	['skedʒa]
sweat (perspiration)	**sudore** (m)	[su'dore]
to sweat (perspire)	**sudare** (vi)	[su'dare]
vomiting	**vomito** (m)	['vomito]
convulsions	**convulsioni** (f pl)	[konvul'sjoni]
pregnant (adj)	**incinta**	[in'tʃinta]
to be born	**nascere** (vi)	['naʃere]

delivery, labor	parto (m)	['parto]
to deliver (~ a baby)	essere in travaglio	['essere in tra'vaʎʎo]
abortion	aborto (m)	[a'borto]
breathing, respiration	respirazione (f)	[respira'tsjone]
in-breath (inhalation)	inspirazione (f)	[inspira'tsjone]
out-breath (exhalation)	espirazione (f)	[espira'tsjone]
to exhale (breathe out)	espirare (vi)	[espi'rare]
to inhale (vi)	inspirare (vi)	[inspi'rare]
disabled person	invalido (m)	[in'valido]
cripple	storpio (m)	['storpjo]
drug addict	battaglia (f)	[bat'taʎʎa]
deaf (adj)	sordo	['sordo]
mute (adj)	muto	['muto]
deaf mute (adj)	sordomuto	[sordo'muto]
mad, insane (adj)	matto	['matto]
madman (demented person)	matto (m)	['matto]
madwoman	matta (f)	['matta]
to go insane	impazzire (vi)	[impat'tsire]
gene	gene (m)	['dʒene]
immunity	immunità (f)	[immuni'ta]
hereditary (adj)	ereditario	[eredi'tario]
congenital (adj)	innato	[in'nato]
virus	virus (m)	['virus]
microbe	microbo (m)	['mikrobo]
bacterium	batterio (m)	[bat'terio]
infection	infezione (f)	[infe'tsjone]

71. Symptoms. Treatments. Part 3

hospital	ospedale (m)	[ospe'dale]
patient	paziente (m)	[pa'tsjente]
diagnosis	diagnosi (f)	[di'aɲozi]
cure	cura (f)	['kura]
medical treatment	trattamento (m)	[tratta'mento]
to get treatment	curarsi (vr)	[ku'rarsi]
to treat (~ a patient)	curare (vt)	[ku'rare]
to nurse (look after)	accudire	[akku'dire]
care (nursing ~)	assistenza (f)	[assi'stentsa]
operation, surgery	operazione (f)	[opera'tsjone]
to bandage (head, limb)	bendare (vt)	[ben'dare]
bandaging	fasciatura (f)	[faʃa'tura]

~ vaccination	**vaccinazione** (f)	[vatʃinaˈtsjone]
to vaccinate (vt)	**vaccinare** (vt)	[vatʃiˈnare]
injection, shot	**iniezione** (f)	[injeˈtsjone]
~ to give an injection	**fare una puntura**	[ˈfare ˈuna punˈtura]
Vaccino	*vaccine*	
attack	**attacco** (m)	[atˈtakko]
amputation	**amputazione** (f)	[amputaˈtsjone]
to amputate (vt)	**amputare** (vt)	[ampuˈtare]
coma	**coma** (m)	[ˈkoma]
~ to be in a coma	**essere in coma**	[ˈessere in ˈkoma]
~ intensive care	**rianimazione** (f)	[rianimaˈtsjone]
~ to recover (~ from flu)	**guarire** (vi)	[gwaˈrire]
condition (patient's ~)	**stato** (f)	[ˈstato]
consciousness	**conoscenza** (f)	[konoˈʃentsa]
memory (faculty)	**memoria** (f)	[meˈmoria]
to pull out (tooth)	**estrarre** (vt)	[eˈstrarre]
~ filling	**otturazione** (f)	[otturaˈtsjone]
to fill (a tooth)	**otturare** (vt)	[ottuˈrare]
hypnosis	**ipnosi** (f)	[ipˈnozi]
to hypnotize (vt)	**ipnotizzare** (vt)	[ipnotidˈdzare]

72. Doctors

doctor	**medico** (m)	[ˈmediko]
nurse	**infermiera** (f)	[inferˈmjera]
personal doctor	**medico** (m) **personale**	[ˈmediko persoˈnale]
dentist	**dentista** (m)	[denˈtista]
eye doctor	**oculista** (m)	[okuˈlista]
internist	**internista** (m)	[interˈnista]
~ surgeon	**chirurgo** (m)	[kiˈrurgo]
~ psychiatrist	**psichiatra** (m)	[psikiˈatra]
pediatrician	**pediatra** (m)	[pediˈatra]
psychologist	**psicologo** (m)	[psiˈkologo]
gynecologist	**ginecologo** (m)	[dʒineˈkologo]
cardiologist	**cardiologo** (m)	[karˈdjologo]

73. Medicine. Drugs. Accessories

medicine, drug	**medicina** (f)	[mediˈtʃina]
remedy	**rimedio** (m)	[riˈmedio]
⌐ to prescribe (vt)	**prescrivere** (vt)	[presˈkrivere]
prescription	**prescrizione** (f)	[preskriˈtsjone]
~ tablet, pill	**compressa** (f)	[komˈpressa]

ointment	unguento (m)	[un'gwento]
ampule	fiala (f)	[fi'ala]
mixture, solution	pozione (f)	[po'tsjone]
syrup	sciroppo (m)	[ʃi'roppo]
capsule	pillola (f)	['pillola]
powder	polverina (f)	[polve'rina]

gauze bandage	benda (f)	['benda]
cotton wool	ovatta (f)	[o'vatta]
iodine	iodio (m)	[i'odio]

Band-Aid	cerotto (m)	[tʃe'rotto]
eyedropper	contagocce (m)	[konta'gotʃe]
thermometer	termometro (m)	[ter'mometro]
syringe	siringa (f)	[si'ringa]

| wheelchair | sedia (f) a rotelle | ['sedia a ro'telle] |
| crutches | stampelle (f pl) | [stam'pelle] |

painkiller	analgesico (m)	[anal'dʒeziko]
laxative	lassativo (m)	[lassa'tivo]
spirits (ethanol)	alcol (m)	[al'kol]
medicinal herbs	erba (f) officinale	['erba offitʃi'nale]
herbal (~ tea)	d'erbe	['derbe]

74. Smoking. Tobacco products

tobacco	tabacco (m)	[ta'bakko]
cigarette	sigaretta (f)	[siga'retta]
cigar	sigaro (m)	['sigaro]
pipe	pipa (f)	['pipa]
pack (of cigarettes)	pacchetto (m)	[pak'ketto]

matches	fiammiferi (m pl)	[fjam'miferi]
matchbox	scatola (f) di fiammiferi	['skatola di fjam'miferi]
lighter	accendino (m)	[atʃen'dino]
ashtray	portacenere (m)	[porta·'tʃenere]
cigarette case	portasigarette (m)	[porta·siga'rette]

| cigarette holder | bocchino (m) | [bok'kino] |
| filter (cigarette tip) | filtro (m) | ['filtro] |

to smoke (vi, vt)	fumare (vi, vt)	[fu'mare]
to light a cigarette	accendere una sigaretta	[a'tʃendere 'una siga'retta]
smoking	fumo (m)	['fumo]
smoker	fumatore (m)	[fuma'tore]

stub, butt (of cigarette)	cicca (f)	['tʃikka]
smoke, fumes	fumo (m)	['fumo]
ash	cenere (f)	['tʃenere]

HUMAN HABITAT

City

75. City. Life in the city

city, town	**città** (f)	[tʃit'ta]
capital city	**capitale** (f)	[kapi'tale]
village	**villaggio** (m)	[vil'ladʒo]
city map	**mappa** (f) **della città**	['mappa 'della tʃit'ta]
downtown	**centro** (m) **della città**	['tʃentro 'della tʃit'ta]
suburb	**sobborgo** (m)	[sob'borgo]
suburban (adj)	**suburbano**	[subur'bano]
outskirts	**periferia** (f)	[perife'ria]
environs (suburbs)	**dintorni** (m pl)	[din'torni]
city block	**isolato** (m)	[izo'lato]
residential block (area)	**quartiere** (m) **residenziale**	[kwar'tjere rezidentsjale]
traffic	**traffico** (m)	['traffiko]
traffic lights	**semaforo** (m)	[se'maforo]
public transportation	**trasporti** (m pl) **urbani**	[tras'porti ur'bani]
intersection	**incrocio** (m)	[in'krotʃo]
crosswalk	**passaggio** (m) **pedonale**	[pas'sadʒo pedo'nale]
pedestrian underpass	**sottopassaggio** (m)	[sotto·pas'sadʒo]
to cross (~ the street)	**attraversare** (vt)	[attraver'sare]
pedestrian	**pedone** (m)	[pe'done]
sidewalk	**marciapiede** (m)	[martʃa'pjede]
bridge	**ponte** (m)	['ponte]
embankment (river walk)	**banchina** (f)	[baŋ'kina]
fountain	**fontana** (f)	[fon'tana]
allée (garden walkway)	**vialetto** (m)	[via'letto]
park	**parco** (m)	['parko]
boulevard	**boulevard** (m)	[bul'var]
square	**piazza** (f)	['pjattsa]
avenue (wide street)	**viale** (m), **corso** (m)	[vi'ale], ['korso]
street	**via** (f), **strada** (f)	['via], ['strada]
side street	**vicolo** (m)	['vikolo]
dead end	**vicolo** (m) **cieco**	['vikolo 'tʃjeko]
house	**casa** (f)	['kaza]

| building | edificio (m) | [edi'fitʃo] |
| skyscraper | grattacielo (m) | [gratta'tʃelo] |

facade	facciata (f)	[fa'tʃata]
roof	tetto (m)	['tetto]
window	finestra (f)	[fi'nestra]
arch	arco (m)	['arko]
column	colonna (f)	[ko'lonna]
corner	angolo (m)	['angolo]

store window	vetrina (f)	[ve'trina]
signboard (store sign, etc.)	insegna (f)	[in'seɲa]
poster (e.g., playbill)	cartellone (m)	[kartel'lone]
advertising poster	cartellone (m) pubblicitario	[kartel'lone pubblitʃi'tario]
billboard	tabellone (m) pubblicitario	[tabel'lone pubblitʃi'tario]

garbage, trash	pattume (m), spazzatura (f)	[pat'tume], [spattsa'tura]
trash can (public ~)	pattumiera (f)	[pattu'mjera]
to litter (vi)	sporcare (vi)	[spor'kare]
garbage dump	discarica (f) di rifiuti	[dis'karika di ri'fjuti]

phone booth	cabina (f) telefonica	[ka'bina tele'fonika]
lamppost	lampione (m)	[lam'pjone]
bench (park ~)	panchina (f)	[paŋ'kina]

police officer	poliziotto (m)	[poli'tsjotto]
police	polizia (f)	[poli'tsia]
beggar	mendicante (m)	[mendi'kante]
homeless (n)	barbone (m)	[bar'bone]

76. Urban institutions

store	negozio (m)	[ne'gotsio]
drugstore, pharmacy	farmacia (f)	[farma'tʃia]
eyeglass store	ottica (f)	['ottika]
shopping mall	centro (m) commerciale	['tʃentro kommer'tʃale]
supermarket	supermercato (m)	[supermer'kato]

bakery	panetteria (f)	[panette'ria]
baker	fornaio (m)	[for'najo]
pastry shop	pasticceria (f)	[pastitʃe'ria]
grocery store	drogheria (f)	[droge'ria]
butcher shop	macelleria (f)	[matʃelle'ria]

produce store	fruttivendolo (m)	[frutti'vendolo]
market	mercato (m)	[mer'kato]
coffee house	caffè (m)	[kaf'fe]
restaurant	ristorante (m)	[risto'rante]

pub, bar	**birreria** (f), **pub** (m)	[birre'ria], [pab]
pizzeria	**pizzeria** (f)	[pittse'ria]
hair salon	**salone** (m) **di parrucchiere**	[sa'lone di parruk'kjere]
post office	**ufficio** (m) **postale**	[uf'fitʃo po'stale]
dry cleaners	**lavanderia** (f) **a secco**	[lavande'ria a 'sekko]
photo studio	**studio** (m) **fotografico**	['studio foto'grafiko]
shoe store	**negozio** (m) **di scarpe**	[ne'gotsio di 'skarpe]
bookstore	**libreria** (f)	[libre'ria]
sporting goods store	**negozio** (m) **sportivo**	[ne'gotsio spor'tivo]
clothes repair shop	**riparazione** (f) **di abiti**	[ripara'tsjone di 'abiti]
formal wear rental	**noleggio** (m) **di abiti**	[no'ledʒo di 'abiti]
video rental store	**noleggio** (m) **di film**	[no'ledʒo di film]
circus	**circo** (m)	['tʃirko]
zoo	**zoo** (m)	['dzoo]
movie theater	**cinema** (m)	['tʃinema]
museum	**museo** (m)	[mu'zeo]
library	**biblioteca** (f)	[biblio'teka]
theater	**teatro** (m)	[te'atro]
opera (opera house)	**teatro** (m) **dell'opera**	[te'atro dell 'opera]
nightclub	**locale notturno** (m)	[lo'kale not'turno]
casino	**casinò** (m)	[kazi'no]
mosque	**moschea** (f)	[mos'kea]
synagogue	**sinagoga** (f)	[sina'goga]
cathedral	**cattedrale** (f)	[katte'drale]
temple	**tempio** (m)	['tempjo]
church	**chiesa** (f)	['kjeza]
college	**istituto** (m)	[isti'tuto]
university	**università** (f)	[universi'ta]
school	**scuola** (f)	['skwola]
prefecture	**prefettura** (f)	[prefet'tura]
city hall	**municipio** (m)	[muni'tʃipio]
hotel	**albergo** (m)	[al'bergo]
bank	**banca** (f)	['banka]
embassy	**ambasciata** (f)	[amba'ʃata]
travel agency	**agenzia** (f) **di viaggi**	[adʒen'tsia di 'vjadʒi]
information office	**ufficio** (m) **informazioni**	[uf'fitʃo informa'tsjoni]
currency exchange	**ufficio** (m) **dei cambi**	[uf'fitʃo dei 'kambi]
subway	**metropolitana** (f)	[metropoli'tana]
hospital	**ospedale** (m)	[ospe'dale]
gas station	**distributore** (m) **di benzina**	[distribu'tore di ben'dzina]
parking lot	**parcheggio** (m)	[par'kedʒo]

77. Urban transportation

bus	**autobus** (m)	['autobus]
streetcar	**tram** (m)	[tram]
trolley bus	**filobus** (m)	['filobus]
route (of bus, etc.)	**itinerario** (m)	[itine'rario]
number (e.g., bus ~)	**numero** (m)	['numero]
to go by …	**andare in …**	[an'dare in]
to get on (~ the bus)	**salire su …**	[sa'lire su]
to get off …	**scendere da …**	['ʃendere da]
stop (e.g., bus ~)	**fermata** (f)	[fer'mata]
next stop	**prossima fermata** (f)	['prossima fer'mata]
terminus	**capolinea** (m)	[kapo'linea]
schedule	**orario** (m)	[o'rario]
to wait (vt)	**aspettare** (vt)	[aspet'tare]
ticket	**biglietto** (m)	[biʎ'ʎetto]
fare	**prezzo** (m) **del biglietto**	['prettso del biʎ'ʎetto]
cashier (ticket seller)	**cassiere** (m)	[kas'sjere]
ticket inspection	**controllo** (m) **dei biglietti**	[kon'trollo dei biʎ'ʎeti]
ticket inspector	**bigliettaio** (m)	[biʎʎet'tajo]
to be late (for …)	**essere in ritardo**	['essere in ri'tardo]
to miss (~ the train, etc.)	**perdere** (vt)	['perdere]
to be in a hurry	**avere fretta**	[a'vere 'fretta]
taxi, cab	**taxi** (m)	['taksi]
taxi driver	**taxista** (m)	[ta'ksista]
by taxi	**in taxi**	[in 'taksi]
taxi stand	**parcheggio** (m) **di taxi**	[par'kedʒo di 'taksi]
to call a taxi	**chiamare un taxi**	[kja'mare un 'taksi]
to take a taxi	**prendere un taxi**	['prendere un 'taksi]
traffic	**traffico** (m)	['traffiko]
traffic jam	**ingorgo** (m)	[in'gorgo]
rush hour	**ore** (f pl) **di punta**	['ore di 'punta]
to park (vi)	**parcheggiarsi** (vr)	[parke'dʒarsi]
to park (vt)	**parcheggiare** (vt)	[parke'dʒare]
parking lot	**parcheggio** (m)	[par'kedʒo]
subway	**metropolitana** (f)	[metropoli'tana]
station	**stazione** (f)	[sta'tsjone]
to take the subway	**prendere la metropolitana**	['prendere la metropoli'tana]
train	**treno** (m)	['treno]
train station	**stazione** (f) **ferroviaria**	[sta'tsjone ferro'vjaria]

78. Sightseeing

monument	**monumento** (m)	[monu'mento]
fortress	**fortezza** (f)	[for'tettsa]
palace	**palazzo** (m)	[pa'lattso]
castle	**castello** (m)	[ka'stello]
tower	**torre** (f)	['torre]
mausoleum	**mausoleo** (m)	[mauzo'leo]
architecture	**architettura** (f)	[arkitet'tura]
medieval (adj)	**medievale**	[medje'vale]
ancient (adj)	**antico**	[an'tiko]
national (adj)	**nazionale**	[natsio'nale]
famous (monument, etc.)	**famoso**	[fa'mozo]
tourist	**turista** (m)	[tu'rista]
guide (person)	**guida** (f)	['gwida]
excursion, sightseeing tour	**escursione** (f)	[eskur'sjone]
to show (vt)	**fare vedere**	['fare ve'dere]
to tell (vt)	**raccontare** (vt)	[rakkon'tare]
to find (vt)	**trovare** (vt)	[tro'vare]
to get lost (lose one's way)	**perdersi** (vr)	['perdersi]
map (e.g., subway ~)	**mappa** (f)	['mappa]
map (e.g., city ~)	**piantina** (f)	[pjan'tina]
souvenir, gift	**souvenir** (m)	[suve'nir]
gift shop	**negozio** (m) **di articoli da regalo**	[ne'gotsio di ar'tikoli da re'galo]
to take pictures	**fare foto**	['fare 'foto]
to have one's picture taken	**fotografarsi**	[fotogra'farsi]

79. Shopping

to buy (purchase)	**comprare** (vt)	[kom'prare]
purchase	**acquisto** (m)	[a'kwisto]
to go shopping	**fare acquisti**	['fare a'kwisti]
shopping	**shopping** (m)	['ʃopping]
to be open (ab. store)	**essere aperto**	['essere a'perto]
to be closed	**essere chiuso**	['essere 'kjuzo]
footwear, shoes	**calzature** (f pl)	[kaltsa'ture]
clothes, clothing	**abbigliamento** (m)	[abbiʎʎa'mento]
cosmetics	**cosmetica** (f)	[ko'zmetika]
food products	**alimentari** (m pl)	[alimen'tari]
gift, present	**regalo** (m)	[re'galo]
salesman	**commesso** (m)	[kom'messo]
saleswoman	**commessa** (f)	[kom'messa]

check out, cash desk	cassa (f)	['kassa]
mirror	specchio (m)	['spekkio]
counter (store ~)	banco (m)	['banko]
fitting room	camerino (m)	[kame'rino]
to try on	provare (vt)	[pro'vare]
to fit (ab. dress, etc.)	stare bene	['stare 'bene]
to like (I like …)	piacere (vi)	[pja'tʃere]
price	prezzo (m)	['prettso]
price tag	etichetta (f) del prezzo	[eti'ketta del 'prettso]
to cost (vt)	costare (vt)	[ko'stare]
How much?	Quanto?	['kwanto]
discount	sconto (m)	['skonto]
inexpensive (adj)	no muy caro	[no muj 'karo]
cheap (adj)	a buon mercato	[a bu'on mer'kato]
expensive (adj)	caro	['karo]
It's expensive	È caro	[e 'karo]
rental (n)	noleggio (m)	[no'ledʒo]
to rent (~ a tuxedo)	noleggiare (vt)	[nole'dʒare]
credit (trade credit)	credito (m)	['kredito]
on credit (adv)	a credito	[a 'kredito]

80. Money

money	soldi (m pl)	['soldi]
currency exchange	cambio (m)	['kambio]
exchange rate	corso (m) di cambio	['korso di 'kambio]
ATM	bancomat (m)	['bankomat]
coin	moneta (f)	[mo'neta]
dollar	dollaro (m)	['dollaro]
euro	euro (m)	['euro]
lira	lira (f)	['lira]
Deutschmark	marco (m)	['marko]
franc	franco (m)	['franko]
pound sterling	sterlina (f)	[ster'lina]
yen	yen (m)	[jen]
debt	debito (m)	['debito]
debtor	debitore (m)	[debi'tore]
to lend (money)	prestare (vt)	[pre'stare]
to borrow (vi, vt)	prendere in prestito	['prendere in 'prestito]
bank	banca (f)	['banka]
account	conto (m)	['konto]
to deposit into the account	versare sul conto	[ver'sare sul 'konto]

to withdraw (vt)	**prelevare dal conto**	[prele'vare dal 'konto]
credit card	**carta** (f) **di credito**	['karta di 'kredito]
cash	**contanti** (m pl)	[kon'tanti]
check	**assegno** (m)	[as'seɲo]
to write a check	**emettere un assegno**	[e'mettere un as'seɲo]
checkbook	**libretto** (m) **di assegni**	[li'bretto di as'seɲi]
wallet	**portafoglio** (m)	[porta·'foʎʎo]
change purse	**borsellino** (m)	[borsel'lino]
safe	**cassaforte** (f)	[kassa'forte]
heir	**erede** (m)	[e'rede]
inheritance	**eredità** (f)	[eredi'ta]
fortune (wealth)	**fortuna** (f)	[for'tuna]
lease	**affitto** (m)	[af'fitto]
rent (money)	**affitto** (m)	[af'fitto]
to rent (sth from sb)	**affittare** (vt)	[affit'tare]
price	**prezzo** (m)	['prettso]
cost	**costo** (m), **prezzo** (m)	['kosto], ['prettso]
sum	**somma** (f)	['somma]
to spend (vt)	**spendere** (vt)	['spendere]
expenses	**spese** (f pl)	['speze]
to economize (vi, vt)	**economizzare** (vi, vt)	[ekonomid'dzare]
economical	**economico**	[eko'nomiko]
to pay (vi, vt)	**pagare** (vi, vt)	[pa'gare]
payment	**pagamento** (m)	[paga'mento]
change (give the ~)	**resto** (m)	['resto]
tax	**imposta** (f)	[im'posta]
fine	**multa** (f), **ammenda** (f)	['multa], [am'menda]
to fine (vt)	**multare** (vt)	[mul'tare]

81. Post. Postal service

post office	**posta** (f), **ufficio** (m) **postale**	['posta], [uf'fitʃo po'stale]
mail (letters, etc.)	**posta** (f)	['posta]
mailman	**postino** (m)	[po'stino]
opening hours	**orario** (m) **di apertura**	[o'rario di aper'tura]
letter	**lettera** (f)	['lettera]
registered letter	**raccomandata** (f)	[rakkoman'data]
postcard	**cartolina** (f)	[karto'lina]
telegram	**telegramma** (m)	[tele'gramma]
package (parcel)	**pacco** (m) **postale**	['pakko po'stale]
money transfer	**vaglia** (m) **postale**	['vaʎʎa po'stale]

to receive (vt)	ricevere (vt)	[ri'tʃevere]
to send (vt)	spedire (vt)	[spe'dire]
sending	invio (m)	[in'vio]
address	indirizzo (m)	[indi'rittso]
ZIP code	codice (m) postale	['koditʃe po'stale]
sender	mittente (m)	[mit'tente]
receiver	destinatario (m)	[destina'tario]
name (first name)	nome (m)	['nome]
surname (last name)	cognome (m)	[ko'ɲome]
postage rate	tariffa (f)	[ta'riffa]
standard (adj)	ordinario	[ordi'nario]
economical (adj)	standard	['standar]
weight	peso (m)	['pezo]
to weigh (~ letters)	pesare (vt)	[pe'zare]
envelope	busta (f)	['busta]
postage stamp	francobollo (m)	[franko'bollo]

Dwelling. House. Home

82. House. Dwelling

house	**casa** (f)	['kaza]
at home (adv)	**a casa**	[a 'kaza]
yard	**cortile** (m)	[kor'tile]
fence (iron ~)	**recinto** (m)	[re'tʃinto]
brick (n)	**mattone** (m)	[mat'tone]
brick (as adj)	**di mattoni**	[di mat'toni]
stone (n)	**pietra** (f)	['pjetra]
stone (as adj)	**di pietra**	[di 'pjetra]
concrete (n)	**beton** (m)	[be'ton]
concrete (as adj)	**di beton**	[di be'ton]
new (new-built)	**nuovo**	[nu'ovo]
old (adj)	**vecchio**	['vekkio]
decrepit (house)	**fatiscente**	[fati'ʃente]
modern (adj)	**moderno**	[mo'derno]
multistory (adj)	**a molti piani**	[a 'molti 'pjani]
tall (~ building)	**alto**	['alto]
floor, story	**piano** (m)	['pjano]
single-story (adj)	**di un piano**	[di un 'pjano]
1st floor	**pianoterra** (m)	[pjano'terra]
top floor	**ultimo piano** (m)	['ultimo 'pjano]
roof	**tetto** (m)	['tetto]
chimney	**ciminiera** (f)	[tʃimi'njera]
roof tiles	**tegola** (f)	['tegola]
tiled (adj)	**di tegole**	[di 'tegole]
attic (storage place)	**soffitta** (f)	[sof'fitta]
window	**finestra** (f)	[fi'nestra]
glass	**vetro** (m)	['vetro]
window ledge	**davanzale** (m)	[davan'tsale]
shutters	**imposte** (f pl)	[im'poste]
wall	**muro** (m)	['muro]
balcony	**balcone** (m)	[bal'kone]
downspout	**tubo** (m) **pluviale**	['tubo plu'vjale]
upstairs (to be ~)	**su, di sopra**	[su], [di 'sopra]
to go upstairs	**andare di sopra**	[an'dare di 'sopra]

| to come down (the stairs) | scendere (vi) | ['ʃendere] |
| to move (to new premises) | trasferirsi (vr) | [trasfe'rirsi] |

83. House. Entrance. Lift

entrance	entrata (f)	[en'trata]
stairs (stairway)	scala (f)	['skala]
steps	gradini (m pl)	[gra'dini]
banister	ringhiera (f)	[rin'gjera]
lobby (hotel ~)	hall (f)	[oll]
mailbox	cassetta (f) della posta	[kas'setta 'della 'posta]
garbage can	secchio (m) della spazzatura	['sekkio 'della spattsa'tura]
trash chute	scivolo (m) per la spazzatura	['ʃivolo per la spattsa'tura]
elevator	ascensore (m)	[aʃen'sore]
freight elevator	montacarichi (m)	[monta'kariki]
elevator cage	cabina (f) di ascensore	[ka'bina de aʃen'sore]
to take the elevator	prendere l'ascensore	['prendere laʃen'sore]
apartment	appartamento (m)	[apparta'mento]
residents (~ of a building)	inquilini (m pl)	[inkwi'lini]
neighbor (masc.)	vicino (m)	[vi'tʃino]
neighbor (fem.)	vicina (f)	[vi'tʃina]
neighbors	vicini (m pl)	[vi'tʃini]

84. House. Doors. Locks

door	porta (f)	['porta]
gate (vehicle ~)	cancello (m)	[kan'tʃello]
handle, doorknob	maniglia (f)	[ma'niʎʎa]
to unlock (unbolt)	togliere il catenaccio	['toʎʎere il kate'natʃo]
to open (vt)	aprire (vt)	[a'prire]
to close (vt)	chiudere (vt)	['kjudere]
key	chiave (f)	['kjave]
bunch (of keys)	mazzo (m)	['mattso]
to creak (door, etc.)	cigolare (vi)	[tʃigo'lare]
creak	cigolio (m)	[tʃigo'lio]
hinge (door ~)	cardine (m)	['kardine]
doormat	zerbino (m)	[dzer'bino]
door lock	serratura (f)	[serra'tura]
keyhole	buco (m) della serratura	['buko 'della serra'tura]
crossbar (sliding bar)	chiavistello (m)	[kjavi'stello]
door latch	catenaccio (m)	[kate'natʃo]

padlock	lucchetto (m)	[luk'ketto]
to ring (~ the door bell)	suonare (vt)	[suo'nare]
ringing (sound)	suono (m)	[su'ono]
doorbell	campanello (m)	[kampa'nello]
doorbell button	pulsante (m)	[pul'sante]
knock (at the door)	bussata (f)	[bus'sata]
to knock (vi)	bussare (vi)	[bus'sare]

code	codice (m)	['koditʃe]
combination lock	serratura (f) a codice	[serra'tura a 'koditʃe]
intercom	citofono (m)	[tʃi'tofono]
number (on the door)	numero (m)	['numero]
doorplate	targhetta (f)	[tar'getta]
peephole	spioncino (m)	[spion'tʃino]

85. Country house

village	villaggio (m)	[vil'ladʒo]
vegetable garden	orto (m)	['orto]
fence	recinto (m)	[re'tʃinto]
picket fence	steccato (m)	[stek'kato]
wicket gate	cancelletto (m)	[kantʃel'letto]

granary	granaio (m)	[gra'najo]
root cellar	cantina (f), scantinato (m)	[kan'tina], [skanti'nato]
shed (garden ~)	capanno (m)	[ka'panno]
water well	pozzo (m)	['pottso]

stove (wood-fired ~)	stufa (f)	['stufa]
to stoke the stove	attizzare (vt)	[attid'dzare]
firewood	legna (f) da ardere	['leɲa da 'ardere]
log (firewood)	ciocco (m)	['tʃokko]

veranda	veranda (f)	[ve'randa]
deck (terrace)	terrazza (f)	[ter'rattsa]
stoop (front steps)	scala (f) d'ingresso	['skala din'gresso]
swing (hanging seat)	altalena (f)	[alta'lena]

86. Castle. Palace

castle	castello (m)	[ka'stello]
palace	palazzo (m)	[pa'lattso]
fortress	fortezza (f)	[for'tettsa]

wall (round castle)	muro (m)	['muro]
tower	torre (f)	['torre]
keep, donjon	torre (f) principale	['torre printʃi'pale]
portcullis	saracinesca (f)	[saratʃi'neska]

underground passage	tunnel (m)	['tunnel]
moat	fossato (m)	[fos'sato]
chain	catena (f)	[ka'tena]
arrow loop	feritoia (f)	[feri'toja]

magnificent (adj)	magnifico	[ma'ɲifiko]
majestic (adj)	maestoso	[mae'stozo]
impregnable (adj)	inespugnabile	[inespu'ɲabile]
medieval (adj)	medievale	[medje'vale]

87. Apartment

apartment	appartamento (m)	[apparta'mento]
room	camera (f), stanza (f)	['kamera], ['stantsa]
bedroom	camera (f) da letto	['kamera da 'letto]
dining room	sala (f) da pranzo	['sala da 'prantso]
living room	salotto (m)	[sa'lotto]
study (home office)	studio (m)	['studio]

entry room	ingresso (m)	[in'gresso]
bathroom (room with a bath or shower)	bagno (m)	['baɲo]
half bath	gabinetto (m)	[gabi'netto]

ceiling	soffitto (m)	[sof'fitto]
floor	pavimento (m)	[pavi'mento]
corner	angolo (m)	['angolo]

88. Apartment. Cleaning

to clean (vi, vt)	pulire (vt)	[pu'lire]
to put away (to stow)	mettere via	['mettere 'via]
dust	polvere (f)	['polvere]
dusty (adj)	impolverato	[impolve'rato]
to dust (vt)	spolverare (vt)	[spolve'rare]
vacuum cleaner	aspirapolvere (m)	[aspira·'polvere]
to vacuum (vt)	passare l'aspirapolvere	[pas'sare laspira·'polvere]

to sweep (vi, vt)	spazzare (vi, vt)	[spat'tsare]
sweepings	spazzatura (f)	[spattsa'tura]

order	ordine (m)	['ordine]
disorder, mess	disordine (m)	[di'sordine]

mop	frettazzo (m)	[fret'tattso]
dust cloth	strofinaccio (m)	[strofi'natʃo]
short broom	scopa (f)	['skopa]
dustpan	paletta (f)	[pa'letta]

89. Furniture. Interior

furniture	mobili (m pl)	['mobili]
table	tavolo (m)	['tavolo]
chair	sedia (f)	['sedia]
bed	letto (m)	['letto]
couch, sofa	divano (m)	[di'vano]
armchair	poltrona (f)	[pol'trona]
bookcase	libreria (f)	[libre'ria]
shelf	ripiano (m)	[ri'pjano]
wardrobe	armadio (m)	[ar'madio]
coat rack (wall-mounted ~)	attaccapanni (m) da parete	[attakka'panni da pa'rete]
coat stand	appendiabiti (m) da terra	[apen'djabiti da terra]
bureau, dresser	comò (m)	[ko'mo]
coffee table	tavolino (m) da salotto	[tavo'lina da sa'lotto]
mirror	specchio (m)	['spekkio]
carpet	tappeto (m)	[tap'peto]
rug, small carpet	tappetino (m)	[tappe'tino]
fireplace	camino (m)	[ka'mino]
candle	candela (f)	[kan'dela]
candlestick	candeliere (m)	[kande'ljere]
drapes	tende (f pl)	['tende]
wallpaper	carta (f) da parati	['karta da pa'rati]
blinds (jalousie)	tende (f pl) alla veneziana	['tende alla vene'tsjana]
table lamp	lampada (f) da tavolo	['lampada da 'tavolo]
wall lamp (sconce)	lampada (f) da parete	['lampada da pa'rete]
floor lamp	lampada (f) a stelo	['lampada a 'stelo]
chandelier	lampadario (m)	[lampa'dario]
leg (of chair, table)	gamba (f)	['gamba]
armrest	bracciolo (m)	['bratʃolo]
back (backrest)	spalliera (f)	[spal'ljera]
drawer	cassetto (m)	[kas'setto]

90. Bedding

bedclothes	biancheria (f) da letto	[bjanke'ria da 'letto]
pillow	cuscino (m)	[ku'ʃino]
pillowcase	federa (f)	['federa]
duvet, comforter	coperta (f)	[ko'perta]
sheet	lenzuolo (m)	[lentsu'olo]
bedspread	copriletto (m)	[kopri'letto]

91. Kitchen

kitchen	cucina (f)	[ku'tʃina]
gas	gas (m)	[gas]
gas stove (range)	fornello (m) a gas	[for'nello a gas]
electric stove	fornello (m) elettrico	[for'nello e'lettriko]
oven	forno (m)	['forno]
microwave oven	forno (m) a microonde	['forno a mikro'onde]
refrigerator	frigorifero (m)	[frigo'rifero]
freezer	congelatore (m)	[kondʒela'tore]
dishwasher	lavastoviglie (f)	[lavasto'viʎʎe]
meat grinder	tritacarne (m)	[trita'karne]
juicer	spremifrutta (m)	[spremi'frutta]
toaster	tostapane (m)	[tosta'pane]
mixer	mixer (m)	['mikser]
coffee machine	macchina (f) da caffè	['makkina da kaf'fe]
coffee pot	caffettiera (f)	[kaffet'tjera]
coffee grinder	macinacaffè (m)	[matʃinakaf'fe]
kettle	bollitore (m)	[bolli'tore]
teapot	teiera (f)	[te'jera]
lid	coperchio (m)	[ko'perkio]
tea strainer	colino (m) da tè	[ko'lino da te]
spoon	cucchiaio (m)	[kuk'kjajo]
teaspoon	cucchiaino (m) da tè	[kuk'kjajno da 'te]
soup spoon	cucchiaio (m)	[kuk'kjajo]
fork	forchetta (f)	[for'ketta]
knife	coltello (m)	[kol'tello]
tableware (dishes)	stoviglie (f pl)	[sto'viʎʎe]
plate (dinner ~)	piatto (m)	['pjatto]
saucer	piattino (m)	[pjat'tino]
shot glass	cicchetto (m)	[tʃik'ketto]
glass (tumbler)	bicchiere (m)	[bik'kjere]
cup	tazzina (f)	[tat'tsina]
sugar bowl	zuccheriera (f)	[dzukke'rjera]
salt shaker	saliera (f)	[sa'ljera]
pepper shaker	pepiera (f)	[pe'pjera]
butter dish	burriera (f)	[bur'rjera]
stock pot (soup pot)	pentola (f)	['pentola]
frying pan (skillet)	padella (f)	[pa'della]
ladle	mestolo (m)	['mestolo]
colander	colapasta (m)	[kola'pasta]
tray (serving ~)	vassoio (m)	[vas'sojo]

bottle	**bottiglia** (f)	[bot'tiʎʎa]
jar (glass)	**barattolo** (m) **di vetro**	[ba'rattolo di 'vetro]
can	**latta** (f), **lattina** (f)	['latta], [lat'tina]
bottle opener	**apribottiglie** (m)	[apribot'tiʎʎe]
can opener	**apriscatole** (m)	[apri'skatole]
corkscrew	**cavatappi** (m)	[kava'tappi]
filter	**filtro** (m)	['filtro]
to filter (vt)	**filtrare** (vt)	[fil'trare]
trash, garbage (food waste, etc.)	**spazzatura** (f)	[spattsa'tura]
trash can (kitchen ~)	**pattumiera** (f)	[pattu'mjera]

92. Bathroom

bathroom	**bagno** (m)	['baɲo]
water	**acqua** (f)	['akwa]
faucet	**rubinetto** (m)	[rubi'netto]
hot water	**acqua** (f) **calda**	['akwa 'kalda]
cold water	**acqua** (f) **fredda**	['akwa 'fredda]
toothpaste	**dentifricio** (m)	[denti'fritʃo]
to brush one's teeth	**lavarsi i denti**	[la'varsi i 'denti]
toothbrush	**spazzolino** (m) **da denti**	[spatso'lino da 'denti]
to shave (vi)	**rasarsi** (vr)	[ra'zarsi]
shaving foam	**schiuma** (f) **da barba**	['skjuma da 'barba]
razor	**rasoio** (m)	[ra'zojo]
to wash (one's hands, etc.)	**lavare** (vt)	[la'vare]
to take a bath	**fare un bagno**	['fare un 'baɲo]
shower	**doccia** (f)	['dotʃa]
to take a shower	**fare una doccia**	['fare 'una 'dotʃa]
bathtub	**vasca** (f) **da bagno**	['vaska da 'baɲo]
toilet (toilet bowl)	**water** (m)	['vater]
sink (washbasin)	**lavandino** (m)	[lavan'dino]
soap	**sapone** (m)	[sa'pone]
soap dish	**porta** (m) **sapone**	['porta sa'pone]
sponge	**spugna** (f)	['spuɲa]
shampoo	**shampoo** (m)	['ʃampo]
towel	**asciugamano** (m)	[aʃuga'mano]
bathrobe	**accappatoio** (m)	[akkappa'tojo]
laundry (laundering)	**bucato** (m)	[bu'kato]
washing machine	**lavatrice** (f)	[lava'tritʃe]
to do the laundry	**fare il bucato**	['fare il bu'kato]

laundry detergent	detersivo (m) per il bucato	[deter'sivo per il bu'kato]

93. Household appliances

TV set	televisore (m)	[televi'zore]
tape recorder	registratore (m) a nastro	[redʒistra'tore a 'nastro]
VCR (video recorder)	videoregistratore (m)	[video·redʒistra'tore]
radio	radio (f)	['radio]
player (CD, MP3, etc.)	lettore (m)	[let'tore]

video projector	videoproiettore (m)	[video·projet'tore]
home movie theater	home cinema (m)	['om 'tʃinema]
DVD player	lettore (m) DVD	[let'tore divu'di]
amplifier	amplificatore (m)	[amplifika'tore]
video game console	console (f) video giochi	['konsole 'video 'dʒoki]

video camera	videocamera (f)	[video·'kamera]
camera (photo)	macchina (f) fotografica	['makkina foto'grafika]
digital camera	fotocamera (f) digitale	[foto'kamera didʒi'tale]

vacuum cleaner	aspirapolvere (m)	[aspira·'polvere]
iron (e.g., steam ~)	ferro (m) da stiro	['ferro da 'stiro]
ironing board	asse (f) da stiro	['asse da 'stiro]

telephone	telefono (m)	[te'lefono]
cell phone	telefonino (m)	[telefo'nino]
typewriter	macchina (f) da scrivere	['makkina da 'skrivere]
sewing machine	macchina (f) da cucire	['makkina da ku'tʃire]

microphone	microfono (m)	[mi'krofono]
headphones	cuffia (f)	['kuffia]
remote control (TV)	telecomando (m)	[teleko'mando]

CD, compact disc	CD (m)	[tʃi'di]
cassette, tape	cassetta (f)	[kas'setta]
vinyl record	disco (m)	['disko]

94. Repairs. Renovation

renovations	lavori (m pl) di restauro	[la'vori di re'stauro]
to renovate (vt)	rinnovare (vt)	[rinno'vare]
to repair, to fix (vt)	riparare (vt)	[ripa'rare]
to put in order	mettere in ordine	['mettere in 'ordine]
to redo (do again)	rifare (vt)	[ri'fare]

paint	vernice (f), pittura (f)	[ver'nitʃe], [pit'tura]
to paint (~ a wall)	pitturare (vt)	[pittu'rare]

house painter	**imbianchino** (m)	[imbjaŋ'kino]
paintbrush	**pennello** (m)	[pen'nello]
whitewash	**imbiancatura** (f)	[imbjanka'tura]
to whitewash (vt)	**imbiancare** (vt)	[imbjan'kare]
wallpaper	**carta** (f) **da parati**	['karta da pa'rati]
to wallpaper (vt)	**tappezzare** (vt)	[tappet'tsare]
varnish	**vernice** (f)	[ver'nitʃe]
to varnish (vt)	**verniciare** (vt)	[verni'tʃare]

95. Plumbing

water	**acqua** (f)	['akwa]
hot water	**acqua** (f) **calda**	['akwa 'kalda]
cold water	**acqua** (f) **fredda**	['akwa 'fredda]
faucet	**rubinetto** (m)	[rubi'netto]
drop (of water)	**goccia** (f)	['gotʃa]
to drip (vi)	**gocciolare** (vi)	[gotʃo'lare]
to leak (ab. pipe)	**perdere** (vi)	['perdere]
leak (pipe ~)	**perdita** (f)	['perdita]
puddle	**pozza** (f)	['pottsa]
pipe	**tubo** (m)	['tubo]
valve (e.g., ball ~)	**valvola** (f)	['valvola]
to be clogged up	**intasarsi** (vr)	[inta'zarsi]
tools	**strumenti** (m pl)	[stru'menti]
adjustable wrench	**chiave** (f) **inglese**	['kjave in'gleze]
to unscrew (lid, filter, etc.)	**svitare** (vt)	[zvi'tare]
to screw (tighten)	**avvitare** (vt)	[avvi'tare]
to unclog (vt)	**stasare** (vt)	[sta'zare]
plumber	**idraulico** (m)	[i'drauliko]
basement	**seminterrato** (m)	[seminter'rato]
sewerage (system)	**fognatura** (f)	[foɲa'tura]

96. Fire. Conflagration

fire (accident)	**fuoco** (m)	[fu'oko]
flame	**fiamma** (f)	['fjamma]
spark	**scintilla** (f)	[ʃin'tilla]
smoke (from fire)	**fumo** (m)	['fumo]
torch (flaming stick)	**fiaccola** (f)	['fjakkola]
campfire	**falò** (m)	[fa'lo]
gas, gasoline	**benzina** (f)	[ben'dzina]
kerosene (type of fuel)	**cherosene** (m)	[kero'zene]

flammable (adj)	combustibile	[kombu'stibile]
explosive (adj)	esplosivo	[esplo'zivo]
NO SMOKING	VIETATO FUMARE!	[vje'tato fu'mare]

safety	sicurezza (f)	[siku'rettsa]
danger	pericolo (m)	[pe'rikolo]
dangerous (adj)	pericoloso	[periko'lozo]

to catch fire	prendere fuoco	['prendere fu'oko]
explosion	esplosione (f)	[esplo'zjone]
to set fire	incendiare (vt)	[intʃen'djare]
arsonist	incendiario (m)	[intʃen'djario]
arson	incendio (m) doloso	[in'tʃendio do'lozo]

to blaze (vi)	divampare (vi)	[divam'pare]
to burn (be on fire)	bruciare (vi)	[bru'tʃare]
to burn down	bruciarsi (vr)	[bru'tʃarsi]

to call the fire department	chiamare i pompieri	[kja'mare i pom'pjeri]
firefighter, fireman	pompiere (m)	[pom'pjere]
fire truck	autopompa (f)	[auto'pompa]
fire department	corpo (m) dei pompieri	['korpo dei pom'pjeri]
fire truck ladder	autoscala (f) da pompieri	[auto'skala da pom'pjeri]

fire hose	manichetta (f)	[mani'ketta]
fire extinguisher	estintore (m)	[estin'tore]
helmet	casco (m)	['kasko]
siren	sirena (f)	[si'rena]

to cry (for help)	gridare (vi)	[gri'dare]
to call for help	chiamare in aiuto	[kja'mare in a'juto]
rescuer	soccorritore (m)	[sokkorri'tore]
to rescue (vt)	salvare (vt)	[sal'vare]

to arrive (vi)	arrivare (vi)	[arri'vare]
to extinguish (vt)	spegnere (vt)	['speɲere]
water	acqua (f)	['akwa]
sand	sabbia (f)	['sabbia]

ruins (destruction)	rovine (f pl)	[ro'vine]
to collapse (building, etc.)	crollare (vi)	[krol'lare]
to fall down (vi)	cadere (vi)	[ka'dere]
to cave in (ceiling, floor)	collassare (vi)	[kolla'sare]

| piece of debris | frammento (m) | [fram'mento] |
| ash | cenere (f) | ['tʃenere] |

| to suffocate (die) | asfissiare (vi) | [asfis'sjare] |
| to be killed (perish) | morire, perire (vi) | [mo'rire], [pe'rire] |

HUMAN ACTIVITIES

Job. Business. Part 1

97. Banking

bank	banca (f)	['banka]
branch (of bank, etc.)	filiale (f)	[fi'ljale]
bank clerk, consultant	consulente (m)	[konsu'lente]
manager (director)	direttore (m)	[diret'tore]
bank account	conto (m) bancario	['konto ban'kario]
account number	numero (m) del conto	['numero del 'konto]
checking account	conto (m) corrente	['konto kor'rente]
savings account	conto (m) di risparmio	['konto di ris'parmio]
to open an account	aprire un conto	[a'prire un 'konto]
to close the account	chiudere il conto	['kjudere il 'konto]
to deposit into the account	versare sul conto	[ver'sare sul 'konto]
to withdraw (vt)	prelevare dal conto	[prele'vare dal 'konto]
deposit	deposito (m)	[de'pozito]
to make a deposit	depositare (vt)	[depozi'tare]
wire transfer	trasferimento (m) telegrafico	[trasferi'mento tele'grafiko]
to wire, to transfer	rimettere i soldi	[ri'mettere i 'soldi]
sum	somma (f)	['somma]
How much?	Quanto?	['kwanto]
signature	firma (f)	['firma]
to sign (vt)	firmare (vt)	[fir'mare]
credit card	carta (f) di credito	['karta di 'kredito]
code (PIN code)	codice (m)	['koditʃe]
credit card number	numero (m) della carta di credito	['numero 'della 'karta di 'kredito]
ATM	bancomat (m)	['bankomat]
check	assegno (m)	[as'seɲo]
to write a check	emettere un assegno	[e'mettere un as'seɲo]
checkbook	libretto (m) di assegni	[li'bretto di as'seɲi]
loan (bank ~)	prestito (m)	['prestito]
to apply for a loan	fare domanda per un prestito	['fare do'manda per un 'prestito]

to get a loan	ottenere un prestito	[otte'nere un 'prestito]
to give a loan	concedere un prestito	[kon'tʃedere un 'prestito]
guarantee	garanzia (f)	[garan'tsia]

98. Telephone. Phone conversation

telephone	telefono (m)	[te'lefono]
cell phone	telefonino (m)	[telefo'nino]
answering machine	segreteria (f) telefonica	[segrete'ria tele'fonika]
to call (by phone)	telefonare (vi, vt)	[telefo'nare]
phone call	chiamata (f)	[kja'mata]
to dial a number	comporre un numero	[kom'porre un 'numero]
Hello!	Pronto!	['pronto]
to ask (vt)	chiedere, domandare	['kjedere], [doman'dare]
to answer (vi, vt)	rispondere (vi, vt)	[ris'pondere]
to hear (vt)	udire, sentire (vt)	[u'dire], [sen'tire]
well (adv)	bene	['bene]
not well (adv)	male	['male]
noises (interference)	disturbi (m pl)	[di'sturbi]
receiver	cornetta (f)	[kor'netta]
to pick up (~ the phone)	alzare la cornetta	[al'tsare la kor'netta]
to hang up (~ the phone)	riattaccare la cornetta	[riattak'kare la kor'netta]
busy (engaged)	occupato	[okku'pato]
to ring (ab. phone)	squillare (vi)	[skwil'lare]
telephone book	elenco (m) telefonico	[e'lenko tele'foniko]
local (adj)	locale	[lo'kale]
local call	chiamata (f) locale	[kja'mata lo'kale]
long distance (~ call)	interurbano	[interur'bano]
long-distance call	chiamata (f) interurbana	[kja'mata interur'bana]
international (adj)	internazionale	[internatsjo'nale]
international call	chiamata (f) internazionale	[kja'mata internatsjo'nale]

99. Cell phone

cell phone	telefonino (m)	[telefo'nino]
display	schermo (m)	['skermo]
button	tasto (m)	['tasto]
SIM card	scheda SIM (f)	['skeda 'sim]
battery	pila (f)	['pila]
to be dead (battery)	essere scarico	['essere 'skariko]

charger	caricabatteria (m)	[karika·batte'ria]
menu	menù (m)	[me'nu]
settings	impostazioni (f pl)	[imposta'tsjoni]
tune (melody)	melodia (f)	[melo'dia]
to select (vt)	scegliere (vt)	['ʃeʎʎere]

calculator	calcolatrice (f)	[kalkola'tritʃe]
voice mail	segreteria (f) telefonica	[segre'tria tele'fonika]
alarm clock	sveglia (f)	['zveʎʎa]
contacts	contatti (m pl)	[kon'tatti]

SMS (text message)	messaggio (m) SMS	[mes'sadʒo ese'mese]
subscriber	abbonato (m)	[abbo'nato]

100. Stationery

ballpoint pen	penna (f) a sfera	[penna a 'sfera]
fountain pen	penna (f) stilografica	['penna stilo'grafika]

pencil	matita (f)	[ma'tita]
highlighter	evidenziatore (m)	[evidentsja'tore]
felt-tip pen	pennarello (m)	[penna'rello]

notepad	taccuino (m)	[tak'kwino]
agenda (diary)	agenda (f)	[a'dʒenda]

ruler	righello (m)	[ri'gello]
calculator	calcolatrice (f)	[kalkola'tritʃe]
eraser	gomma (f) per cancellare	['gomma per kantʃel'lare]
thumbtack	puntina (f)	[pun'tina]
paper clip	graffetta (f)	[graf'fetta]

glue	colla (f)	['kolla]
stapler	pinzatrice (f)	[pintsa'tritʃe]
hole punch	perforatrice (f)	[perfora'tritʃe]
pencil sharpener	temperamatite (m)	[temperama'tite]

Job. Business. Part 2

101. Mass Media

newspaper	giornale (m)	[dʒor'nale]
magazine	rivista (f)	[ri'vista]
press (printed media)	stampa (f)	['stampa]
radio	radio (f)	['radio]
radio station	stazione (f) radio	[sta'tsjone 'radio]
television	televisione (f)	[televi'zjone]

presenter, host	presentatore (m)	[prezenta'tore]
newscaster	annunciatore (m)	[annuntʃa'tore]
commentator	commentatore (m)	[kommenta'tore]

journalist	giornalista (m)	[dʒorna'lista]
correspondent (reporter)	corrispondente (m)	[korrispon'dente]
press photographer	fotocronista (m)	[fotokro'nista]
reporter	cronista (m)	[kro'nista]

editor	redattore (m)	[redat'tore]
editor-in-chief	redattore capo (m)	[redat'tore 'kapo]

to subscribe (to ...)	abbonarsi a ...	[abbo'narsi]
subscription	abbonamento (m)	[abbona'mento]
subscriber	abbonato (m)	[abbo'nato]
to read (vi, vt)	leggere (vi, vt)	['ledʒere]
reader	lettore (m)	[let'tore]

circulation (of newspaper)	tiratura (f)	[tira'tura]
monthly (adj)	mensile	[men'sile]
weekly (adj)	settimanale	[settima'nale]
issue (edition)	numero (m)	['numero]
new (~ issue)	fresco (m)	['fresko]

headline	testata (f)	[te'stata]
short article	trafiletto (m)	[trafi'letto]
column (regular article)	rubrica (f)	[ru'brika]
article	articolo (m)	[ar'tikolo]
page	pagina (f)	['padʒina]

reportage, report	servizio (m)	[ser'vitsio]
event (happening)	evento (m)	[e'vento]
sensation (news)	sensazione (f)	[sensa'tsjone]
scandal	scandalo (m)	['skandalo]
scandalous (adj)	scandaloso	[skanda'lozo]

great (~ scandal)	enorme, grande	[e'norme], ['grande]
show (e.g., cooking ~)	trasmissione (f)	[trazmis'sjone]
interview	intervista (f)	[inter'vista]
live broadcast	trasmissione (f) in diretta	[trazmis'sjone in di'retta]
channel	canale (m)	[ka'nale]

102. Agriculture

agriculture	agricoltura (f)	[agrikol'tura]
peasant (masc.)	contadino (m)	[konta'dino]
peasant (fem.)	contadina (f)	[konta'dina]
farmer	fattore (m)	[fat'tore]
tractor (farm ~)	trattore (m)	[trat'tore]
combine, harvester	mietitrebbia (f)	[mjeti'trebbia]
plow	aratro (m)	[a'ratro]
to plow (vi, vt)	arare (vt)	[a'rare]
plowland	terreno (m) coltivato	[ter'reno kolti'vato]
furrow (in field)	solco (m)	['solko]
to sow (vi, vt)	seminare (vt)	[semi'nare]
seeder	seminatrice (f)	[semina'tritʃe]
sowing (process)	semina (f)	['semina]
scythe	falce (f)	['faltʃe]
to mow, to scythe	falciare (vt)	[fal'tʃare]
spade (tool)	pala (f)	['pala]
to till (vt)	scavare (vt)	[ska'vare]
hoe	zappa (f)	['tsappa]
to hoe, to weed	zappare (vt)	[tsap'pare]
weed (plant)	erbaccia (f)	[er'batʃa]
watering can	innaffiatoio (m)	[innaffja'tojo]
to water (plants)	innaffiare (vt)	[innaf'fjare]
watering (act)	innaffiamento (m)	[innaffja'mento]
pitchfork	forca (f)	['forka]
rake	rastrello (m)	[ra'strello]
fertilizer	concime (m)	[kon'tʃime]
to fertilize (vt)	concimare (vt)	[kontʃi'mare]
manure (fertilizer)	letame (m)	[le'tame]
field	campo (m)	['kampo]
meadow	prato (m)	['prato]
vegetable garden	orto (m)	['orto]
orchard (e.g., apple ~)	frutteto (m)	[frut'teto]

to graze (vt)	pascolare (vt)	[pasko'lare]
herder (herdsman)	pastore (m)	[pa'store]
pasture	pascolo (m)	['paskolo]

| cattle breeding | allevamento (m) di bestiame | [alleva'mento di bes'tjame] |
| sheep farming | allevamento (m) di pecore | [alleva'mento di 'pekore] |

plantation	piantagione (f)	[pjanta'dʒone]
row (garden bed ~s)	filare (m)	[fi'lare]
hothouse	serra (f) da orto	['serra da 'orto]

| drought (lack of rain) | siccità (f) | [sitʃi'ta] |
| dry (~ summer) | secco, arido | ['sekko], ['arrido] |

| cereal crops | cereali (m pl) | [tʃere'ali] |
| to harvest, to gather | raccogliere (vt) | [rak'koʎʎere] |

miller (person)	mugnaio (m)	[mu'ɲajo]
mill (e.g., gristmill)	mulino (m)	[mu'lino]
to grind (grain)	macinare (vt)	[matʃi'nare]
flour	farina (f)	[fa'rina]
straw	paglia (f)	['paʎʎa]

103. Building. Building process

construction site	cantiere (m) edile	[kan'tjere 'edile]
to build (vt)	costruire (vt)	[kostru'ire]
construction worker	operaio (m) edile	[ope'rajo e'dile]

project	progetto (m)	[pro'dʒetto]
architect	architetto (m)	[arki'tetto]
worker	operaio (m)	[ope'rajo]

foundation (of a building)	fondamenta (f pl)	[fonda'menta]
roof	tetto (m)	['tetto]
foundation pile	palo (m) di fondazione	['palo di fonda'tsjone]
wall	muro (m)	['muro]

| reinforcing bars | barre (f pl) di rinforzo | ['barre di rin'fortso] |
| scaffolding | impalcatura (f) | [impalka'tura] |

concrete	beton (m)	[be'ton]
granite	granito (m)	[gra'nito]
stone	pietra (f)	['pjetra]
brick	mattone (m)	[mat'tone]

| sand | sabbia (f) | ['sabbia] |
| cement | cemento (m) | [tʃe'mento] |

plaster (for walls)	intonaco (m)	[in'tonako]
to plaster (vt)	intonacare (vt)	[intona'kare]
paint	pittura (f)	[pit'tura]
to paint (~ a wall)	pitturare (vt)	[pittu'rare]
barrel	botte (f)	['botte]
crane	gru (f)	[gru]
to lift, to hoist (vt)	sollevare (vt)	[solle'vare]
to lower (vt)	abbassare (vt)	[abbas'sare]
bulldozer	bulldozer (m)	[bulldo'dzer]
excavator	scavatrice (f)	[skava'tritʃe]
scoop, bucket	cucchiaia (f)	[kuk'kjaja]
to dig (excavate)	scavare (vt)	[ska'vare]
hard hat	casco (m)	['kasko]

Professions and occupations

104. Job search. Dismissal

job	lavoro (m)	[la'voro]
staff (work force)	organico (m)	[or'ganiko]
personnel	personale (m)	[perso'nale]
career	carriera (f)	[kar'rjera]
prospects (chances)	prospettiva (f)	[prospet'tiva]
skills (mastery)	abilità (f pl)	[abili'ta]
selection (screening)	selezione (f)	[sele'tsjone]
employment agency	agenzia (f) di collocamento	[adʒen'tsia di kolloka'mento]
résumé	curriculum vitae (f)	[kur'rikulum 'vite]
job interview	colloquio (m)	[kol'lokwio]
vacancy, opening	posto (m) vacante	['posto va'kante]
salary, pay	salario (m)	[sa'lario]
fixed salary	stipendio (m) fisso	[sti'pendio 'fisso]
pay, compensation	compenso (m)	[kom'penso]
position (job)	carica (f)	['karika]
duty (of employee)	mansione (f)	[man'sjone]
range of duties	mansioni (f pl) di lavoro	[man'sjoni di la'voro]
busy (I'm ~)	occupato	[okku'pato]
to fire (dismiss)	licenziare (vt)	[litʃen'tsjare]
dismissal	licenziamento (m)	[litʃentsja'mento]
unemployment	disoccupazione (f)	[disokkupa'tsjone]
unemployed (n)	disoccupato (m)	[disokku'pato]
retirement	pensionamento (m)	[pensjona'mento]
to retire (from job)	andare in pensione	[an'dare in pen'sjone]

105. Business people

director	direttore (m)	[diret'tore]
manager (director)	dirigente (m)	[diri'dʒente]
boss	capo (m)	['kapo]
superior	capo (m), superiore (m)	['kapo], [supe'rjore]
superiors	capi (m pl)	['kapi]

| president | presidente (m) | [prezi'dente] |
| chairman | presidente (m) | [prezi'dente] |

deputy (substitute)	vice (m)	['vitʃe]
assistant	assistente (m)	[assi'stente]
secretary	segretario (m)	[segre'tario]
personal assistant	assistente (m) personale	[assi'stente perso'nale]

businessman	uomo (m) d'affari	[u'omo daf'fari]
entrepreneur	imprenditore (m)	[imprendi'tore]
founder	fondatore (m)	[fonda'tore]
to found (vt)	fondare (vt)	[fon'dare]

incorporator	socio (m)	['sotʃo]
partner	partner (m)	['partner]
stockholder	azionista (m)	[atsio'nista]

millionaire	milionario (m)	[miljo'nario]
billionaire	miliardario (m)	[miljar'dario]
owner, proprietor	proprietario (m)	[proprie'tario]
landowner	latifondista (m)	[latifon'dista]

| client | cliente (m) | [kli'ente] |
| regular client | cliente (m) abituale | [kli'ente abitu'ale] |

| buyer (customer) | compratore (m) | [kompra'tore] |
| visitor | visitatore (m) | [vizita'tore] |

professional (n)	professionista (m)	[professjo'nista]
expert	esperto (m)	[e'sperto]
specialist	specialista (m)	[spetʃa'lista]

| banker | banchiere (m) | [baŋ'kjere] |
| broker | broker (m) | ['broker] |

cashier, teller	cassiere (m)	[kas'sjere]
accountant	contabile (m)	[kon'tabile]
security guard	guardia (f) giurata	['gwardia dʒu'rata]

| investor | investitore (m) | [investi'tore] |
| debtor | debitore (m) | [debi'tore] |

| creditor | creditore (m) | [kredi'tore] |
| borrower | mutuatario (m) | [mutua'tario] |

| importer | importatore (m) | [importa'tore] |
| exporter | esportatore (m) | [esporta'tore] |

manufacturer	produttore (m)	[produt'tore]
distributor	distributore (m)	[distribu'tore]
middleman	intermediario (m)	[interme'djario]
consultant	consulente (m)	[konsu'lente]

sales representative	rappresentante (m)	[rapprezen'tante]
agent	agente (m)	[a'dʒente]
insurance agent	assicuratore (m)	[assikura'tore]

106. Service professions

cook	cuoco (m)	[ku'oko]
chef (kitchen chef)	capocuoco (m)	[kapo·ku'oko]
baker	fornaio (m)	[for'najo]

bartender	barista (m)	[ba'rista]
waiter	cameriere (m)	[kame'rjere]
waitress	cameriera (f)	[kame'rjera]

lawyer, attorney	avvocato (m)	[avvo'kato]
lawyer (legal expert)	esperto (m) legale	[e'sperto le'gale]
notary public	notaio (m)	[no'tajo]

electrician	elettricista (m)	[elettri'tʃista]
plumber	idraulico (m)	[i'drauliko]
carpenter	falegname (m)	[fale'ɲame]

masseur	massaggiatore (m)	[massadʒa'tore]
masseuse	massaggiatrice (f)	[massadʒa'tritʃe]
doctor	medico (m)	['mediko]

taxi driver	taxista (m)	[ta'ksista]
driver	autista (m)	[au'tista]
delivery man	fattorino (m)	[fatto'rino]

chambermaid	cameriera (f)	[kame'rjera]
security guard	guardia (f) giurata	['gwardia dʒu'rata]
flight attendant (fem.)	hostess (f)	['ostess]

schoolteacher	insegnante (m, f)	[inse'ɲante]
librarian	bibliotecario (m)	[bibliote'kario]
translator	traduttore (m)	[tradut'tore]

| interpreter | interprete (m) | [in'terprete] |
| guide | guida (f) | ['gwida] |

hairdresser	parrucchiere (m)	[parruk'kjere]
mailman	postino (m)	[po'stino]
salesman (store staff)	commesso (m)	[kom'messo]

| gardener | giardiniere (m) | [dʒardi'njere] |
| domestic servant | domestico (m) | [do'mestiko] |

| maid (female servant) | domestica (f) | [do'mestika] |
| cleaner (cleaning lady) | donna (f) delle pulizie | ['donna 'delle puli'tsie] |

107. Military professions and ranks

private	**soldato** (m) **semplice**	[sol'dato 'semplitʃe]
sergeant	**sergente** (m)	[ser'dʒente]
lieutenant	**tenente** (m)	[te'nente]
captain	**capitano** (m)	[kapi'tano]
major	**maggiore** (m)	[ma'dʒore]
colonel	**colonnello** (m)	[kolon'nello]
general	**generale** (m)	[dʒene'rale]
marshal	**maresciallo** (m)	[mare'ʃallo]
admiral	**ammiraglio** (m)	[ammi'raʎʎo]
military (n)	**militare** (m)	[mili'tare]
soldier	**soldato** (m)	[sol'dato]
officer	**ufficiale** (m)	[uffi'tʃale]
commander	**comandante** (m)	[koman'dante]
border guard	**guardia** (f) **di frontiera**	['gwardia di fron'tjera]
radio operator	**marconista** (m)	[marko'nista]
scout (searcher)	**esploratore** (m)	[esplora'tore]
pioneer (sapper)	**geniere** (m)	[dʒe'njere]
marksman	**tiratore** (m)	[tira'tore]
navigator	**navigatore** (m)	[naviga'tore]

108. Officials. Priests

king	**re** (m)	[re]
queen	**regina** (f)	[re'dʒina]
prince	**principe** (m)	['printʃipe]
princess	**principessa** (f)	[printʃi'pessa]
czar	**zar** (m)	[tsar]
czarina	**zarina** (f)	[tsa'rina]
president	**presidente** (m)	[prezi'dente]
Secretary (minister)	**ministro** (m)	[mi'nistro]
prime minister	**primo ministro** (m)	['primo mi'nistro]
senator	**senatore** (m)	[sena'tore]
diplomat	**diplomatico** (m)	[diplo'matiko]
consul	**console** (m)	['konsole]
ambassador	**ambasciatore** (m)	[ambaʃa'tore]
counselor (diplomatic officer)	**consigliere** (m)	[konsiʎ'ʎere]
official, functionary (civil servant)	**funzionario** (m)	[funtsio'nario]

| prefect | prefetto (m) | [pre'fetto] |
| mayor | sindaco (m) | ['sindako] |

| judge | giudice (m) | ['dʒuditʃe] |
| prosecutor (e.g., district attorney) | procuratore (m) | [prokura'tore] |

missionary	missionario (m)	[missio'nario]
monk	monaco (m)	['monako]
abbot	abate (m)	[a'bate]
rabbi	rabbino (m)	[rab'bino]

vizier	visir (m)	[vi'zir]
shah	scià (m)	['ʃa]
sheikh	sceicco (m)	[ʃe'ikko]

109. Agricultural professions

beekeeper	apicoltore (m)	[apikol'tore]
herder, shepherd	pastore (m)	[pa'store]
agronomist	agronomo (m)	[a'gronomo]
cattle breeder	allevatore (m) di bestiame	[alleva'tore di bes'tjame]
veterinarian	veterinario (m)	[veteri'nario]

farmer	fattore (m)	[fat'tore]
winemaker	vinificatore (m)	[vinifika'tore]
zoologist	zoologo (m)	[dzo'ologo]
cowboy	cowboy (m)	[kaw'boj]

110. Art professions

| actor | attore (m) | [at'tore] |
| actress | attrice (f) | [at'tritʃe] |

| singer (masc.) | cantante (m) | [kan'tante] |
| singer (fem.) | cantante (f) | [kan'tante] |

| dancer (masc.) | danzatore (m) | [dantsa'tore] |
| dancer (fem.) | ballerina (f) | [balle'rina] |

| performer (masc.) | artista (m) | [ar'tista] |
| performer (fem.) | artista (f) | [ar'tista] |

musician	musicista (m)	[muzi'tʃista]
pianist	pianista (m)	[pia'nista]
guitar player	chitarrista (m)	[kitar'rista]
conductor (orchestra ~)	direttore (m) d'orchestra	[diret'tore dor'kestra]

composer	compositore (m)	[kompozi'tore]
impresario	impresario (m)	[impre'zario]
film director	regista (m)	[re'dʒista]
producer	produttore (m)	[produt'tore]
scriptwriter	sceneggiatore (m)	[ʃenedʒa'tore]
critic	critico (m)	['kritiko]
writer	scrittore (m)	[skrit'tore]
poet	poeta (m)	[po'eta]
sculptor	scultore (m)	[skul'tore]
artist (painter)	pittore (m)	[pit'tore]
⁓ juggler	giocoliere (m)	[dʒoko'ljere]
⁓ clown	pagliaccio (m)	[paʎ'ʎatʃo]
⁓ acrobat	acrobata (m)	[a'krobata]
⁓ magician	prestigiatore (m)	[prestidʒa'tore]

111. Various professions

doctor	medico (m)	['mediko]
nurse	infermiera (f)	[infer'mjera]
psychiatrist	psichiatra (m)	[psiki'atra]
dentist	dentista (m)	[den'tista]
⁓ surgeon	chirurgo (m)	[ki'rurgo]
astronaut	astronauta (m)	[astro'nauta]
astronomer	astronomo (m)	[a'stronomo]
driver (of taxi, etc.)	autista (m)	[au'tista]
engineer (train driver)	macchinista (m)	[makki'nista]
mechanic	meccanico (m)	[mek'kaniko]
⁓ miner	minatore (m)	[mina'tore]
⁓ worker	operaio (m)	[ope'rajo]
locksmith	operaio (m) metallurgico	[ope'rajo metal'lurdʒiko]
⁓ joiner (carpenter)	falegname (m)	[fale'ɲame]
turner (lathe operator)	tornitore (m)	[torni'tore]
⁓ construction worker	operaio (m) edile	[ope'rajo e'dile]
⁓ welder	saldatore (m)	[salda'tore]
professor (title)	professore (m)	[profes'sore]
architect	architetto (m)	[arki'tetto]
historian	storico (m)	['storiko]
scientist	scienziato (m)	[ʃien'tsjato]
physicist	fisico (m)	['fiziko]
chemist (scientist)	chimico (m)	['kimiko]
archeologist	archeologo (m)	[arke'ologo]
geologist	geologo (m)	[dʒe'ologo]

researcher (scientist)	ricercatore (m)	[ritʃerka'tore]
babysitter	baby-sitter (f)	[bebi'siter]
teacher, educator	insegnante (m, f)	[inse'ɲante]

editor	redattore (m)	[redat'tore]
editor-in-chief	redattore capo (m)	[redat'tore 'kapo]
correspondent	corrispondente (m)	[korrispon'dente]
typist (fem.)	dattilografa (f)	[datti'lografa]

designer	designer (m)	[di'zajner]
computer expert	esperto (m) informatico	[e'sperto infor'matiko]
programmer	programmatore (m)	[programma'tore]
engineer (designer)	ingegnere (m)	[indʒe'ɲere]

sailor	marittimo (m)	[ma'rittimo]
seaman	marinaio (m)	[mari'najo]
rescuer	soccorritore (m)	[sokkorri'tore]

fireman	pompiere (m)	[pom'pjere]
police officer	poliziotto (m)	[poli'tsjotto]
watchman	guardiano (m)	[gwar'djano]
detective	detective (m)	[de'tektiv]

customs officer	doganiere (m)	[doga'njere]
bodyguard	guardia (f) del corpo	['gwardia del 'korpo]
prison guard	guardia (f) carceraria	['gwardia kartʃe'raria]
inspector	ispettore (m)	[ispet'tore]

sportsman	sportivo (m)	[spor'tivo]
trainer, coach	allenatore (m)	[allena'tore]
butcher	macellaio (m)	[matʃel'lajo]
cobbler (shoe repairer)	calzolaio (m)	[kaltso'lajo]
merchant	uomo (m) d'affari	[u'omo daf'fari]
loader (person)	caricatore (m)	[karika'tore]

| fashion designer | stilista (m) | [sti'lista] |
| model (fem.) | modella (f) | [mo'della] |

112. Occupations. Social status

| schoolboy | scolaro (m) | [sko'laro] |
| student (college ~) | studente (m) | [stu'dente] |

philosopher	filosofo (m)	[fi'lozofo]
economist	economista (m)	[ekono'mista]
inventor	inventore (m)	[inven'tore]

unemployed (n)	disoccupato (m)	[disokku'pato]
retiree	pensionato (m)	[pensjo'nato]
spy, secret agent	spia (f)	['spia]

prisoner	**detenuto** (m)	[dete'nuto]
striker	**scioperante** (m)	[ʃope'rante]
bureaucrat	**burocrate** (m)	[bu'rokrate]
traveler (globetrotter)	**viaggiatore** (m)	[vjadʒa'tore]
gay, homosexual (n)	**omosessuale** (m)	[omosessu'ale]
hacker	**hacker** (m)	['aker]
hippie	**hippy**	['ippi]
bandit	**bandito** (m)	[ban'dito]
hit man, killer	**sicario** (m)	[si'kario]
drug addict	**drogato** (m)	[dro'gato]
drug dealer	**trafficante** (m) **di droga**	[traffi'kante di 'droga]
prostitute (fem.)	**prostituta** (f)	[prosti'tuta]
pimp	**magnaccia** (m)	[ma'ɲatʃa]
sorcerer	**stregone** (m)	[stre'gone]
sorceress (evil ~)	**strega** (f)	['strega]
pirate	**pirata** (m)	[pi'rata]
slave	**schiavo** (m)	['skjavo]
samurai	**samurai** (m)	[samu'raj]
savage (primitive)	**selvaggio** (m)	[sel'vadʒo]

Sports

113. Kinds of sports. Sportspersons

sportsman	**sportivo** (m)	[spor'tivo]
kind of sports	**sport** (m)	[sport]
basketball	**pallacanestro** (m)	[pallaka'nestro]
basketball player	**cestista** (m)	[ʧes'tista]
baseball	**baseball** (m)	['bejzbol]
baseball player	**giocatore** (m) **di baseball**	[ʤoka'tore di 'bejzbol]
soccer	**calcio** (m)	['kalʧo]
soccer player	**calciatore** (m)	[kalʧa'tore]
goalkeeper	**portiere** (m)	[por'tjere]
hockey	**hockey** (m)	['okkej]
hockey player	**hockeista** (m)	[okke'ista]
volleyball	**pallavolo** (m)	[palla'volo]
volleyball player	**pallavolista** (m)	[pallavo'lista]
boxing	**pugilato** (m)	[puʤi'lato]
boxer	**pugile** (m)	['puʤile]
wrestling	**lotta** (f)	['lotta]
wrestler	**lottatore** (m)	[lotta'tore]
karate	**karate** (m)	[ka'rate]
karate fighter	**karateka** (m)	[kara'teka]
judo	**judo** (m)	['ʤudo]
judo athlete	**judoista** (m)	[ʤudo'ista]
tennis	**tennis** (m)	['tennis]
tennis player	**tennista** (m)	[ten'nista]
swimming	**nuoto** (m)	[nu'oto]
swimmer	**nuotatore** (m)	[nuota'tore]
fencing	**scherma** (f)	['skerma]
fencer	**schermitore** (m)	[skermi'tore]
chess	**scacchi** (m pl)	['skakki]
chess player	**scacchista** (m)	[skak'kista]

alpinism	**alpinismo** (m)	[alpi'nizmo]
alpinist	**alpinista** (m)	[alpi'nista]
running	**corsa** (f)	['korsa]
runner	**corridore** (m)	[korri'dore]
athletics	**atletica** (f) **leggera**	[a'tletika le'dʒera]
athlete	**atleta** (m)	[a'tleta]
horseback riding	**ippica** (f)	['ippika]
horse rider	**fantino** (m)	[fan'tino]
figure skating	**pattinaggio** (m) **artistico**	[patti'nadʒo ar'tistiko]
figure skater (masc.)	**pattinatore** (m)	[pattina'tore]
figure skater (fem.)	**pattinatrice** (f)	[pattina'tritʃe]
powerlifting	**pesistica** (f)	[pe'zistika]
powerlifter	**pesista** (m)	[pe'zista]
car racing	**automobilismo** (m)	[automobi'lizmo]
racer (driver)	**pilota** (m)	[pi'lota]
cycling	**ciclismo** (m)	[tʃik'lizmo]
cyclist	**ciclista** (m)	[tʃik'lista]
broad jump	**salto** (m) **in lungo**	['salto in 'lungo]
pole vault	**salto** (m) **con l'asta**	['salto kon 'lasta]
jumper	**saltatore** (m)	[salta'tore]

114. Kinds of sports. Miscellaneous

football	**football** (m) **americano**	['futboll ameri'kano]
badminton	**badminton** (m)	['badminton]
biathlon	**biathlon** (m)	['biatlon]
billiards	**biliardo** (m)	[bi'ljardo]
bobsled	**bob** (m)	[bob]
bodybuilding	**culturismo** (m)	[kultu'rizmo]
water polo	**pallanuoto** (m)	[pallanu'oto]
handball	**pallamano** (m)	[palla'mano]
golf	**golf** (m)	[golf]
rowing, crew	**canottaggio** (m)	[kanot'tadʒo]
scuba diving	**immersione** (f) **subacquea**	[immer'sjone su'bakvea]
cross-country skiing	**sci** (m) **di fondo**	[ʃi di 'fondo]
table tennis (ping-pong)	**tennis** (m) **da tavolo**	['tennis da 'tavolo]
sailing	**vela** (f)	['vela]
rally racing	**rally** (m)	['relli]
rugby	**rugby** (m)	['ragbi]

| snowboarding | snowboard (m) | ['znobord] |
| archery | tiro (m) con l'arco | ['tiro kon 'larko] |

115. Gym

barbell	bilanciere (m)	[bilan'tʃere]
dumbbells	manubri (m pl)	[ma'nubri]
training machine	attrezzo (m) sportivo	[at'trettso spor'tivo]
exercise bicycle	cyclette (f)	[si'klett]
treadmill	tapis roulant (m)	[ta'pi ru'lan]
horizontal bar	sbarra (f)	['zbarra]
parallel bars	parallele (f pl)	[paral'lele]
vault (vaulting horse)	cavallo (m)	[ka'vallo]
mat (exercise ~)	materassino (m)	[materas'sino]
jump rope	corda (f) per saltare	['korda per sal'tare]
aerobics	aerobica (f)	[ae'robika]
yoga	yoga (m)	['joga]

116. Sports. Miscellaneous

Olympic Games	Giochi (m pl) Olimpici	['dʒoki o'limpitʃi]
winner	vincitore (m)	[vintʃi'tore]
to be winning	ottenere la vittoria	[otte'nere la vit'toria]
to win (vi)	vincere (vi)	['vintʃere]
leader	leader (m), capo (m)	['lider], ['kapo]
to lead (vi)	essere alla guida	['essere 'alla 'gwida]
first place	primo posto (m)	['primo 'posto]
second place	secondo posto (m)	[se'kondo 'posto]
third place	terzo posto (m)	['tertso 'posto]
medal	medaglia (f)	[me'daʎʎa]
trophy	trofeo (m)	[tro'feo]
prize cup (trophy)	coppa (f)	['koppa]
prize (in game)	premio (m)	['premio]
main prize	primo premio (m)	['primo 'premio]
record	record (m)	['rekord]
to set a record	stabilire un record	[stabi'lire un 'rekord]
final	finale (m)	[fi'nale]
final (adj)	finale	[fi'nale]
champion	campione (m)	[kam'pjone]
championship	campionato (m)	[kampjo'nato]

stadium	**stadio** (m)	['stadio]
stand (bleachers)	**tribuna** (f)	[tri'buna]
fan, supporter	**tifoso, fan** (m)	[ti'fozo], [fan]
opponent, rival	**avversario** (m)	[avver'sario]
start (start line)	**partenza** (f)	[par'tentsa]
finish line	**traguardo** (m)	[tra'gwardo]
defeat	**sconfitta** (f)	[skon'fitta]
to lose (not win)	**perdere** (vt)	['perdere]
referee	**arbitro** (m)	['arbitro]
jury (judges)	**giuria** (f)	[dʒu'ria]
score	**punteggio** (m)	[pun'tedʒo]
tie	**pareggio** (m)	[pa'redʒo]
to tie (vi)	**pareggiare** (vi)	[pare'dʒare]
point	**punto** (m)	['punto]
result (final score)	**risultato** (m)	[rizul'tato]
period	**tempo** (m)	['tempo]
half-time	**intervallo** (m)	[inter'vallo]
doping	**doping** (m)	['doping]
to penalize (vt)	**penalizzare** (vt)	[penalid'dzare]
to disqualify (vt)	**squalificare** (vt)	[skwalifi'kare]
apparatus	**attrezzatura** (f)	[attrettsa'tura]
javelin	**giavellotto** (m)	[dʒavel'lotto]
shot (metal ball)	**peso** (m)	['pezo]
ball (snooker, etc.)	**biglia** (f)	['biʎʎa]
aim (target)	**obiettivo** (m)	[objet'tivo]
target	**bersaglio** (m)	[ber'saʎʎo]
to shoot (vi)	**sparare** (vi)	[spa'rare]
accurate (~ shot)	**preciso**	[pre'tʃizo]
trainer, coach	**allenatore** (m)	[allena'tore]
to train (sb)	**allenare** (vt)	[alle'nare]
to train (vi)	**allenarsi** (vr)	[alle'narsi]
training	**allenamento** (m)	[allena'mento]
gym	**palestra** (f)	[pa'lestra]
exercise (physical)	**esercizio** (m)	[ezer'tʃitsio]
warm-up (athlete ~)	**riscaldamento** (m)	[riskalda'mento]

Education

117. School

school	scuola (f)	['skwola]
principal (headmaster)	direttore (m) di scuola	[diret'tore di 'skwola]
pupil (boy)	allievo (m)	[al'ljevo]
pupil (girl)	allieva (f)	[al'ljeva]
schoolboy	scolaro (m)	[sko'laro]
schoolgirl	scolara (f)	[sko'lara]
to teach (sb)	insegnare	[inse'ɲare]
to learn (language, etc.)	imparare (vt)	[impa'rare]
to learn by heart	imparare a memoria	[impa'rare a me'moria]
to learn (~ to count, etc.)	studiare (vi)	[stu'djare]
to be in school	frequentare la scuola	[frekwen'tare la 'skwola]
to go to school	andare a scuola	[an'dare a 'skwola]
alphabet	alfabeto (m)	[alfa'beto]
subject (at school)	materia (f)	[ma'teria]
classroom	classe (f)	['klasse]
lesson	lezione (f)	[le'tsjone]
recess	ricreazione (f)	[rikrea'tsjone]
school bell	campanella (f)	[kampa'nella]
school desk	banco (m)	['banko]
chalkboard	lavagna (f)	[la'vaɲa]
grade	voto (m)	['voto]
good grade	voto (m) alto	['voto 'alto]
bad grade	voto (m) basso	['voto 'basso]
to give a grade	dare un voto	['dare un 'voto]
mistake, error	errore (m)	[er'rore]
to make mistakes	fare errori	['fare er'rori]
to correct (an error)	correggere (vt)	[kor'redʒere]
cheat sheet	bigliettino (m)	[biʎʎet'tino]
homework	compiti (m pl)	['kompiti]
exercise (in education)	esercizio (m)	[ezer'tʃitsio]
to be present	essere presente	['essere pre'zente]
to be absent	essere assente	['essere as'sente]
to miss school	mancare le lezioni	[man'kare le le'tsjoni]

to punish (vt)	punire (vt)	[pu'nire]
punishment	punizione (f)	[puni'tsjone]
conduct (behavior)	comportamento (m)	[komporta'mento]
~ report card	pagella (f)	[pa'dʒella]
~ pencil	matita (f)	[ma'tita]
~ eraser	gomma (f) per cancellare	['gomma per kantʃel'lare]
~ chalk	gesso (m)	['dʒesso]
~ pencil case	astuccio (m) portamatite	[as'tutʃo portama'tite]
~ schoolbag	cartella (f)	[kar'tella]
pen	penna (f)	['penna]
school notebook	quaderno (m)	[kwa'derno]
~ textbook	manuale (m)	[manu'ale]
~ drafting compass	compasso (m)	[kom'passo]
to make technical drawings	disegnare (vt)	[dize'ɲare]
technical drawing	disegno (m) tecnico	[di'zeɲo 'tekniko]
poem	poesia (f)	[poe'zia]
by heart (adv)	a memoria	[a me'moria]
to learn by heart	imparare a memoria	[impa'rare a me'moria]
school vacation	vacanze (f pl) scolastiche	[va'kantse sko'lastike]
to be on vacation	essere in vacanza	['essere in va'kantsa]
to spend one's vacation	passare le vacanze	[pas'sare le va'kantse]
~ test (written math ~)	prova (f) scritta	['prova 'skritta]
~ essay (composition)	composizione (f)	[kompozi'tsjone]
~ dictation	dettato (m)	[det'tato]
exam (examination)	esame (m)	[e'zame]
~ to take an exam	sostenere un esame	[soste'neme un e'zame]
experiment (e.g., chemistry ~)	esperimento (m)	[esperi'mento]

118. College. University

academy	accademia (f)	[akka'demia]
university	università (f)	[universi'ta]
faculty (e.g., ~ of Medicine)	facoltà (f)	[fakol'ta]
student (masc.)	studente (m)	[stu'dente]
student (fem.)	studentessa (f)	[studen'tessa]
lecturer (teacher)	docente (m. f)	[do'tʃente]
~ lecture hall, room	aula (f)	['aula]
~ graduate	diplomato (m)	[diplo'mato]
diploma	diploma (m)	[di'ploma]

dissertation	tesi (f)	['tezi]
study (report)	ricerca (f)	[ri'tʃerka]
laboratory	laboratorio (m)	[labora'torio]
lecture	lezione (f)	[le'tsjone]
coursemate	compagno (m) di corso	[kom'paɲo di 'korso]
scholarship	borsa (f) di studio	['borsa di 'studio]
academic degree	titolo (m) accademico	['titolo akka'demiko]

119. Sciences. Disciplines

mathematics	matematica (f)	[mate'matika]
algebra	algebra (f)	['aldʒebra]
geometry	geometria (f)	[dʒeome'tria]
astronomy	astronomia (f)	[astrono'mia]
biology	biologia (f)	[biolo'dʒia]
geography	geografia (f)	[dʒeogra'fia]
geology	geologia (f)	[dʒeolo'dʒia]
history	storia (f)	['storia]
medicine	medicina (f)	[medi'tʃina]
pedagogy	pedagogia (f)	[pedago'dʒia]
law	diritto (m)	[di'ritto]
physics	fisica (f)	['fizika]
chemistry	chimica (f)	['kimika]
philosophy	filosofia (f)	[filozo'fia]
psychology	psicologia (f)	[psikolo'dʒia]

120. Writing system. Orthography

grammar	grammatica (f)	[gram'matika]
vocabulary	lessico (m)	['lessiko]
phonetics	fonetica (f)	[fo'netika]
noun	sostantivo (m)	[sostan'tivo]
adjective	aggettivo (m)	[adʒet'tivo]
verb	verbo (m)	['verbo]
adverb	avverbio (m)	[av'verbio]
pronoun	pronome (m)	[pro'nome]
interjection	interiezione (f)	[interje'tsjone]
preposition	preposizione (f)	[prepozi'tsjone]
root	radice (f)	[ra'ditʃe]
ending	desinenza (f)	[dezi'nentsa]
prefix	prefisso (m)	[pre'fisso]

~ syllable	**sillaba** (f)	['sillaba]
suffix	**suffisso** (m)	[suf'fisso]
stress mark	**accento** (m)	[a'tʃento]
apostrophe	**apostrofo** (m)	[a'postrofo]
period, dot	**punto** (m)	['punto]
~ comma	**virgola** (f)	['virgola]
semicolon	**punto** (m) **e virgola**	['punto e 'virgola]
~ colon	**due punti**	['due 'punti]
ellipsis	**puntini** (m pl) **di sospensione**	[pun'tini di sospen'sjone]
question mark	**punto** (m) **interrogativo**	['punto interroga'tivo]
exclamation point	**punto** (m) **esclamativo**	['punto esklama'tivo]
quotation marks	**virgolette** (f pl)	[virgo'lette]
in quotation marks	**tra virgolette**	[tra virgo'lette]
parenthesis	**parentesi** (f pl)	[pa'rentezi]
in parenthesis	**tra parentesi**	[tra pa'rentezi]
~ hyphen	**trattino** (m)	[trat'tino]
~ dash	**lineetta** (f)	[line'etta]
space (between words)	**spazio** (m)	['spatsio]
letter	**lettera** (f)	['lettera]
capital letter	**lettera** (f) **maiuscola**	['lettera ma'juskola]
~ vowel (n)	**vocale** (f)	[vo'kale]
~ consonant (n)	**consonante** (f)	[konso'nante]
sentence	**proposizione** (f)	[propozi'tsjone]
subject	**soggetto** (m)	[so'dʒetto]
predicate	**predicato** (m)	[predi'kato]
line	**riga** (f)	['riga]
~ on a new line	**a capo**	[a 'kapo]
~ paragraph	**capoverso** (m)	[kapo'verso]
word	**parola** (f)	[pa'rola]
group of words	**gruppo** (m) **di parole**	['gruppo di pa'role]
expression	**espressione** (f)	[espres'sjone]
synonym	**sinonimo** (m)	[si'nonimo]
~ antonym	**antonimo** (m)	[an'tonimo]
rule	**regola** (f)	['regola]
exception	**eccezione** (f)	[etʃe'tsjone]
correct (adj)	**corretto**	[kor'retto]
conjugation	**coniugazione** (f)	[konjuga'tsjone]
declension	**declinazione** (f)	[deklina'tsjone]
~ nominal case	**caso** (m) **nominativo**	['kazo nomina'tivo]

question	domanda (f)	[do'manda]
to underline (vt)	sottolineare (vt)	[sottoline'are]
dotted line	linea (f) tratteggiata	['linea tratte'dʒata]

121. Foreign languages

language	lingua (f)	['lingua]
foreign (adj)	straniero	[stra'njero]
foreign language	lingua (f) straniera	['lingua stra'njera]
to study (vt)	studiare (vt)	[stu'djare]
to learn (language, etc.)	imparare (vt)	[impa'rare]

to read (vi, vt)	leggere (vi, vt)	['ledʒere]
to speak (vi, vt)	parlare (vi, vt)	[par'lare]
to understand (vt)	capire (vt)	[ka'pire]
to write (vt)	scrivere (vi, vt)	['skrivere]

fast (adv)	rapidamente	[rapida'mente]
slowly (adv)	lentamente	[lenta'mente]
fluently (adv)	correntemente	[korrente'mente]

rules	regole (f pl)	['regole]
grammar	grammatica (f)	[gram'matika]
vocabulary	lessico (m)	['lessiko]
phonetics	fonetica (f)	[fo'netika]

textbook	manuale (m)	[manu'ale]
dictionary	dizionario (m)	[ditsjo'nario]
teach-yourself book	manuale (m) autodidattico	[manu'ale autodi'dattiko]
phrasebook	frasario (m)	[fra'zario]

cassette, tape	cassetta (f)	[kas'setta]
videotape	videocassetta (f)	[video·kas'setta]
CD, compact disc	CD (m)	[tʃi'di]
DVD	DVD (m)	[divu'di]

alphabet	alfabeto (m)	[alfa'beto]
to spell (vt)	compitare (vt)	[kompi'tare]
pronunciation	pronuncia (f)	[pro'nuntʃa]

accent	accento (m)	[a'tʃento]
with an accent	con un accento	[kon un a'tʃento]
without an accent	senza accento	['sentsa a'tʃento]

| word | vocabolo (m) | [vo'kabolo] |
| meaning | significato (m) | [siɲifi'kato] |

| course (e.g., a French ~) | corso (m) | ['korso] |
| to sign up | iscriversi (vr) | [is'kriversi] |

teacher	insegnante (m, f)	[inse'ɲante]
translation (process)	traduzione (f)	[tradu'tsjone]
translation (text, etc.)	traduzione (f)	[tradu'tsjone]
translator	traduttore (m)	[tradut'tore]
interpreter	interprete (m)	[in'terprete]
polyglot	poliglotta (m)	[poli'glotta]
memory	memoria (f)	[me'moria]

122. Fairy tale characters

Santa Claus	Babbo Natale (m)	['babbo na'tale]
Cinderella	Cenerentola (f)	[tʃene'rentola]
mermaid	sirena (f)	[si'rena]
Neptune	Nettuno (m)	[net'tuno]
magician, wizard	mago (m)	['mago]
fairy	fata (f)	['fata]
magic (adj)	magico	['madʒiko]
magic wand	bacchetta (f) magica	[bak'ketta 'madʒika]
fairy tale	fiaba (f), favola (f)	['fjaba], ['favola]
miracle	miracolo (m)	[mi'rakolo]
dwarf	nano (m)	['nano]
to turn into ...	trasformarsi in ...	[trasfor'marsi in]
ghost	spettro (m)	['spettro]
phantom	fantasma (m)	[fan'tazma]
monster	mostro (m)	['mostro]
dragon	drago (m)	['drago]
giant	gigante (m)	[dʒi'gante]

123. Zodiac Signs

Aries	Ariete (m)	[a'rjete]
Taurus	Toro (m)	['toro]
Gemini	Gemelli (m pl)	[dʒe'melli]
Cancer	Cancro (m)	['kankro]
Leo	Leone (m)	[le'one]
Virgo	Vergine (f)	['verdʒine]
Libra	Bilancia (f)	[bi'lantʃa]
Scorpio	Scorpione (m)	[skor'pjone]
Sagittarius	Sagittario (m)	[sadʒit'tario]
Capricorn	Capricorno (m)	[kapri'korno]
Aquarius	Acquario (m)	[a'kwario]
Pisces	Pesci (m pl)	['peʃi]
character	carattere (m)	[ka'rattere]

character traits	**tratti** (m pl) **del carattere**	['tratti del ka'rattere]
behavior	**comportamento** (m)	[komporta'mento]
to tell fortunes	**predire il futuro**	[pre'dire il fu'turo]
fortune-teller	**cartomante** (f)	[karto'mante]
horoscope	**oroscopo** (m)	[o'roskopo]

Arts

124. Theater

theater	**teatro** (m)	[te'atro]
opera	**opera** (f)	['opera]
operetta	**operetta** (f)	[ope'retta]
ballet	**balletto** (m)	[bal'letto]
theater poster	**cartellone** (m)	[kartel'lone]
troupe	**compagnia** (f) **teatrale**	[kompa'ɲia tea'trale]
(theatrical company)		
tour	**tournée** (f)	[tur'ne]
to be on tour	**andare in tournée**	[an'dare in tur'ne]
to rehearse (vi, vt)	**fare le prove**	['fare le 'prove]
rehearsal	**prova** (f)	['prova]
repertoire	**repertorio** (m)	[reper'torio]
performance	**rappresentazione** (f)	[rapprezenta'tsjone]
theatrical show	**spettacolo** (m)	[spet'takolo]
play	**opera** (f) **teatrale**	['opera tea'trale]
ticket	**biglietto** (m)	[biʎ'ʎetto]
box office (ticket booth)	**botteghino** (m)	[botte'gino]
lobby, foyer	**hall** (f)	[oll]
coat check (cloakroom)	**guardaroba** (f)	[gwarda'roba]
coat check tag	**cartellino** (m)	[kartel'lino
	del guardaroba	del gwarda'roba]
binoculars	**binocolo** (m)	[bi'nokolo]
usher	**maschera** (f)	['maskera]
orchestra seats	**platea** (f)	['platea]
balcony	**balconata** (f)	[balko'nata]
dress circle	**prima galleria** (f)	['prima galle'ria]
box	**palco** (m)	['palko]
row	**fila** (f)	['fila]
seat	**posto** (m)	['posto]
audience	**pubblico** (m)	['pubbliko]
spectator	**spettatore** (m)	[spetta'tore]
to clap (vi, vt)	**battere le mani**	['battere le 'mani]
applause	**applauso** (m)	[app'lauzo]
ovation	**ovazione** (f)	[ova'tsjone]
stage	**palcoscenico** (m)	[palko'ʃeniko]
curtain	**sipario** (m)	[si'pario]
scenery	**scenografia** (f)	[ʃenogra'fia]

backstage	quinte (f pl)	['kwinte]
scene (e.g., the last ~)	scena (f)	['ʃena]
act	atto (m)	['atto]
intermission	intervallo (m)	[inter'vallo]

125. Cinema

actor	attore (m)	[at'tore]
actress	attrice (f)	[at'tritʃe]
movies (industry)	cinema (m)	['tʃinema]
movie	film (m)	[film]
episode	puntata (f)	[pun'tata]
detective movie	film (m) giallo	[film 'dʒallo]
action movie	film (m) d'azione	[film da'tsjone]
adventure movie	film (m) d'avventure	[film davven'ture]
sci-fi movie	film (m) di fantascienza	['film de fanta'ʃentsa]
horror movie	film (m) d'orrore	[film dor'rore]
comedy movie	film (m) comico	[film 'komiko]
melodrama	melodramma (m)	[melo'dramma]
drama	dramma (m)	['dramma]
fictional movie	film (m) a soggetto	[film a so'dʒetto]
documentary	documentario (m)	[dokumen'tario]
cartoon	cartoni (m pl) animati	[kar'toni ani'mati]
silent movies	cinema (m) muto	['tʃinema 'muto]
role (part)	parte (f)	['parte]
leading role	parte (f) principale	['parte printʃi'pale]
to play (vi, vt)	recitare (vi, vt)	[retʃi'tare]
movie star	star (f), stella (f)	[star], ['stella]
well-known (adj)	noto	['noto]
famous (adj)	famoso	[fa'mozo]
popular (adj)	popolare	[popo'lare]
script (screenplay)	sceneggiatura (m)	[ʃenedʒa'tura]
scriptwriter	sceneggiatore (m)	[ʃenedʒa'tore]
movie director	regista (m)	[re'dʒista]
producer	produttore (m)	[produt'tore]
assistant	assistente (m)	[assi'stente]
cameraman	cameraman (m)	[kamera'men]
stuntman	cascatore (m)	[kaska'tore]
double (stand-in)	controfigura (f)	[kontrofi'gura]
to shoot a movie	girare un film	[dʒi'rare un film]
audition, screen test	provino (m)	[pro'vino]
shooting	ripresa (f)	[ri'preza]

movie crew	troupe (f) cinematografica	[trup tʃinemato'grafika]
movie set	set (m)	[set]
camera	cinepresa (f)	[tʃine'preza]
movie theater	cinema (m)	['tʃinema]
screen (e.g., big ~)	schermo (m)	['skermo]
to show a movie	proiettare un film	[projet'tare un film]
soundtrack	colonna (f) sonora	[ko'lonna so'nora]
special effects	effetti (m pl) speciali	[ef'fetti spe'tʃali]
subtitles	sottotitoli (m pl)	[sotto'titoli]
credits	titoli (m pl) di coda	['titoli di 'koda]
translation	traduzione (f)	[tradu'tsjone]

126. Painting

art	arte (f)	['arte]
fine arts	belle arti (f pl)	['belle 'arti]
art gallery	galleria (f) d'arte	[galle'ria 'darte]
art exhibition	mostra (f)	['mostra]
painting (art)	pittura (f)	[pit'tura]
graphic art	grafica (f)	['grafika]
abstract art	astrattismo (m)	[astrat'tizmo]
impressionism	impressionismo (m)	[impressio'nizmo]
picture (painting)	quadro (m)	['kwadro]
drawing	disegno (m)	[di'zeɲo]
poster	cartellone (m)	[kartel'lone]
illustration (picture)	illustrazione (f)	[illustra'tsjone]
miniature	miniatura (f)	[minia'tura]
copy (of painting, etc.)	copia (f)	['kopia]
reproduction	riproduzione (f)	[riprodu'tsjone]
mosaic	mosaico (m)	[mo'zaiko]
stained glass window	vetrata (f)	[ve'trata]
fresco	affresco (m)	[af'fresko]
engraving	incisione (f)	[intʃi'zjone]
bust (sculpture)	busto (m)	['busto]
sculpture	scultura (f)	[skul'tura]
statue	statua (f)	['statua]
plaster of Paris	gesso (m)	['dʒesso]
plaster (as adj)	in gesso	[in 'dʒesso]
portrait	ritratto (m)	[ri'tratto]
self-portrait	autoritratto (m)	[autori'tratto]
landscape painting	paesaggio (m)	[pae'zadʒo]

still life	natura (f) morta	[na'tura 'morta]
caricature	caricatura (f)	[karika'tura]
sketch	abbozzo (m)	[ab'bottso]

paint	colore (m)	[ko'lore]
watercolor paint	acquerello (m)	[akwe'rello]
oil (paint)	olio (m)	['oljo]
pencil	matita (f)	[ma'tita]
India ink	inchiostro (m) di china	[in'kjostro di 'kina]
charcoal	carbone (m)	[kar'bone]

| to draw (vi, vt) | disegnare (vt) | [dize'ɲare] |
| to paint (vi, vt) | dipingere (vt) | [di'pindʒere] |

to pose (vi)	posare (vi)	[po'zare]
artist's model (masc.)	modello (m)	[mo'dello]
artist's model (fem.)	modella (f)	[mo'della]

artist (painter)	pittore (m)	[pit'tore]
work of art	opera (f) d'arte	['opera 'darte]
masterpiece	capolavoro (m)	[kapo·la'voro]
studio (artist's workroom)	laboratorio (m)	[labora'torio]

canvas (cloth)	tela (f)	['tela]
easel	cavalletto (m)	[kaval'letto]
palette	tavolozza (f)	[tavo'lottsa]

frame (picture ~, etc.)	cornice (f)	[kor'nitʃe]
restoration	restauro (m)	[re'stauro]
to restore (vt)	restaurare (vt)	[restau'rare]

127. Literature & Poetry

literature	letteratura (f)	[lettera'tura]
author (writer)	autore (m)	[au'tore]
pseudonym	pseudonimo (m)	[pseu'donimo]

book	libro (m)	['libro]
volume	volume (m)	[vo'lume]
table of contents	sommario (m), indice (m)	[som'mario], ['inditʃe]
page	pagina (f)	['padʒina]
main character	protagonista (m)	[protago'nista]
autograph	autografo (m)	[au'tografo]

short story	racconto (m)	[rak'konto]
story (novella)	romanzo (m) breve	[ro'mandzo 'breve]
novel	romanzo (m)	[ro'mandzo]
work (writing)	opera (f)	['opera]
fable	favola (f)	['favola]
detective novel	giallo (m)	['dʒallo]

poem (verse)	**verso** (m)	['verso]
poetry	**poesia** (f)	[poe'zia]
poem (epic, ballad)	**poema** (m)	[po'ema]
poet	**poeta** (m)	[po'eta]
fiction	**narrativa** (f)	[narra'tiva]
science fiction	**fantascienza** (f)	[fanta'ʃentsa]
adventures	**avventure** (f pl)	[avven'ture]
educational literature	**letteratura** (f) **formativa**	[lettera'tura forma'tiva]
children's literature	**libri** (m pl) **per l'infanzia**	['libri per lin'fansia]

128. Circus

circus	**circo** (m)	['tʃirko]
traveling circus	**tendone** (m) **del circo**	[ten'done del 'tʃirko]
program	**programma** (m)	[pro'gramma]
performance	**spettacolo** (m)	[spet'takolo]
act (circus ~)	**numero** (m)	['numero]
circus ring	**arena** (f)	[a'rena]
pantomime (act)	**pantomima** (m)	[panto'mima]
clown	**pagliaccio** (m)	[paʎ'ʎatʃo]
acrobat	**acrobata** (m)	[a'krobata]
acrobatics	**acrobatica** (f)	[akro'batika]
gymnast	**ginnasta** (m)	[dʒin'nasta]
acrobatic gymnastics	**ginnastica** (m)	[dʒin'nastika]
somersault	**salto** (m) **mortale**	['salto mor'tale]
athlete (strongman)	**forzuto** (m)	[for'tsuto]
tamer (e.g., lion ~)	**domatore** (m)	[doma'tore]
rider (circus horse ~)	**cavallerizzo** (m)	[kavalle'riddzo]
assistant	**assistente** (m)	[assi'stente]
stunt	**acrobazia** (f)	[akroba'tsia]
magic trick	**gioco** (m) **di prestigio**	['dʒoko di pre'stidʒo]
conjurer, magician	**prestigiatore** (m)	[prestidʒa'tore]
juggler	**giocoliere** (m)	[dʒoko'ljere]
to juggle (vi, vt)	**giocolare** (vi)	[dʒoko'lare]
animal trainer	**ammaestratore** (m)	[ammaestra'tore]
animal training	**ammaestramento** (m)	[ammaestra'mento]
to train (animals)	**ammaestrare** (vt)	[ammae'strare]

129. Music. Pop music

music	**musica** (f)	['muzika]
musician	**musicista** (m)	[muzi'tʃista]

musical instrument	strumento (m) musicale	[stru'mento muzi'kale]
to play ...	suonare ...	[suo'nare]
guitar	chitarra (f)	[ki'tarra]
violin	violino (m)	[vio'lino]
cello	violoncello (m)	[violon'tʃello]
double bass	contrabbasso (m)	[kontrab'basso]
harp	arpa (f)	['arpa]
piano	pianoforte (m)	[pjano'forte]
grand piano	pianoforte (m) a coda	[pjano'forte a 'koda]
organ	organo (m)	['organo]
wind instruments	strumenti (m pl) a fiato	[stru'menti a 'fjato]
oboe	oboe (m)	['oboe]
saxophone	sassofono (m)	[sas'sofono]
clarinet	clarinetto (m)	[klari'netto]
flute	flauto (m)	['flauto]
trumpet	tromba (f)	['tromba]
accordion	fisarmonica (f)	[fizar'monika]
drum	tamburo (m)	[tam'buro]
duo	duetto (m)	[du'etto]
trio	trio (m)	['trio]
quartet	quartetto (m)	[kwar'tetto]
choir	coro (m)	['koro]
orchestra	orchestra (f)	[or'kestra]
pop music	musica (f) pop	['muzika pop]
rock music	musica (f) rock	['muzika rok]
rock group	gruppo (m) rock	['gruppo rok]
jazz	jazz (m)	[dʒaz]
idol	idolo (m)	['idolo]
admirer, fan	ammiratore (m)	[ammira'tore]
concert	concerto (m)	[kon'tʃerto]
symphony	sinfonia (f)	[sinfo'nia]
composition	composizione (f)	[kompozi'tsjone]
to compose (write)	comporre (vt)	[kom'porre]
singing (n)	canto (m)	['kanto]
song	canzone (f)	[kan'tsone]
tune (melody)	melodia (f)	[melo'dia]
rhythm	ritmo (m)	['ritmo]
blues	blues (m)	[bluz]
sheet music	note (f pl)	['note]
baton	bacchetta (f)	[bak'ketta]
bow	arco (m)	['arko]
string	corda (f)	['korda]
case (e.g., guitar ~)	custodia (f)	[ku'stodia]

Rest. Entertainment. Travel

130. Trip. Travel

tourism, travel	**turismo** (m)	[tu'rizmo]
tourist	**turista** (m)	[tu'rista]
trip, voyage	**viaggio** (m)	['vjaʤo]
adventure	**avventura** (f)	[avven'tura]
trip, journey	**viaggio** (m)	['vjaʤo]
vacation	**vacanza** (f)	[va'kantsa]
to be on vacation	**essere in vacanza**	['essere in va'kantsa]
rest	**riposo** (m)	[ri'pozo]
train	**treno** (m)	['treno]
by train	**in treno**	[in 'treno]
airplane	**aereo** (m)	[a'ereo]
by airplane	**in aereo**	[in a'ereo]
by car	**in macchina**	[in 'makkina]
by ship	**in nave**	[in 'nave]
luggage	**bagaglio** (m)	[ba'gaʎʎo]
suitcase	**valigia** (f)	[va'liʤa]
luggage cart	**carrello** (m)	[kar'rello]
passport	**passaporto** (m)	[passa'porto]
visa	**visto** (m)	['visto]
ticket	**biglietto** (m)	[biʎ'ʎetto]
air ticket	**biglietto** (m) **aereo**	[biʎ'ʎetto a'ereo]
guidebook	**guida** (f)	['gwida]
map (tourist ~)	**carta** (f) **geografica**	['karta ʤeo'grafika]
area (rural ~)	**località** (f)	[lokali'ta]
place, site	**luogo** (m)	[lu'ogo]
exotica (n)	**ogetti** (m pl) **esotici**	[o'ʤetti e'zotiʧi]
exotic (adj)	**esotico**	[e'zotiko]
amazing (adj)	**sorprendente**	[sorpren'dente]
group	**gruppo** (m)	['gruppo]
excursion, sightseeing tour	**escursione** (f)	[eskur'sjone]
guide (person)	**guida** (f)	['gwida]

131. Hotel

hotel	**albergo, hotel** (m)	[al'bergo], [o'tel]
motel	**motel** (m)	[mo'tel]
three-star (~ hotel)	**tre stelle**	[tre 'stelle]
five-star	**cinque stelle**	['tʃinkwe 'stelle]
to stay (in a hotel, etc.)	**alloggiare** (vi)	[allo'dʒare]
room	**camera** (f)	['kamera]
single room	**camera** (f) **singola**	['kamera 'singola]
double room	**camera** (f) **doppia**	['kamera 'doppia]
to book a room	**prenotare una camera**	[preno'tare 'una 'kamera]
half board	**mezza pensione** (f)	['meddza pen'sjone]
full board	**pensione** (f) **completa**	[pen'sjone kom'pleta]
with bath	**con bagno**	[kon 'baɲo]
with shower	**con doccia**	[kon 'dotʃa]
satellite television	**televisione** (f) **satellitare**	[televi'zjone satelli'tare]
air-conditioner	**condizionatore** (m)	[konditsiona'tore]
towel	**asciugamano** (m)	[aʃuga'mano]
key	**chiave** (f)	['kjave]
administrator	**amministratore** (m)	[amministra'tore]
chambermaid	**cameriera** (f)	[kame'rjera]
porter, bellboy	**portabagagli** (m)	[porta·ba'gaʎʎi]
doorman	**portiere** (m)	[por'tjere]
restaurant	**ristorante** (m)	[risto'rante]
pub, bar	**bar** (m)	[bar]
breakfast	**colazione** (f)	[kola'tsjone]
dinner	**cena** (f)	['tʃena]
buffet	**buffet** (m)	[buf'fe]
lobby	**hall** (f)	[oll]
elevator	**ascensore** (m)	[aʃen'sore]
DO NOT DISTURB	**NON DISTURBARE**	[non distur'bare]
NO SMOKING	**VIETATO FUMARE!**	[vje'tato fu'mare]

132. Books. Reading

book	**libro** (m)	['libro]
author	**autore** (m)	[au'tore]
writer	**scrittore** (m)	[skrit'tore]
to write (~ a book)	**scrivere** (vi, vt)	['skrivere]
reader	**lettore** (m)	[let'tore]
to read (vi, vt)	**leggere** (vi, vt)	['ledʒere]

reading (activity)	**lettura** (f)	[let'tura]
silently (to oneself)	**in silenzio**	[in si'lentsio]
aloud (adv)	**ad alta voce**	[ad 'alta 'votʃe]

to publish (vt)	**pubblicare** (vt)	[pubbli'kare]
publishing (process)	**pubblicazione** (f)	[publika'tsjone]
publisher	**editore** (m)	[edi'tore]
publishing house	**casa** (f) **editrice**	['kaza edi'tritʃe]

to come out (be released)	**uscire** (vi)	[u'ʃire]
release (of a book)	**uscita** (f)	[u'ʃita]
print run	**tiratura** (f)	[tira'tura]

| bookstore | **libreria** (f) | [libre'ria] |
| library | **biblioteca** (f) | [biblio'teka] |

story (novella)	**romanzo** (m) **breve**	[ro'mandzo 'breve]
short story	**racconto** (m)	[rak'konto]
novel	**romanzo** (m)	[ro'mandzo]
detective novel	**giallo** (m)	['dʒallo]

memoirs	**memorie** (f pl)	[me'morie]
legend	**leggenda** (f)	[le'dʒenda]
myth	**mito** (m)	['mito]

poetry, poems	**poesia** (f), **versi** (m pl)	[poe'zia], ['versi]
autobiography	**autobiografia** (f)	[auto·biogra'fia]
selected works	**opere** (f pl) **scelte**	['opere 'ʃelte]
science fiction	**fantascienza** (f)	[fanta'ʃentsa]

title	**titolo** (m)	['titolo]
introduction	**introduzione** (f)	[introdu'tsjone]
title page	**frontespizio** (m)	[fronte'spitsio]

chapter	**capitolo** (m)	[ka'pitolo]
extract	**frammento** (m)	[fram'mento]
episode	**episodio** (m)	[epi'zodio]

plot (storyline)	**soggetto** (m)	[so'dʒetto]
contents	**contenuto** (m)	[konte'nuto]
table of contents	**sommario** (m)	[som'mario]
main character	**protagonista** (m)	[protago'nista]

volume	**volume** (m)	[vo'lume]
cover	**copertina** (f)	[koper'tina]
binding	**rilegatura** (f)	[rilega'tura]
bookmark	**segnalibro** (m)	[seɲa'libro]
page	**pagina** (f)	['padʒina]
to page through	**sfogliare** (vt)	[sfoʎ'ʎare]
margins	**margini** (m pl)	['mardʒini]
annotation	**annotazione** (f)	[annota'tsjone]
(marginal note, etc.)		

footnote	nota (f)	['nota]
text	testo (m)	['testo]
type, font	carattere (m)	[ka'rattere]
misprint, typo	refuso (m)	[re'fuzo]
translation	traduzione (f)	[tradu'tsjone]
to translate (vt)	tradurre (vt)	[tra'durre]
original (n)	originale (m)	[oridʒi'nale]
famous (adj)	famoso	[fa'mozo]
unknown (not famous)	sconosciuto	[skono'ʃuto]
interesting (adj)	interessante	[interes'sante]
bestseller	best seller (m)	[best 'seller]
dictionary	dizionario (m)	[ditsjo'nario]
textbook	manuale (m)	[manu'ale]
encyclopedia	enciclopedia (f)	[entʃiklope'dia]

133. Hunting. Fishing

hunting	caccia (f)	['katʃa]
to hunt (vi, vt)	cacciare (vt)	[ka'tʃare]
hunter	cacciatore (m)	[katʃa'tore]
to shoot (vi)	sparare (vi)	[spa'rare]
rifle	fucile (m)	[fu'tʃile]
bullet (shell)	cartuccia (f)	[kar'tutʃa]
shot (lead balls)	pallini (m pl)	[pal'lini]
steel trap	tagliola (f)	[taʎ'ʎoʎa]
snare (for birds, etc.)	trappola (f)	['trappola]
to fall into the steel trap	cadere in trappola	[ka'dere in 'trappola]
to lay a steel trap	tendere una trappola	['tendere 'una 'trappola]
poacher	bracconiere (m)	[brakko'njere]
game (in hunting)	cacciagione (m)	[katʃa'dʒone]
hound dog	cane (m) da caccia	['kane da 'katʃa]
safari	safari (m)	[sa'fari]
mounted animal	animale (m) impagliato	[ani'male impaʎ'ʎato]
fisherman, angler	pescatore (m)	[peska'tore]
fishing (angling)	pesca (f)	['peska]
to fish (vi)	pescare (vi)	[pe'skare]
fishing rod	canna (f) da pesca	['kanna da 'peska]
fishing line	lenza (f)	['lentsa]
hook	amo (m)	['amo]
float, bobber	galleggiante (m)	[galle'dʒante]
bait	esca (f)	['eska]
to cast a line	lanciare la canna	[lan'tʃare la 'kanna]

to bite (ab. fish)	abboccare (vi)	[abbok'kare]
catch (of fish)	pescato (m)	[pe'skato]
ice-hole	buco (m) nel ghiaccio	['buko nel 'gjatʃo]

fishing net	rete (f)	['rete]
boat	barca (f)	['barka]
to net (to fish with a net)	prendere con la rete	['prendere kon la 'rete]
to cast[throw] the net	gettare la rete	[dʒet'tare la 'rete]
to haul the net in	tirare le reti	[ti'rare le 'reti]
to fall into the net	cadere nella rete	[ka'dere 'nella 'rete]

whaler (person)	baleniere (m)	[bale'njere]
whaleboat	baleniera (f)	[bale'njera]
harpoon	rampone (m)	[ram'pone]

134. Games. Billiards

billiards	biliardo (m)	[bi'ljardo]
billiard room, hall	sala (f) da biliardo	['sala da bi'ljardo]
ball (snooker, etc.)	bilia (f)	['bilia]

to pocket a ball	imbucare (vt)	[imbu'kare]
cue	stecca (f) da biliardo	['stekka da bi'ljardo]
pocket	buca (f)	['buka]

135. Games. Playing cards

diamonds	quadri (m pl)	['kwadri]
spades	picche (f pl)	['pikke]
hearts	cuori (m pl)	[ku'ori]
clubs	fiori (m pl)	['fjori]

ace	asso (m)	['asso]
king	re (m)	[re]
queen	donna (f)	['donna]
jack, knave	fante (m)	['fante]

| playing card | carta (f) da gioco | ['karta da 'dʒoko] |
| cards | carte (f pl) | ['karte] |

| trump | briscola (f) | ['briskola] |
| deck of cards | mazzo (m) di carte | ['mattso di 'karte] |

point	punto (m)	['punto]
to deal (vi, vt)	dare le carte	['dare le 'karte]
to shuffle (cards)	mescolare (vt)	[mesko'lare]
lead, turn (n)	turno (m)	['turno]
cardsharp	baro (m)	['baro]

136. Rest. Games. Miscellaneous

to stroll (vi, vt)	passeggiare (vi)	[passe'dʒare]
stroll (leisurely walk)	passeggiata (f)	[passe'dʒata]
car ride	gita (f)	['dʒita]
adventure	avventura (f)	[avven'tura]
picnic	picnic (m)	['piknik]
game (chess, etc.)	gioco (m)	['dʒoko]
player	giocatore (m)	[dʒoka'tore]
game (one ~ of chess)	partita (f)	[par'tita]
collector (e.g., philatelist)	collezionista (m)	[kolletsjo'nista]
to collect (stamps, etc.)	collezionare (vt)	[kolletsio'nare]
collection	collezione (f)	[kolle'tsjone]
crossword puzzle	cruciverba (m)	[krutʃi'verba]
racetrack	ippodromo (m)	[ip'podromo]
(horse racing venue)		
disco (discotheque)	discoteca (f)	[disko'teka]
sauna	sauna (f)	['sauna]
lottery	lotteria (f)	[lotte'ria]
camping trip	campeggio (m)	[kam'pedʒo]
camp	campo (m)	['kampo]
tent (for camping)	tenda (f) da campeggio	['tenda da kam'pedʒo]
compass	bussola (f)	['bussola]
camper	campeggiatore (m)	[kampedʒa'tore]
to watch (movie, etc.)	guardare (vt)	[gwar'dare]
viewer	telespettatore (m)	[telespetta'tore]
TV show (TV program)	trasmissione (f)	[trazmis'sjone]

137. Photography

camera (photo)	macchina (f) fotografica	['makkina foto'grafika]
photo, picture	fotografia (f)	[fotogra'fia]
photographer	fotografo (m)	[fo'tografo]
photo studio	studio (m) fotografico	['studio foto'grafiko]
photo album	album (m) di fotografie	['album di fotogra'fie]
camera lens	obiettivo (m)	[objet'tivo]
telephoto lens	teleobiettivo (m)	[teleobjet'tivo]
filter	filtro (m)	['filtro]
lens	lente (f)	['lente]
optics (high-quality ~)	ottica (f)	['ottika]
diaphragm (aperture)	diaframma (m)	[dia'framma]

| exposure time (shutter speed) | tempo (m) di esposizione | ['tempo di espozi'tsjone] |
| viewfinder | mirino (m) | [mi'rino] |

digital camera	fotocamera (f) digitale	[foto'kamera didʒi'tale]
tripod	cavalletto (m)	[kaval'letto]
flash	flash (m)	[fleʃ]

to photograph (vt)	fotografare (vt)	[fotogra'fare]
to take pictures	fare foto	['fare 'foto]
to have one's picture taken	fotografarsi	[fotogra'farsi]

focus	fuoco (m)	[fu'oko]
to focus	mettere a fuoco	['mettere a fu'oko]
sharp, in focus (adj)	nitido	['nitido]
sharpness	nitidezza (f)	[niti'dettsa]

| contrast | contrasto (m) | [kon'trasto] |
| contrast (as adj) | contrastato | [kontra'stato] |

picture (photo)	foto (f)	['foto]
negative (n)	negativa (f)	[nega'tiva]
film (a roll of ~)	pellicola (f) fotografica	[pel'likola foto'grafika]
frame (still)	fotogramma (m)	[foto'gramma]
to print (photos)	stampare (vt)	[stam'pare]

138. Beach. Swimming

beach	spiaggia (f)	['spjadʒa]
sand	sabbia (f)	['sabbia]
deserted (beach)	deserto	[de'zerto]

suntan	abbronzatura (f)	[abbrondza'tura]
to get a tan	abbronzarsi (vr)	[abbron'dzarsi]
tan (adj)	abbronzato	[abbron'dzato]
sunscreen	crema (f) solare	['krema so'lare]

bikini	bikini (m)	[bi'kini]
bathing suit	costume (m) da bagno	[ko'stume da 'baɲo]
swim trunks	slip (m) da bagno	[zlip da 'baɲo]

swimming pool	piscina (f)	[pi'ʃina]
to swim (vi)	nuotare (vi)	[nuo'tare]
shower	doccia (f)	['dotʃa]
to change (one's clothes)	cambiarsi (vr)	[kam'bjarsi]
towel	asciugamano (m)	[aʃuga'mano]

boat	barca (f)	['barka]
motorboat	motoscafo (m)	[moto'skafo]
water ski	sci (m) nautico	[ʃi 'nautiko]

paddle boat	**pedalò** (m)	[peda'lo]
surfing	**surf** (m)	[serf]
surfer	**surfista** (m)	[sur'fista]
scuba set	**autorespiratore** (m)	[autorespira'tore]
flippers (swim fins)	**pinne** (f pl)	['pinne]
mask (diving ~)	**maschera** (f)	['maskera]
diver	**subacqueo** (m)	[su'bakveo]
to dive (vi)	**tuffarsi** (vr)	[tuf'farsi]
underwater (adv)	**sott'acqua**	[so'takva]
beach umbrella	**ombrellone** (m)	[ombrel'lone]
sunbed (lounger)	**sdraio** (f)	['zdrajo]
sunglasses	**occhiali** (m pl) **da sole**	[ok'kjali da 'sole]
air mattress	**materasso** (m) **ad aria**	[mate'rasso ad 'aria]
to play (amuse oneself)	**giocare** (vi)	[dʒo'kare]
to go for a swim	**fare il bagno**	['fare il 'baɲo]
beach ball	**pallone** (m)	[pal'lone]
to inflate (vt)	**gonfiare** (vt)	[gon'fjare]
inflatable, air (adj)	**gonfiabile**	[gon'fjabile]
wave	**onda** (f)	['onda]
buoy (line of ~s)	**boa** (f)	['boa]
to drown (ab. person)	**annegare** (vi)	[anne'gare]
to save, to rescue	**salvare** (vt)	[sal'vare]
life vest	**giubbotto** (m) **di salvataggio**	[dʒub'botto di salva'tadʒo]
to observe, to watch	**osservare** (vt)	[osser'vare]
lifeguard	**bagnino** (m)	[ba'ɲino]

TECHNICAL EQUIPMENT. TRANSPORTATION

Technical equipment

139. Computer

computer	computer (m)	[kom'pjuter]
notebook, laptop	computer (m) portatile	[kom'pjuter por'tatile]
to turn on	accendere (vt)	[a'tʃendere]
to turn off	spegnere (vt)	['speɲere]
keyboard	tastiera (f)	[tas'tjera]
key	tasto (m)	['tasto]
mouse	mouse (m)	['maus]
mouse pad	tappetino (m) del mouse	[tappe'tino del 'maus]
button	tasto (m)	['tasto]
cursor	cursore (m)	[kur'sore]
monitor	monitor (m)	['monitor]
screen	schermo (m)	['skermo]
hard disk	disco (m) rigido	['disko 'ridʒido]
hard disk capacity	spazio (m) sul disco rigido	['spatsio sul 'disko 'ridʒido]
memory	memoria (f)	[me'moria]
random access memory	memoria (f) operativa	[me'moria opera'tiva]
file	file (m)	[fajl]
folder	cartella (f)	[kar'tella]
to open (vt)	aprire (vt)	[a'prire]
to close (vt)	chiudere (vt)	['kjudere]
to save (vt)	salvare (vt)	[sal'vare]
to delete (vt)	eliminare (vt)	[elimi'nare]
to copy (vt)	copiare (vt)	[ko'pjare]
to sort (vt)	ordinare (vt)	[ordi'nare]
to transfer (copy)	trasferire (vt)	[trasfe'rire]
program	programma (m)	[pro'gramma]
software	software (m)	['softwea]
programmer	programmatore (m)	[programma'tore]
to program (vt)	programmare (vt)	[program'mare]
hacker	hacker (m)	['aker]

password	password (f)	['password]
virus	virus (m)	['virus]
to find, to detect	trovare (vt)	[tro'vare]
byte	byte (m)	[bajt]
megabyte	megabyte (m)	['megabajt]
data	dati (m pl)	['dati]
database	database (m)	['databejz]
cable (USB, etc.)	cavo (m)	['kavo]
to disconnect (vt)	sconnettere (vt)	[skon'nettere]
to connect (sth to sth)	collegare (vt)	[kolle'gare]

140. Internet. E-mail

Internet	internet (f)	['internet]
browser	navigatore (m)	[naviga'tore]
search engine	motore (m) di ricerca	[mo'tore di ri'tʃerka]
provider	provider (m)	[pro'vajder]
webmaster	webmaster (m)	web'master]
website	sito web (m)	['sito web]
webpage	pagina web (f)	['padʒina web]
address (e-mail ~)	indirizzo (m)	[indi'rittso]
address book	rubrica (f) indirizzi	[ru'brika indi'rittsi]
mailbox	casella (f) di posta	[ka'zella di 'posta]
mail	posta (f)	['posta]
full (adj)	battaglia (f)	[bat'taʎʎa]
message	messaggio (m)	[mes'sadʒo]
incoming messages	messaggi (m pl) in arrivo	[mes'sadʒi in ar'rivo]
outgoing messages	messaggi (m pl) in uscita	[mes'sadʒo in u'ʃita]
sender	mittente (m)	[mit'tente]
to send (vt)	inviare (vt)	[in'vjare]
sending (of mail)	invio (m)	[in'vio]
receiver	destinatario (m)	[destina'tario]
to receive (vt)	ricevere (vt)	[ri'tʃevere]
correspondence	corrispondenza (f)	[korrispon'dentsa]
to correspond (vi)	essere in corrispondenza	['essere in korrispon'dentsa]
file	file (m)	[fajl]
to download (vt)	scaricare (vt)	[skari'kare]
to create (vt)	creare (vt)	[kre'are]
to delete (vt)	eliminare (vt)	[elimi'nare]

deleted (adj)	eliminato	[elimi'nato]
connection (ADSL, etc.)	connessione (f)	[konne'sjone]
speed	velocità (f)	[veloʧi'ta]
modem	modem (m)	['modem]
access	accesso (m)	[a'ʧesso]
port (e.g., input ~)	porta (f)	['porta]
connection (make a ~)	collegamento (m)	[kollega'mento]
to connect to ... (vi)	collegarsi a ...	[kolle'garsi a]
to select (vt)	scegliere (vt)	['ʃeʎʎere]
to search (for ...)	cercare (vt)	[ʧer'kare]

Transportation

141. Airplane

airplane	aereo (m)	[a'ereo]
air ticket	biglietto (m) aereo	[biʎ'ʎetto a'ereo]
airline	compagnia (f) aerea	[kompa'ɲia a'erea]
airport	aeroporto (m)	[aero'porto]
supersonic (adj)	supersonico	[super'soniko]
captain	comandante (m)	[koman'dante]
crew	equipaggio (m)	[ekwi'padʒo]
pilot	pilota (m)	[pi'lota]
flight attendant (fem.)	hostess (f)	['ostess]
navigator	navigatore (m)	[naviga'tore]
wings	ali (f pl)	['ali]
tail	coda (f)	['koda]
cockpit	cabina (f)	[ka'bina]
engine	motore (m)	[mo'tore]
undercarriage (landing gear)	carrello (m) d'atterraggio	[kar'rello datter'radʒo]
turbine	turbina (f)	[tur'bina]
propeller	elica (f)	['elika]
black box	scatola (f) nera	['skatola 'nera]
yoke (control column)	barra (f) di comando	['barra di ko'mando]
fuel	combustibile (m)	[kombu'stibile]
safety card	safety card (f)	['sejfti kard]
oxygen mask	maschera (f) ad ossigeno	['maskera ad os'sidʒeno]
uniform	uniforme (f)	[uni'forme]
life vest	giubbotto (m) di salvataggio	[dʒub'botto di salva'tadʒo]
parachute	paracadute (m)	[paraka'dute]
takeoff	decollo (m)	[de'kollo]
to take off (vi)	decollare (vi)	[dekol'lare]
runway	pista (f) di decollo	['pista di de'kollo]
visibility	visibilità (f)	[vizibili'ta]
flight (act of flying)	volo (m)	['volo]
altitude	altitudine (f)	[alti'tudine]
air pocket	vuoto (m) d'aria	[vu'oto 'daria]
seat	posto (m)	['posto]
headphones	cuffia (f)	['kuffia]

folding tray (tray table)	**tavolinetto** (m) **pieghevole**	[tavoli'netto pje'gevole]
airplane window	**oblò** (m), **finestrino** (m)	[ob'lo], [fine'strino]
aisle	**corridoio** (m)	[korri'dojo]

142. Train

train	**treno** (m)	['treno]
commuter train	**elettrotreno** (m)	[elettro'treno]
express train	**treno** (m) **rapido**	['treno 'rapido]
diesel locomotive	**locomotiva** (f) **diesel**	[lokomo'tiva 'dizel]
steam locomotive	**locomotiva** (f) **a vapore**	[lokomo'tiva a va'pore]
passenger car	**carrozza** (f)	[kar'rottsa]
dining car	**vagone** (m) **ristorante**	[va'gone risto'rante]
rails	**rotaie** (f pl)	[ro'taje]
railroad	**ferrovia** (f)	[ferro'via]
railway tie	**traversa** (f)	[tra'versa]
platform (railway ~)	**banchina** (f)	[baŋ'kina]
track (~ 1, 2, etc.)	**binario** (m)	[bi'nario]
semaphore	**semaforo** (m)	[se'maforo]
station	**stazione** (f)	[sta'tsjone]
engineer (train driver)	**macchinista** (m)	[makki'nista]
porter (of luggage)	**portabagagli** (m)	[porta·ba'gaʎʎi]
car attendant	**cuccettista** (m, f)	[kutʃet'tista]
passenger	**passeggero** (m)	[passe'dʒero]
conductor (ticket inspector)	**controllore** (m)	[kontrol'lore]
corridor (in train)	**corridoio** (m)	[korri'dojo]
emergency brake	**freno** (m) **di emergenza**	['freno di emer'dʒentsa]
compartment	**scompartimento** (m)	[skomparti'mento]
berth	**cuccetta** (f)	[ku'tʃetta]
upper berth	**cuccetta** (f) **superiore**	[ku'tʃetta supe'rjore]
lower berth	**cuccetta** (f) **inferiore**	[ku'tʃetta infe'rjore]
bed linen, bedding	**biancheria** (f) **da letto**	[bjanke'ria da 'letto]
ticket	**biglietto** (m)	[biʎ'ʎetto]
schedule	**orario** (m)	[o'rario]
information display	**tabellone** (m) **orari**	[tabel'lone o'rari]
to leave, to depart	**partire** (vi)	[par'tire]
departure (of train)	**partenza** (f)	[par'tentsa]
to arrive (ab. train)	**arrivare** (vi)	[arri'vare]
arrival	**arrivo** (m)	[ar'rivo]
to arrive by train	**arrivare con il treno**	[arri'vare kon il 'treno]
to get on the train	**salire sul treno**	[sa'lire sul 'treno]

to get off the train	scendere dal treno	['ʃendere dal 'treno]
train wreck	deragliamento (m)	[deraʎʎa'mento]
to derail (vi)	deragliare (vi)	[deraʎ'ʎare]
steam locomotive	locomotiva (f) a vapore	[lokomo'tiva a va'pore]
stoker, fireman	fuochista (m)	[fo'kista]
firebox	forno (m)	['forno]
coal	carbone (m)	[kar'bone]

143. Ship

ship	nave (f)	['nave]
vessel	imbarcazione (f)	[imbarka'tsjone]
steamship	piroscafo (m)	[pi'roskafo]
riverboat	barca (f) fluviale	['barka flu'vjale]
cruise ship	transatlantico (m)	[transat'lantiko]
cruiser	incrociatore (m)	[inkrotʃa'tore]
yacht	yacht (m)	[jot]
tugboat	rimorchiatore (m)	[rimorkja'tore]
barge	chiatta (f)	['kjatta]
ferry	traghetto (m)	[tra'getto]
sailing ship	veliero (m)	[ve'ljero]
brigantine	brigantino (m)	[brigan'tino]
ice breaker	rompighiaccio (m)	[rompi'gjatʃo]
submarine	sottomarino (m)	[sottoma'rino]
boat (flat-bottomed ~)	barca (f)	['barka]
dinghy	scialuppa (f)	[ʃa'luppa]
lifeboat	scialuppa (f) di salvataggio	[ʃa'luppa di salva'tadʒo]
motorboat	motoscafo (m)	[moto'skafo]
captain	capitano (m)	[kapi'tano]
seaman	marittimo (m)	[ma'rittimo]
sailor	marinaio (m)	[mari'najo]
crew	equipaggio (m)	[ekwi'padʒo]
boatswain	nostromo (m)	[no'stromo]
ship's boy	mozzo (m) di nave	['mottso di 'nave]
cook	cuoco (m)	[ku'oko]
ship's doctor	medico (m) di bordo	['mediko di 'bordo]
deck	ponte (m)	['ponte]
mast	albero (m)	['albero]
sail	vela (f)	['vela]
hold	stiva (f)	['stiva]

bow (prow)	**prua** (f)	['prua]
stern	**poppa** (f)	['poppa]
oar	**remo** (m)	['remo]
screw propeller	**elica** (f)	['elika]
cabin	**cabina** (f)	[ka'bina]
wardroom	**quadrato** (m) **degli ufficiali**	[kwa'drato 'deʎʎi uffi'ʧali]
engine room	**sala** (f) **macchine**	['sala 'makkine]
bridge	**ponte** (m) **di comando**	['ponte di ko'mando]
radio room	**cabina** (f) **radiotelegrafica**	[ka'bina radiotele'grafika]
wave (radio)	**onda** (f)	['onda]
logbook	**giornale** (m) **di bordo**	[ʤor'nale di 'bordo]
spyglass	**cannocchiale** (m)	[kannok'kjale]
bell	**campana** (f)	[kam'pana]
flag	**bandiera** (f)	[ban'djera]
hawser (mooring ~)	**cavo** (m) **d'ormeggio**	['kavo dor'meʤo]
knot (bowline, etc.)	**nodo** (m)	['nodo]
deckrails	**ringhiera** (f)	[rin'gjera]
gangway	**passerella** (f)	[passe'rella]
anchor	**ancora** (f)	['ankora]
to weigh anchor	**levare l'ancora**	[le'vare 'lankora]
to drop anchor	**gettare l'ancora**	[ʤet'tare 'lankora]
anchor chain	**catena** (f) **dell'ancora**	[ka'tena dell 'ankora]
port (harbor)	**porto** (m)	['porto]
quay, wharf	**banchina** (f)	[baŋ'kina]
to berth (moor)	**ormeggiarsi** (vr)	[orme'ʤarsi]
to cast off	**salpare** (vi)	[sal'pare]
trip, voyage	**viaggio** (m)	['vjaʤo]
cruise (sea trip)	**crociera** (f)	[kro'ʧera]
course (route)	**rotta** (f)	['rotta]
route (itinerary)	**itinerario** (m)	[itine'rario]
fairway (safe water channel)	**tratto** (m) **navigabile**	['tratto navi'gabile]
shallows	**secca** (f)	['sekka]
to run aground	**arenarsi** (vr)	[are'narsi]
storm	**tempesta** (f)	[tem'pesta]
signal	**segnale** (m)	[se'nale]
to sink (vi)	**affondare** (vi)	[affon'dare]
Man overboard!	**Uomo in mare!**	[u'omo in 'mare]
SOS (distress signal)	**SOS**	['esse o 'esse]
ring buoy	**salvagente** (m) **anulare**	[salva'ʤente anu'lare]

144. Airport

airport	aeroporto (m)	[aero'porto]
airplane	aereo (m)	[a'ereo]
airline	compagnia (f) aerea	[kompa'ɲia a'erea]
air traffic controller	controllore (m) di volo	[kontrol'lore di 'volo]
departure	partenza (f)	[par'tentsa]
arrival	arrivo (m)	[ar'rivo]
to arrive (by plane)	arrivare (vi)	[arri'vare]
departure time	ora (f) di partenza	['ora di par'tentsa]
arrival time	ora (f) di arrivo	['ora di ar'rivo]
to be delayed	essere ritardato	['essere ritar'dato]
flight delay	volo (m) ritardato	['volo ritar'dato]
information board	tabellone (m) orari	[tabel'lone o'rari]
information	informazione (f)	[informa'tsjone]
to announce (vt)	annunciare (vt)	[annun'tʃare]
flight (e.g., next ~)	volo (m)	['volo]
customs	dogana (f)	[do'gana]
customs officer	doganiere (m)	[doga'njere]
customs declaration	dichiarazione (f)	[dikjara'tsjone]
to fill out (vt)	riempire (vt)	[riem'pire]
to fill out the declaration	riempire una dichiarazione	[riem'pire 'una dikjara'tsjone]
passport control	controllo (m) passaporti	[kon'trollo passa'porti]
luggage	bagaglio (m)	[ba'gaʎʎo]
hand luggage	bagaglio (m) a mano	[ba'gaʎʎo a 'mano]
luggage cart	carrello (m)	[kar'rello]
landing	atterraggio (m)	[atter'radʒo]
landing strip	pista (f) di atterraggio	['pista di atter'radʒo]
to land (vi)	atterrare (vi)	[atter'rare]
airstair (passenger stair)	scaletta (f) dell'aereo	[ska'letta dell a'ereo]
check-in	check-in (m)	[tʃek-in]
check-in counter	banco (m) del check-in	['banko del tʃek-in]
to check-in (vi)	fare il check-in	['fare il tʃek-in]
boarding pass	carta (f) d'imbarco	['karta dim'barko]
departure gate	porta (f) d'imbarco	['porta dim'barko]
transit	transito (m)	['tranzito]
to wait (vt)	aspettare (vt)	[aspet'tare]
departure lounge	sala (f) d'attesa	['sala dat'teza]
to see off	accompagnare (vt)	[akkompa'ɲare]
to say goodbye	congedarsi (vr)	[kondʒe'darsi]

145. Bicycle. Motorcycle

bicycle	**bicicletta** (f)	[bitʃi'kletta]
scooter	**motorino** (m)	[moto'rino]
motorcycle, bike	**motocicletta** (f)	[mototʃi'kletta]
to go by bicycle	**andare in bicicletta**	[an'dare in bitʃi'kletta]
handlebars	**manubrio** (m)	[ma'nubrio]
pedal	**pedale** (m)	[pe'dale]
brakes	**freni** (m pl)	['freni]
bicycle seat (saddle)	**sellino** (m)	[sel'lino]
pump	**pompa** (f)	['pompa]
luggage rack	**portabagagli** (m)	[porta·ba'gaʎʎi]
front lamp	**fanale** (m) **anteriore**	[fa'nale ante'rjore]
helmet	**casco** (m)	['kasko]
wheel	**ruota** (f)	[ru'ota]
fender	**parafango** (m)	[para'fango]
rim	**cerchione** (m)	[tʃer'kjone]
spoke	**raggio** (m)	['radʒo]

Cars

146. Types of cars

automobile, car	**automobile** (f)	[auto'mobile]
sports car	**auto** (f) **sportiva**	['auto spor'tiva]
limousine	**limousine** (f)	[limu'zin]
off-road vehicle	**fuoristrada** (m)	[fuori'strada]
convertible (n)	**cabriolet** (m)	[kabrio'le]
minibus	**pulmino** (m)	[pul'mino]
ambulance	**ambulanza** (f)	[ambu'lantsa]
snowplow	**spazzaneve** (m)	[spattsa'neve]
truck	**camion** (m)	['kamjon]
tanker truck	**autocisterna** (f)	[auto·ʧi'sterna]
van (small truck)	**furgone** (m)	[fur'gone]
road tractor (trailer truck)	**motrice** (f)	[mo'triʧe]
trailer	**rimorchio** (m)	[ri'morkio]
comfortable (adj)	**confortevole**	[konfor'tevole]
used (adj)	**di seconda mano**	[di se'konda 'mano]

147. Cars. Bodywork

hood	**cofano** (m)	['kofano]
fender	**parafango** (m)	[para'fango]
roof	**tetto** (m)	['tetto]
windshield	**parabrezza** (m)	[para'breddza]
rear-view mirror	**retrovisore** (m)	[retrovi'zore]
windshield washer	**lavacristallo** (m)	[lava kris'tallo]
windshield wipers	**tergicristallo** (m)	[terdʒikris'tallo]
side window	**finestrino** (m) **laterale**	[fine'strino late'rale]
window lift (power window)	**alzacristalli** (m)	[altsa·kri'stalli]
antenna	**antenna** (f)	[an'tenna]
sunroof	**tettuccio** (m) **apribile**	[tet'tutʃo a'pribile]
bumper	**paraurti** (m)	[para'urti]
trunk	**bagagliaio** (m)	[bagaʎ'ʎajo]
roof luggage rack	**portapacchi** (m)	[porta'pakki]
door	**portiera** (f)	[por'tjera]

door handle	maniglia (f)	[ma'niʎʎa]
door lock	serratura (f)	[serra'tura]
license plate	targa (f)	['targa]
muffler	marmitta (f)	[mar'mitta]
gas tank	serbatoio (m) della benzina	[serba'tojo della ben'dzina]
tailpipe	tubo (m) di scarico	['tubo di 'skariko]
gas, accelerator	acceleratore (m)	[atʃelera'tore]
pedal	pedale (m)	[pe'dale]
gas pedal	pedale (m) dell'acceleratore	[pe'dale dell atʃelera'tore]
brake	freno (m)	['freno]
brake pedal	pedale (m) del freno	[pe'dale del 'freno]
to brake (use the brake)	frenare (vi)	[fre'nare]
parking brake	freno (m) a mano	['freno a 'mano]
clutch	frizione (f)	[fri'tsjone]
clutch pedal	pedale (m) della frizione	[pe'dale 'della fri'tsjone]
clutch disc	disco (m) della frizione	['disko 'della fri'tsjone]
shock absorber	ammortizzatore (m)	[ammortiddza'tore]
wheel	ruota (f)	[ru'ota]
spare tire	ruota (f) di scorta	[ru'ota di 'skorta]
tire	pneumatico (m)	[pneu'matiko]
hubcap	copriruota (m)	[kopri·ru'ota]
driving wheels	ruote (f pl) motrici	[ru'ote mo'tritʃi]
front-wheel drive (as adj)	a trazione anteriore	[a tra'tsjone ante'rjore]
rear-wheel drive (as adj)	a trazione posteriore	[a tra'tsjone poste'rjore]
all-wheel drive (as adj)	a trazione integrale	[a tra'tsjone inte'grale]
gearbox	scatola (f) del cambio	['skatola del 'kambio]
automatic (adj)	automatico	[auto'matiko]
mechanical (adj)	meccanico	[mek'kaniko]
gear shift	leva (f) del cambio	['leva del 'kambio]
headlight	faro (m)	['faro]
headlights	luci (f pl), fari (m pl)	['lutʃi], ['fari]
low beam	luci (f pl) anabbaglianti	['lutʃi anabbaʎ'ʎanti]
high beam	luci (f pl) abbaglianti	['lutʃi abbaʎ'ʎanti]
brake light	luci (f pl) di arresto	['lutʃi di ar'resto]
parking lights	luci (f pl) di posizione	['lutʃi di pozi'tsjone]
hazard lights	luci (f pl) di emergenza	['lutʃi di emer'dʒentsa]
fog lights	fari (m pl) antinebbia	['fari anti'nebbia]
turn signal	freccia (f)	['fretʃa]
back-up light	luci (f pl) di retromarcia	['lutʃi di retro'martʃa]

148. Cars. Passenger compartment

car inside (interior)	abitacolo (m)	[abi'takolo]
leather (as adj)	di pelle	[di 'pelle]
velour (as adj)	in velluto	[in vel'luto]
upholstery	rivestimento (m)	[rivesti'mento]
instrument (gage)	strumento (m) di bordo	[stru'mento di 'bordo]
dashboard	cruscotto (m)	[kru'skotto]
speedometer	tachimetro (m)	[ta'kimetro]
needle (pointer)	lancetta (f)	[lan'tʃetta]
odometer	contachilometri (m)	[kontaki'lometri]
indicator (sensor)	indicatore (m)	[indika'tore]
level	livello (m)	[li'vello]
warning light	spia (f) luminosa	['spia lumi'noza]
steering wheel	volante (m)	[vo'lante]
horn	clacson (m)	['klakson]
button	pulsante (m)	[pul'sante]
switch	interruttore (m)	[interrut'tore]
seat	sedile (m)	[se'dile]
backrest	spalliera (f)	[spal'ljera]
headrest	appoggiatesta (m)	[appodʒa'testa]
seat belt	cintura (f) di sicurezza	[tʃin'tura di siku'rettsa]
to fasten the belt	allacciare la cintura	[ala'tʃare la tʃin'tura]
adjustment (of seats)	regolazione (f)	[regola'tsjone]
airbag	airbag (m)	['erbeg]
air-conditioner	condizionatore (m)	[konditsiona'tore]
radio	radio (f)	['radio]
CD player	lettore (m) CD	[let'tore tʃi'di]
to turn on	accendere (vt)	[a'tʃendere]
antenna	antenna (f)	[an'tenna]
glove box	vano (m) portaoggetti	['vano porta·o'dʒetti]
ashtray	portacenere (m)	[porta·'tʃenere]

149. Cars. Engine

engine, motor	motore (m)	[mo'tore]
diesel (as adj)	a diesel	[a 'dizel]
gasoline (as adj)	a benzina	[a ben'dzina]
engine volume	cilindrata (f)	[tʃilin'drata]
power	potenza (f)	[po'tentsa]
horsepower	cavallo vapore (m)	[ka'vallo va'pore]
piston	pistone (m)	[pi'stone]

| cylinder | cilindro (m) | [tʃi'lindro] |
| valve | valvola (f) | ['valvola] |

injector	iniettore (m)	[injet'tore]
generator (alternator)	generatore (m)	[dʒenera'tore]
carburetor	carburatore (m)	[karbura'tore]
motor oil	olio (m) motore	['olio mo'tore]

radiator	radiatore (m)	[radia'tore]
coolant	liquido (m) di raffreddamento	['likwido di raffredda'mento]
cooling fan	ventilatore (m)	[ventila'tore]

battery (accumulator)	batteria (m)	[batte'ria]
starter	motorino (m) d'avviamento	[moto'rino davvja'mento]
ignition	accensione (f)	[atʃen'sjone]
spark plug	candela (f) d'accensione	[kan'dela datʃen'sjone]

terminal (of battery)	morsetto (m)	[mor'setto]
positive terminal	più (m)	['pju]
negative terminal	meno (m)	['meno]
fuse	fusibile (m)	[fu'zibile]

air filter	filtro (m) dell'aria	['filtro dell 'aria]
oil filter	filtro (m) dell'olio	['filtro dell 'olio]
fuel filter	filtro (m) del carburante	['filtro del karbu'rante]

150. Cars. Crash. Repair

car crash	incidente (m)	[intʃi'dente]
traffic accident	incidente (m) stradale	[intʃi'dente stra'dale]
to crash (into the wall, etc.)	sbattere contro ...	['zbattere 'kontro]
to get smashed up	avere un incidente	[a'vere un intʃi'dente]
damage	danno (m)	['danno]
intact (unscathed)	illeso	[il'lezo]

breakdown	guasto (m), avaria (f)	['gwasto], [ava'ria]
to break down (vi)	essere rotto	['essere 'rotto]
towrope	cavo (m) di rimorchio	['kavo di ri'morkio]

puncture	foratura (f)	[fora'tura]
to be flat	essere a terra	['essere a 'terra]
to pump up	gonfiare (vt)	[gon'fjare]
pressure	pressione (f)	[pres'sjone]
to check (to examine)	verificare (vt)	[verifi'kare]

| repair | riparazione (f) | [ripara'tsjone] |
| auto repair shop | officina (f) meccanica | [offi'tʃina me'kanika] |

spare part	**pezzo** (m) **di ricambio**	['pettso di ri'kambio]
part	**pezzo** (m)	['pettso]
bolt (with nut)	**bullone** (m)	[bul'lone]
screw (fastener)	**bullone** (m) **a vite**	[bul'lone a 'vite]
nut	**dado** (m)	['dado]
washer	**rondella** (f)	[ron'della]
bearing (e.g., ball ~)	**cuscinetto** (m)	[kuʃi'netto]
tube	**tubo** (m)	['tubo]
gasket (head ~)	**guarnizione** (f)	[gwarni'tsjone]
cable, wire	**filo** (m), **cavo** (m)	['filo], ['kavo]
jack	**cric** (m)	[krik]
wrench	**chiave** (f)	['kjave]
hammer	**martello** (m)	[mar'tello]
pump	**pompa** (f)	['pompa]
screwdriver	**giravite** (m)	[dʒira'vite]
fire extinguisher	**estintore** (m)	[estin'tore]
warning triangle	**triangolo** (m) **di emergenza**	[tri'angolo di emer'dʒentsa]
to stall (vi)	**spegnersi** (vr)	['speɲersi]
stall (n)	**spegnimento** (m) **motore**	[speɲi'mento mo'tore]
to be broken	**essere rotto**	['essere 'rotto]
to overheat (vi)	**surriscaldarsi** (vr)	[surriskal'darsi]
to be clogged up	**intasarsi** (vr)	[inta'zarsi]
to freeze up (pipes, etc.)	**ghiacciarsi** (vr)	[gja'tʃarsi]
to burst (vi, ab. tube)	**spaccarsi** (vr)	[spak'karsi]
pressure	**pressione** (f)	[pres'sjone]
level	**livello** (m)	[li'vello]
slack (~ belt)	**lento**	['lento]
dent	**ammaccatura** (f)	[ammakka'tura]
knocking noise (engine)	**battito** (m)	['battito]
crack	**fessura** (f)	[fes'sura]
scratch	**graffiatura** (f)	[graffja'tura]

151. Cars. Road

road	**strada** (f)	['strada]
highway	**superstrada** (f)	[super'strada]
freeway	**autostrada** (f)	[auto'strada]
direction (way)	**direzione** (f)	[dire'tsjone]
distance	**distanza** (f)	[di'stantsa]
bridge	**ponte** (m)	['ponte]
parking lot	**parcheggio** (m)	[par'kedʒo]

square	piazza (f)	['pjattsa]
interchange	svincolo (m)	['zvinkolo]
tunnel	galleria (f), tunnel (m)	[galle'ria], ['tunnel]

gas station	distributore (m) di benzina	[distribu'tore di ben'dzina]
parking lot	parcheggio (m)	[par'kedʒo]
gas pump (fuel dispenser)	pompa (f) di benzina	['pompa di ben'dzina]
auto repair shop	officina (f) meccanica	[offi'tʃina me'kanika]
to get gas (to fill up)	fare benzina	['fare ben'dzina]
fuel	carburante (m)	[karbu'rante]
jerrycan	tanica (f)	['tanika]

asphalt	asfalto (m)	[as'falto]
road markings	segnaletica (f) stradale	[seɲa'letika stra'dale]
curb	cordolo (m)	['kordolo]
guardrail	barriera (f) di sicurezza	[bar'rjera di siku'rettsa]
ditch	fosso (m)	['fosso]
roadside (shoulder)	ciglio (m) della strada	['tʃiʎʎo della 'strada]
lamppost	lampione (m)	[lam'pjone]

to drive (a car)	guidare, condurre	[gwi'dare], [kon'durre]
to turn (e.g., ~ left)	girare (vi)	[dʒi'rare]
to make a U-turn	fare un'inversione a U	['fare un inver'sjone a u:]
reverse (~ gear)	retromarcia (m)	[retro'martʃa]

to honk (vi)	suonare il clacson	[suo'nare il 'klakson]
honk (sound)	colpo (m) di clacson	['kolpo di 'klakson]
to get stuck (in the mud, etc.)	incastrarsi (vr)	[inka'strarsi]
to spin the wheels	impantanarsi (vr)	[impanta'narsi]
to cut, to turn off (vt)	spegnere (vt)	['speɲere]

speed	velocità (f)	[velotʃi'ta]
to exceed the speed limit	superare i limiti di velocità	[supe'rare i 'limiti di velotʃi'ta]
to give a ticket	multare (vt)	[mul'tare]
traffic lights	semaforo (m)	[se'maforo]
driver's license	patente (f) di guida	[pa'tente di 'gwida]

grade crossing	passaggio (m) a livello	[pas'sadʒo a li'vello]
intersection	incrocio (m)	[in'krotʃo]
crosswalk	passaggio (m) pedonale	[pas'sadʒo pedo'nale]
bend, curve	curva (f)	['kurva]
pedestrian zone	zona (f) pedonale	['dzona pedo'nale]

PEOPLE. LIFE EVENTS

Life events

152. Holidays. Event

celebration, holiday	**festa** (f)	['festa]
national day	**festa** (f) **nazionale**	['festa natsjo'nale]
public holiday	**festività** (f) **civile**	[festivi'ta tʃi'vile]
to commemorate (vt)	**festeggiare** (vt)	[feste'dʒare]
event (happening)	**avvenimento** (m)	[avveni'mento]
event (organized activity)	**evento** (m)	[e'vento]
banquet (party)	**banchetto** (m)	[baŋ'ketto]
reception (formal party)	**ricevimento** (m)	[ritʃevi'mento]
feast	**festino** (m)	[fes'tino]
anniversary	**anniversario** (m)	[anniver'sario]
jubilee	**giubileo** (m)	[dʒubi'leo]
to celebrate (vt)	**festeggiare** (vt)	[feste'dʒare]
New Year	**Capodanno** (m)	[kapo'danno]
Happy New Year!	**Buon Anno!**	[buo'nanno]
Christmas	**Natale** (m)	[na'tale]
Merry Christmas!	**Buon Natale!**	[bu'on na'tale]
Christmas tree	**Albero** (m) **di Natale**	['albero di na'tale]
fireworks (fireworks show)	**fuochi** (m pl) **artificiali**	[fu'oki artifi'tʃali]
wedding	**nozze** (f pl)	['nottse]
groom	**sposo** (m)	['spozo]
bride	**sposa** (f)	['spoza]
to invite (vt)	**invitare** (vt)	[invi'tare]
invitation card	**invito** (m)	[in'vito]
guest	**ospite** (m)	['ospite]
to visit	**andare a trovare**	[an'dare a tro'vare]
(~ your parents, etc.)		
to meet the guests	**accogliere gli invitati**	[ak'koʎʎere ʎi invi'tati]
gift, present	**regalo** (m)	[re'galo]
to give (sth as present)	**offrire** (vt)	[of'frire]
to receive gifts	**ricevere i regali**	[ri'tʃevere i re'gali]
bouquet (of flowers)	**mazzo** (m) **di fiori**	['mattso di 'fjori]

congratulations	**auguri** (m pl)	[au'guri]
to congratulate (vt)	**augurare** (vt)	[augu'rare]
greeting card	**cartolina** (f)	[karto'lina]
to send a postcard	**mandare una cartolina**	[man'dare 'una karto'lina]
to get a postcard	**ricevere una cartolina**	[ri'tʃevere 'una karto'lina]
toast	**brindisi** (m)	['brindizi]
to offer (a drink, etc.)	**offrire** (vt)	[of'frire]
champagne	**champagne** (m)	[ʃam'paɲ]
to enjoy oneself	**divertirsi** (vr)	[diver'tirsi]
merriment (gaiety)	**allegria** (f)	[alle'gria]
joy (emotion)	**gioia** (f)	['dʒoja]
dance	**danza** (f), **ballo** (m)	['dantsa], ['ballo]
to dance (vi, vt)	**ballare** (vi, vt)	[bal'lare]
waltz	**valzer** (m)	['valtser]
tango	**tango** (m)	['tango]

153. Funerals. Burial

cemetery	**cimitero** (m)	[tʃimi'tero]
grave, tomb	**tomba** (f)	['tomba]
cross	**croce** (f)	['krotʃe]
gravestone	**pietra** (f) **tombale**	['pjetra tom'bale]
fence	**recinto** (m)	[re'tʃinto]
chapel	**cappella** (f)	[kap'pella]
death	**morte** (f)	['morte]
to die (vi)	**morire** (vi)	[mo'rire]
the deceased	**defunto** (m)	[de'funto]
mourning	**lutto** (m)	['lutto]
to bury (vt)	**seppellire** (vt)	[seppel'lire]
funeral home	**sede** (f)	['sede
	di pompe funebri	di 'pompe 'funebri]
funeral	**funerale** (m)	[fune'rale]
wreath	**corona** (f) **di fiori**	[ko'rona di 'fjori]
casket, coffin	**bara** (f)	['bara]
hearse	**carro** (m) **funebre**	['karro 'funebre]
shroud	**lenzuolo** (m) **funebre**	[lentsu'olo 'funebre]
funeral procession	**corteo** (m) **funebre**	[kor'teo 'funebre]
funerary urn	**urna** (f) **funeraria**	['urna fune'raria]
crematory	**crematorio** (m)	[krema'torio]
obituary	**necrologio** (m)	[nekro'lodʒo]
to cry (weep)	**piangere** (vi)	['pjandʒere]
to sob (vi)	**singhiozzare** (vi)	[singjot'tsare]

154. War. Soldiers

platoon	**plotone** (m)	[plo'tone]
company	**compagnia** (f)	[kompa'nia]
regiment	**reggimento** (m)	[redʒi'mento]
army	**esercito** (m)	[e'zertʃito]
division	**divisione** (f)	[divi'zjone]
section, squad	**distaccamento** (m)	[distakka'mento]
host (army)	**armata** (f)	[ar'mata]
soldier	**soldato** (m)	[sol'dato]
officer	**ufficiale** (m)	[uffi'tʃale]
private	**soldato** (m) **semplice**	[sol'dato 'semplitʃe]
sergeant	**sergente** (m)	[ser'dʒente]
lieutenant	**tenente** (m)	[te'nente]
captain	**capitano** (m)	[kapi'tano]
major	**maggiore** (m)	[ma'dʒore]
colonel	**colonnello** (m)	[kolon'nello]
general	**generale** (m)	[dʒene'rale]
sailor	**marinaio** (m)	[mari'najo]
captain	**capitano** (m)	[kapi'tano]
boatswain	**nostromo** (m)	[no'stromo]
artilleryman	**artigliere** (m)	[artiʎ'ʎere]
paratrooper	**paracadutista** (m)	[parakadu'tista]
pilot	**pilota** (m)	[pi'lota]
navigator	**navigatore** (m)	[naviga'tore]
mechanic	**meccanico** (m)	[mek'kaniko]
pioneer (sapper)	**geniere** (m)	[dʒe'njere]
parachutist	**paracadutista** (m)	[parakadu'tista]
reconnaissance scout	**esploratore** (m)	[esplora'tore]
sniper	**cecchino** (m)	[tʃek'kino]
patrol (group)	**pattuglia** (f)	[pat'tuʎʎa]
to patrol (vt)	**pattugliare** (vt)	[pattuʎ'ʎare]
sentry, guard	**sentinella** (f)	[senti'nella]
warrior	**guerriero** (m)	[gwer'rjero]
patriot	**patriota** (m)	[patri'ota]
hero	**eroe** (m)	[e'roe]
heroine	**eroina** (f)	[ero'ina]
traitor	**traditore** (m)	[tradi'tore]
deserter	**disertore** (m)	[dizer'tore]
to desert (vi)	**disertare** (vi)	[dizer'tare]
mercenary	**mercenario** (m)	[mertʃe'nario]
recruit	**recluta** (f)	['rekluta]

volunteer	**volontario** (m)	[volon'tario]
dead (n)	**ucciso** (m)	[u'tʃizo]
wounded (n)	**ferito** (m)	[fe'rito]
prisoner of war	**prigioniero** (m) **di guerra**	[pridʒo'njero di 'gwerra]

155. War. Military actions. Part 1

war	**guerra** (f)	['gwerra]
to be at war	**essere in guerra**	['essere in 'gwerra]
civil war	**guerra** (f) **civile**	['gwerra tʃi'vile]
treacherously (adv)	**perfidamente**	[perfida'mente]
declaration of war	**dichiarazione** (f) **di guerra**	[dikjara'tsjone di 'gwerra]
to declare (~ war)	**dichiarare** (vt)	[dikja'rare]
aggression	**aggressione** (f)	[aggres'sjone]
to attack (invade)	**attaccare** (vt)	[attak'kare]
to invade (vt)	**invadere** (vt)	[in'vadere]
invader	**invasore** (m)	[inva'zore]
conqueror	**conquistatore** (m)	[konkwista'tore]
defense	**difesa** (f)	[di'feza]
to defend (a country, etc.)	**difendere** (vt)	[di'fendere]
to defend (against …)	**difendersi** (vr)	[di'fendersi]
enemy	**nemico** (m)	[ne'miko]
foe, adversary	**avversario** (m)	[avver'sario]
enemy (as adj)	**ostile**	[o'stile]
strategy	**strategia** (f)	[strate'dʒia]
tactics	**tattica** (f)	['tattika]
order	**ordine** (m)	['ordine]
command (order)	**comando** (m)	[ko'mando]
to order (vt)	**ordinare** (vt)	[ordi'nare]
mission	**missione** (f)	[mis'sjone]
secret (adj)	**segreto**	[se'greto]
battle	**battaglia** (f)	[bat'taʎʎa]
combat	**combattimento** (m)	[kombatti'mento]
attack	**attacco** (m)	[at'takko]
charge (assault)	**assalto** (m)	[as'salto]
to storm (vt)	**assalire** (vt)	[assa'lire]
siege (to be under ~)	**assedio** (m)	[as'sedio]
offensive (n)	**offensiva** (f)	[offen'siva]
to go on the offensive	**passare all'offensiva**	[pas'sare all ofen'siva]
retreat	**ritirata** (f)	[riti'rata]
to retreat (vi)	**ritirarsi** (vr)	[riti'rarsi]

encirclement	**accerchiamento** (m)	[atʃerkja'mento]
to encircle (vt)	**accerchiare** (vt)	[atʃer'kjare]
bombing (by aircraft)	**bombardamento** (m)	[bombarda'mento]
to drop a bomb	**lanciare una bomba**	[lan'tʃare 'una 'bomba]
to bomb (vt)	**bombardare** (vt)	[bomar'dare]
explosion	**esplosione** (f)	[esplo'zjone]
shot	**sparo** (m)	['sparo]
to fire (~ a shot)	**sparare un colpo**	[spa'rare un 'kolpo]
firing (burst of ~)	**sparatoria** (f)	[spara'toria]
to aim (to point a weapon)	**puntare su ...**	[pun'tare su]
to point (a gun)	**puntare** (vt)	[pun'tare]
to hit (the target)	**colpire** (vt)	[kol'pire]
to sink (~ a ship)	**affondare** (vt)	[affon'dare]
hole (in a ship)	**falla** (f)	['falla]
to founder, to sink (vi)	**affondare** (vi)	[affon'dare]
front (war ~)	**fronte** (m)	['fronte]
evacuation	**evacuazione** (f)	[evakua'tsjone]
to evacuate (vt)	**evacuare** (vt)	[evaku'are]
trench	**trincea** (f)	[trin'tʃea]
barbwire	**filo** (m) **spinato**	['filo spi'nato]
barrier (anti tank ~)	**sbarramento** (m)	[zbarra'mento]
watchtower	**torretta** (f) **di osservazione**	[tor'retta di oserva'tsjone]
military hospital	**ospedale** (m) **militare**	[ospe'dale mili'tare]
to wound (vt)	**ferire** (vt)	[fe'rire]
wound	**ferita** (f)	[fe'rita]
wounded (n)	**ferito** (m)	[fe'rito]
to be wounded	**rimanere ferito**	[rima'nere fe'rito]
serious (wound)	**grave**	['grave]

156. Weapons

weapons	**armi** (f pl)	['armi]
firearms	**arma** (f) **da fuoco**	['arma da fu'oko]
cold weapons (knives, etc.)	**arma** (f) **bianca**	['arma 'bjanka]
chemical weapons	**armi** (f pl) **chimiche**	['armi 'kimike]
nuclear (adj)	**nucleare**	[nukle'are]
nuclear weapons	**armi** (f pl) **nucleari**	['armi nukle'ari]
bomb	**bomba** (f)	['bomba]
atomic bomb	**bomba** (f) **atomica**	['bomba a'tomika]

pistol (gun)	**pistola** (f)	[pi'stola]
rifle	**fucile** (m)	[fu'tʃile]
submachine gun	**mitra** (m)	['mitra]
machine gun	**mitragliatrice** (f)	[mitraʎʎa'tritʃe]
muzzle	**bocca** (f)	['bokka]
barrel	**canna** (f)	['kanna]
caliber	**calibro** (m)	['kalibro]
trigger	**grilletto** (m)	[gril'letto]
sight (aiming device)	**mirino** (m)	[mi'rino]
magazine	**caricatore** (m)	[karika'tore]
butt (shoulder stock)	**calcio** (m)	['kaltʃo]
hand grenade	**bomba** (f) **a mano**	['bomba a 'mano]
explosive	**esplosivo** (m)	[esplo'zivo]
bullet	**pallottola** (f)	[pal'lottola]
cartridge	**cartuccia** (f)	[kar'tutʃa]
charge	**carica** (f)	['karika]
ammunition	**munizioni** (f pl)	[muni'tsjoni]
bomber (aircraft)	**bombardiere** (m)	[bombar'djere]
fighter	**aereo** (m) **da caccia**	[a'ereo da 'katʃa]
helicopter	**elicottero** (m)	[eli'kottero]
anti-aircraft gun	**cannone** (m) **antiaereo**	[kan'none anti·a'ereo]
tank	**carro** (m) **armato**	['karro ar'mato]
tank gun	**cannone** (m)	[kan'none]
artillery	**artiglieria** (f)	[artiʎʎe'ria]
gun (cannon, howitzer)	**cannone** (m)	[kan'none]
to lay (a gun)	**mirare a ...**	[mi'rare a]
shell (projectile)	**proiettile** (m)	[pro'jettile]
mortar bomb	**granata** (f) **da mortaio**	[gra'nata da mor'tajo]
mortar	**mortaio** (m)	[mor'tajo]
splinter (shell fragment)	**scheggia** (f)	['skedʒa]
submarine	**sottomarino** (m)	[sottoma'rino]
torpedo	**siluro** (m)	[si'luro]
missile	**missile** (m)	['missile]
to load (gun)	**caricare** (vt)	[kari'kare]
to shoot (vi)	**sparare** (vi)	[spa'rare]
to point at (the cannon)	**puntare su ...**	[pun'tare su]
bayonet	**baionetta** (f)	[bajo'netta]
rapier	**spada** (f)	['spada]
saber (e.g., cavalry ~)	**sciabola** (f)	['ʃabola]
spear (weapon)	**lancia** (f)	['lantʃa]
bow	**arco** (m)	['arko]

arrow	freccia (f)	['fretʃa]
musket	moschetto (m)	[mos'ketto]
crossbow	balestra (f)	[ba'lestra]

157. Ancient people

primitive (prehistoric)	primitivo	[primi'tivo]
prehistoric (adj)	preistorico	[preis'toriko]
ancient (~ civilization)	antico	[an'tiko]

Stone Age	Età (f) della pietra	[e'ta 'della 'pjetra]
Bronze Age	Età (f) del bronzo	[e'ta del 'brondzo]
Ice Age	epoca (f) glaciale	['epoka gla'tʃale]

tribe	tribù (f)	[tri'bu]
cannibal	cannibale (m)	[kan'nibale]
hunter	cacciatore (m)	[katʃa'tore]
to hunt (vi, vt)	cacciare (vt)	[ka'tʃare]
mammoth	mammut (m)	[mam'mut]

cave	caverna (f), grotta (f)	[ka'verna], ['grotta]
fire	fuoco (m)	[fu'oko]
campfire	falò (m)	[fa'lo]
cave painting	pittura (f) rupestre	[pit'tura ru'pestre]

tool (e.g., stone ax)	strumento (m) di lavoro	[stru'mento di la'voro]
spear	lancia (f)	['lantʃa]
stone ax	ascia (f) di pietra	['aʃa di 'pjetra]
to be at war	essere in guerra	['essere in 'gwerra]
to domesticate (vt)	addomesticare (vt)	[addomesti'kare]

idol	idolo (m)	['idolo]
to worship (vt)	idolatrare (vt)	[idola'trare]
superstition	superstizione (f)	[supersti'tsjone]
rite	rito (m)	['rito]

evolution	evoluzione (f)	[evolu'tsjone]
development	sviluppo (m)	[zvi'luppo]

disappearance (extinction)	estinzione (f)	[estin'tsjone]
to adapt oneself	adattarsi (vr)	[adat'tarsi]

archeology	archeologia (f)	[arkeolo'dʒia]
archeologist	archeologo (m)	[arke'ologo]
archeological (adj)	archeologico	[arkeo'lodʒiko]

excavation site	sito (m) archeologico	['sito arkeo'lodʒiko]
excavations	scavi (m pl)	['skavi]
find (object)	reperto (m)	[re'perto]
fragment	frammento (m)	[fram'mento]

158. Middle Ages

people (ethnic group)	**popolo** (m)	['popolo]
peoples	**popoli** (m pl)	['popoli]
tribe	**tribù** (f)	[tri'bu]
tribes	**tribù** (f pl)	[tri'bu]
barbarians	**barbari** (m pl)	['barbari]
Gauls	**galli** (m pl)	['galli]
Goths	**goti** (m pl)	['goti]
Slavs	**slavi** (m pl)	['zlavi]
Vikings	**vichinghi** (m pl)	[vi'kingi]
Romans	**romani** (m pl)	[ro'mani]
Roman (adj)	**romano**	[ro'mano]
Byzantines	**bizantini** (m pl)	[bidzan'tini]
Byzantium	**Bisanzio** (m)	[bi'zansio]
Byzantine (adj)	**bizantino**	[bidzan'tino]
emperor	**imperatore** (m)	[impera'tore]
leader, chief (tribal ~)	**capo** (m)	['kapo]
powerful (~ king)	**potente**	[po'tente]
king	**re** (m)	[re]
ruler (sovereign)	**governante** (m)	[gover'nante]
knight	**cavaliere** (m)	[kava'ljere]
feudal lord	**feudatario** (m)	[feuda'tario]
feudal (adj)	**feudale**	[feu'dale]
vassal	**vassallo** (m)	[vas'sallo]
duke	**duca** (m)	['duka]
earl	**conte** (m)	['konte]
baron	**barone** (m)	[ba'rone]
bishop	**vescovo** (m)	['veskovo]
armor	**armatura** (f)	[arma'tura]
shield	**scudo** (m)	['skudo]
sword	**spada** (f)	['spada]
visor	**visiera** (f)	[vi'zjera]
chainmail	**cotta** (f) **di maglia**	['kotta di 'maʎʎa]
Crusade	**crociata** (f)	[kro'ʧata]
crusader	**crociato** (m)	[kro'ʧato]
territory	**territorio** (m)	[terri'torio]
to attack (invade)	**attaccare** (vt)	[attak'kare]
to conquer (vt)	**conquistare** (vt)	[konkwi'stare]
to occupy (invade)	**occupare** (vt)	[okku'pare]
siege (to be under ~)	**assedio** (m)	[as'sedio]
besieged (adj)	**assediato**	[asse'djato]

to besiege (vt)	assediare (vt)	[asse'djare]
inquisition	inquisizione (f)	[inkwizi'tsjone]
inquisitor	inquisitore (m)	[inkwizi'tore]
torture	tortura (f)	[tor'tura]
cruel (adj)	crudele	[kru'dele]
heretic	eretico (m)	[e'retiko]
heresy	eresia (f)	[ere'zia]

seafaring	navigazione (f)	[naviga'tsjone]
pirate	pirata (m)	[pi'rata]
piracy	pirateria (f)	[pirate'ria]
boarding (attack)	arrembaggio (m)	[arrem'badʒo]
loot, booty	bottino (m)	[bot'tino]
treasures	tesori (m)	[te'zori]

discovery	scoperta (f)	[sko'perta]
to discover (new land, etc.)	scoprire (vt)	[sko'prire]
expedition	spedizione (f)	[spedi'tsjone]

musketeer	moschettiere (m)	[mosket'tjere]
cardinal	cardinale (m)	[kardi'nale]
heraldry	araldica (f)	[a'raldika]
heraldic (adj)	araldico	[a'raldiko]

159. Leader. Chief. Authorities

king	re (m)	[re]
queen	regina (f)	[re'dʒina]
royal (adj)	reale	[re'ale]
kingdom	regno (m)	['reɲo]

| prince | principe (m) | ['printʃipe] |
| princess | principessa (f) | [printʃi'pessa] |

president	presidente (m)	[prezi'dente]
vice-president	vicepresidente (m)	[vitʃe·prezi'dente]
senator	senatore (m)	[sena'tore]

monarch	monarca (m)	[mo'narka]
ruler (sovereign)	governante (m)	[gover'nante]
dictator	dittatore (m)	[ditta'tore]
tyrant	tiranno (m)	[ti'ranno]
magnate	magnate (m)	[ma'ɲate]

director	direttore (m)	[diret'tore]
chief	capo (m)	['kapo]
manager (director)	dirigente (m)	[diri'dʒente]
boss	capo (m)	['kapo]
owner	proprietario (m)	[proprie'tario]
head (~ of delegation)	capo (m)	['kapo]

| authorities | autorità (f pl) | [autori'ta] |
| superiors | superiori (m pl) | [supe'rjori] |

governor	governatore (m)	[governa'tore]
consul	console (m)	['konsole]
diplomat	diplomatico (m)	[diplo'matiko]
mayor	sindaco (m)	['sindako]
sheriff	sceriffo (m)	[ʃe'riffo]

emperor	imperatore (m)	[impera'tore]
tsar, czar	zar (m)	[tsar]
pharaoh	faraone (m)	[fara'one]
khan	khan (m)	['kan]

160. Breaking the law. Criminals. Part 1

bandit	bandito (m)	[ban'dito]
crime	delitto (m)	[de'litto]
criminal (person)	criminale (m)	[krimi'nale]

thief	ladro (m)	['ladro]
to steal (vi, vt)	rubare (vi, vt)	[ru'bare]
stealing (larceny)	ruberia (f)	[rube'ria]
theft	furto (m)	['furto]

to kidnap (vt)	rapire (vt)	[ra'pire]
kidnapping	rapimento (m)	[rapi'mento]
kidnapper	rapitore (m)	[rapi'tore]

| ransom | riscatto (m) | [ris'katto] |
| to demand ransom | chiedere il riscatto | ['kjedere il ris'katto] |

| to rob (vt) | rapinare (vt) | [rapi'nare] |
| robber | rapinatore (m) | [rapina'tore] |

to extort (vt)	estorcere (vt)	[es'tortʃere]
extortionist	estorsore (m)	[estor'sore]
extortion	estorsione (f)	[estor'sjone]

to murder, to kill	uccidere (vt)	[u'tʃidere]
murder	assassinio (m)	[assas'sinio]
murderer	assassino (m)	[assas'sino]

gunshot	sparo (m)	['sparo]
to fire (~ a shot)	tirare un colpo	[ti'rare un 'kolpo]
to shoot to death	abbattere (vt)	[ab'battere]
to shoot (vi)	sparare (vi)	[spa'rare]
shooting	sparatoria (f)	[spara'toria]
incident (fight, etc.)	incidente (m)	[intʃi'dente]
fight, brawl	rissa (f)	['rissa]

Help!	Aiuto!	[a'juto]
victim	vittima (f)	['vittima]

to damage (vt)	danneggiare (vt)	[danne'dʒare]
damage	danno (m)	['danno]
dead body, corpse	cadavere (m)	[ka'davere]
grave (~ crime)	grave	['grave]

to attack (vt)	aggredire (vt)	[aggre'dire]
to beat (to hit)	picchiare (vt)	[pik'kjare]
to beat up	picchiare (vt)	[pik'kjare]
to take (rob of sth)	sottrarre (vt)	[sot'trarre]
to stab to death	accoltellare a morte	[akkolte'lare a 'morte]
to maim (vt)	mutilare (vt)	[muti'lare]
to wound (vt)	ferire (vt)	[fe'rire]

blackmail	ricatto (m)	[ri'katto]
to blackmail (vt)	ricattare (vt)	[rikat'tare]
blackmailer	ricattatore (m)	[rikatta'tore]

protection racket	estorsione (f)	[estor'sjone]
racketeer	estorsore (m)	[estor'sore]
gangster	gangster (m)	['gangster]
mafia, Mob	mafia (f)	['mafia]

pickpocket	borseggiatore (m)	[borsedʒa'tore]
burglar	scassinatore (m)	[skassina'tore]
smuggling	contrabbando (m)	[kontrab'bando]
smuggler	contrabbandiere (m)	[kontrabban'djere]

forgery	falsificazione (f)	[falsifika'tsjone]
to forge (counterfeit)	falsificare (vt)	[falsifi'kare]
fake (forged)	falso, falsificato	['falso], [falsifi'kato]

161. Breaking the law. Criminals. Part 2

rape	stupro (m)	['stupro]
to rape (vt)	stuprare (vt)	[stu'prare]
rapist	stupratore (m)	[stupra'tore]
maniac	maniaco (m)	[ma'njako]

prostitute (fem.)	prostituta (f)	[prosti'tuta]
prostitution	prostituzione (f)	[prostitu'tsjone]
pimp	magnaccia (m)	[ma'ɲatʃa]

drug addict	drogato (m)	[dro'gato]
drug dealer	trafficante (m) di droga	[traffi'kante di 'droga]

to blow up (bomb)	far esplodere	[far e'splodere]
explosion	esplosione (f)	[esplo'zjone]

to set fire	**incendiare** (vt)	[intʃen'djare]
arsonist	**incendiario** (m)	[intʃen'djario]
terrorism	**terrorismo** (m)	[terro'rizmo]
terrorist	**terrorista** (m)	[terro'rista]
hostage	**ostaggio** (m)	[os'tadʒo]
to swindle (deceive)	**imbrogliare** (vt)	[imbroʎ'ʎare]
swindle, deception	**imbroglio** (m)	[im'broʎʎo]
swindler	**imbroglione** (m)	[imbroʎ'ʎone]
to bribe (vt)	**corrompere** (vt)	[kor'rompere]
bribery	**corruzione** (f)	[korru'tsjone]
bribe	**bustarella** (f)	[busta'rella]
poison	**veleno** (m)	[ve'leno]
to poison (vt)	**avvelenare** (vt)	[avvele'nare]
to poison oneself	**avvelenarsi** (vr)	[avvele'narsi]
suicide (act)	**suicidio** (m)	[sui'tʃidio]
suicide (person)	**suicida** (m)	[sui'tʃida]
to threaten (vt)	**minacciare** (vt)	[mina'tʃare]
threat	**minaccia** (f)	[mi'natʃa]
to make an attempt	**attentare** (vi)	[atten'tare]
attempt (attack)	**attentato** (m)	[atten'tato]
to steal (a car)	**rubare** (vt)	[ru'bare]
to hijack (a plane)	**dirottare** (vt)	[dirot'tare]
revenge	**vendetta** (f)	[ven'detta]
to avenge (get revenge)	**vendicare** (vt)	[vendi'kare]
to torture (vt)	**torturare** (vt)	[tortu'rare]
torture	**tortura** (f)	[tor'tura]
to torment (vt)	**maltrattare** (vt)	[maltrat'tare]
pirate	**pirata** (m)	[pi'rata]
hooligan	**teppista** (m)	[tep'pista]
armed (adj)	**armato**	[ar'mato]
violence	**violenza** (f)	[vio'lentsa]
illegal (unlawful)	**illegale**	[ille'gale]
spying (espionage)	**spionaggio** (m)	[spio'nadʒo]
to spy (vi)	**spiare** (vi)	[spi'are]

162. Police. Law. Part 1

| justice | **giustizia** (f) | [dʒu'stitsia] |
| court (see you in ~) | **tribunale** (m) | [tribu'nale] |

judge	giudice (m)	['dʒuditʃe]
jurors	giurati (m)	[dʒu'rati]
jury trial	processo (m) con giuria	[pro'tʃesso kon dʒu'ria]
to judge, to try (vt)	giudicare (vt)	[dʒudi'kare]

lawyer, attorney	avvocato (m)	[avvo'kato]
defendant	imputato (m)	[impu'tato]
dock	banco (m) degli imputati	['banko 'deʎʎi impu'tati]

| charge | accusa (f) | [ak'kuza] |
| accused | accusato (m) | [akku'zato] |

| sentence | condanna (f) | [kon'danna] |
| to sentence (vt) | condannare (vt) | [kondan'nare] |

guilty (culprit)	colpevole (m)	[kol'pevole]
to punish (vt)	punire (vt)	[pu'nire]
punishment	punizione (f)	[puni'tsjone]

fine (penalty)	multa (f), ammenda (f)	['multa], [am'menda]
life imprisonment	ergastolo (m)	[er'gastolo]
death penalty	pena (f) di morte	['pena di 'morte]
electric chair	sedia (f) elettrica	['sedia e'lettrika]
gallows	impiccagione (f)	[impikka'dʒone]

| to execute (vt) | giustiziare (vt) | [dʒusti'tsjare] |
| execution | esecuzione (f) | [ezeku'tsjone] |

| prison, jail | prigione (f) | [pri'dʒone] |
| cell | cella (f) | ['tʃella] |

escort (convoy)	scorta (f)	['skorta]
prison guard	guardia (f) carceraria	['gwardia kartʃe'raria]
prisoner	prigioniero (m)	[pridʒo'njero]

| handcuffs | manette (f pl) | [ma'nette] |
| to handcuff (vt) | mettere le manette | ['mettere le ma'nette] |

prison break	fuga (f)	['fuga]
to break out (vi)	fuggire (vi)	[fu'dʒire]
to disappear (vi)	scomparire (vi)	[skompa'rire]
to release (from prison)	liberare (vt)	[libe'rare]
amnesty	amnistia (f)	[amni'stia]

police	polizia (f)	[poli'tsia]
police officer	poliziotto (m)	[poli'tsjotto]
police station	commissariato (m)	[kommissa'rjato]
billy club	manganello (m)	[manga'nello]
bullhorn	altoparlante (m)	[altopar'lante]

| patrol car | macchina (f) di pattuglia | ['makkina di pat'tuʎʎa] |
| siren | sirena (f) | [si'rena] |

| to turn on the siren | mettere la sirena | ['mettere la si'rena] |
| siren call | suono (m) della sirena | [su'ono 'della si'rena] |

crime scene	luogo (m) del crimine	[lu'ogo del 'krimine]
witness	testimone (m)	[testi'mone]
freedom	libertà (f)	[liber'ta]
accomplice	complice (m)	['komplitʃe]
to flee (vi)	fuggire (vi)	[fu'dʒire]
trace (to leave a ~)	traccia (f)	['tratʃa]

163. Police. Law. Part 2

search (investigation)	ricerca (f)	[ri'tʃerka]
to look for …	cercare (vt)	[tʃer'kare]
suspicion	sospetto (m)	[so'spetto]
suspicious (e.g., ~ vehicle)	sospetto	[so'spetto]
to stop (cause to halt)	fermare (vt)	[fer'mare]
to detain (keep in custody)	arrestare	[arre'stare]

case (lawsuit)	causa (f)	['kauza]
investigation	inchiesta (f)	[in'kjesta]
detective	detective (m)	[de'tektiv]
investigator	investigatore (m)	[investiga'tore]
hypothesis	versione (f)	[ver'sjone]

motive	movente (m)	[mo'vente]
interrogation	interrogatorio (m)	[interroga'torio]
to interrogate (vt)	interrogare (vt)	[interro'gare]
to question	interrogare (vt)	[interro'gare]
(~ neighbors, etc.)		
check (identity ~)	controllo (m)	[kon'trollo]

round-up (raid)	retata (f)	[re'tata]
search (~ warrant)	perquisizione (f)	[perkwizi'tsjone]
chase (pursuit)	inseguimento (m)	[insegwi'mento]
to pursue, to chase	inseguire (vt)	[inse'gwire]
to track (a criminal)	essere sulle tracce	['essere sulle 'tratʃe]

arrest	arresto (m)	[ar'resto]
to arrest (sb)	arrestare	[arre'stare]
to catch (thief, etc.)	catturare (vt)	[kattu'rare]
capture	cattura (f)	[kat'tura]

document	documento (m)	[doku'mento]
proof (evidence)	prova (f)	['prova]
to prove (vt)	provare (vt)	[pro'vare]
footprint	impronta (f) del piede	[im'pronta del 'pjede]
fingerprints	impronte (f pl) digitali	[im'pronte didʒi'tali]
piece of evidence	elemento (m) di prova	[ele'mento di 'prova]
alibi	alibi (m)	['alibi]

innocent (not guilty)	**innocente**	[inno'tʃente]
injustice	**ingiustizia** (f)	[indʒu'stitsia]
unjust, unfair (adj)	**ingiusto**	[in'dʒusto]

criminal (adj)	**criminale**	[krimi'nale]
to confiscate (vt)	**confiscare** (vt)	[konfis'kare]
drug (illegal substance)	**droga** (f)	['droga]
weapon, gun	**armi** (f pl)	['armi]
to disarm (vt)	**disarmare** (vt)	[dizar'mare]
to order (command)	**ordinare** (vt)	[ordi'nare]
to disappear (vi)	**sparire** (vi)	[spa'rire]

law	**legge** (f)	['ledʒe]
legal, lawful (adj)	**legale**	[le'gale]
illegal, illicit (adj)	**illegale**	[ille'gale]

responsibility (blame)	**responsabilità** (f)	[responsabili'ta]
responsible (adj)	**responsabile**	[respon'sabile]

NATURE

The Earth. Part 1

164. Outer space

space	**cosmo** (m)	['kozmo]
space (as adj)	**cosmico, spaziale**	['kozmiko], [spa'tsjale]
outer space	**spazio** (m) **cosmico**	['spatsio 'kozmiko]
world	**mondo** (m)	['mondo]
universe	**universo** (m)	[uni'verso]
galaxy	**galassia** (f)	[ga'lassia]
star	**stella** (f)	['stella]
constellation	**costellazione** (f)	[kostella'tsjone]
planet	**pianeta** (m)	[pja'neta]
satellite	**satellite** (m)	[sa'tellite]
meteorite	**meteorite** (m)	[meteo'rite]
comet	**cometa** (f)	[ko'meta]
asteroid	**asteroide** (m)	[aste'roide]
orbit	**orbita** (f)	['orbita]
to revolve (~ around the Earth)	**ruotare** (vi)	[ruo'tare]
atmosphere	**atmosfera** (f)	[atmo'sfera]
the Sun	**il Sole**	[il 'sole]
solar system	**sistema** (m) **solare**	[si'stema so'lare]
solar eclipse	**eclisse** (f) **solare**	[e'klisse so'lare]
the Earth	**la Terra**	[la 'terra]
the Moon	**la Luna**	[la 'luna]
Mars	**Marte** (m)	['marte]
Venus	**Venere** (f)	['venere]
Jupiter	**Giove** (m)	['dʒove]
Saturn	**Saturno** (m)	[sa'turno]
Mercury	**Mercurio** (m)	[mer'kurio]
Uranus	**Urano** (m)	[u'rano]
Neptune	**Nettuno** (m)	[net'tuno]
Pluto	**Plutone** (m)	[plu'tone]
Milky Way	**Via** (f) **Lattea**	['via 'lattea]

| Great Bear (Ursa Major) | Orsa (f) Maggiore | ['orsa ma'dʒore] |
| North Star | Stella (f) Polare | ['stella po'lare] |

Martian	marziano (m)	[mar'tsjano]
extraterrestrial (n)	extraterrestre (m)	[ekstrater'restre]
alien	alieno (m)	[a'ljeno]
flying saucer	disco (m) volante	['disko vo'lante]

spaceship	nave (f) spaziale	['nave spa'tsjale]
space station	stazione (f) spaziale	[sta'tsjone spa'tsjale]
blast-off	lancio (m)	['lantʃo]

engine	motore (m)	[mo'tore]
nozzle	ugello (m)	[u'dʒello]
fuel	combustibile (m)	[kombu'stibile]

cockpit, flight deck	cabina (f) di pilotaggio	[ka'bina di pilo'tadʒio]
antenna	antenna (f)	[an'tenna]
porthole	oblò (m)	[ob'lo]
solar panel	batteria (f) solare	[batte'ria so'lare]
spacesuit	scafandro (m)	[ska'fandro]

| weightlessness | imponderabilità (f) | [imponderabili'ta] |
| oxygen | ossigeno (m) | [os'sidʒeno] |

| docking (in space) | aggancio (m) | [ag'gantʃo] |
| to dock (vi, vt) | agganciarsi (vr) | [aggan'tʃarsi] |

observatory	osservatorio (m)	[osserva'torio]
telescope	telescopio (m)	[tele'skopio]
to observe (vt)	osservare (vt)	[osser'vare]
to explore (vt)	esplorare (vt)	[esplo'rare]

165. The Earth

the Earth	la Terra	[la 'terra]
the globe (the Earth)	globo (m) terrestre	['globo ter'restre]
planet	pianeta (m)	[pja'neta]

atmosphere	atmosfera (f)	[atmo'sfera]
geography	geografia (f)	[dʒeogra'fia]
nature	natura (f)	[na'tura]

globe (table ~)	mappamondo (m)	[mappa'mondo]
map	carta (f) geografica	['karta dʒeo'grafika]
atlas	atlante (m)	[a'tlante]

Europe	Europa (f)	[eu'ropa]
Asia	Asia (f)	['azia]
Africa	Africa (f)	['afrika]

Australia	Australia (f)	[au'stralia]
America	America (f)	[a'merika]
North America	America (f) del Nord	[a'merika del nord]
South America	America (f) del Sud	[a'merika del sud]
Antarctica	Antartide (f)	[an'tartide]
the Arctic	Artico (m)	['artiko]

166. Cardinal directions

north	nord (m)	[nord]
to the north	a nord	[a nord]
in the north	al nord	[al nord]
northern (adj)	del nord	[del nord]
south	sud (m)	[sud]
to the south	a sud	[a sud]
in the south	al sud	[al sud]
southern (adj)	del sud	[del sud]
west	ovest (m)	['ovest]
to the west	a ovest	[a 'ovest]
in the west	all'ovest	[all 'ovest]
western (adj)	dell'ovest, occidentale	[dell 'ovest], [otʃiden'tale]
east	est (m)	[est]
to the east	a est	[a est]
in the east	all'est	[all 'est]
eastern (adj)	dell'est, orientale	[dell 'est], [orien'tale]

167. Sea. Ocean

sea	mare (m)	['mare]
ocean	oceano (m)	[o'tʃeano]
gulf (bay)	golfo (m)	['golfo]
straits	stretto (m)	['stretto]
land (solid ground)	terra (f)	['terra]
continent (mainland)	continente (m)	[konti'nente]
island	isola (f)	['izola]
peninsula	penisola (f)	[pe'nizola]
archipelago	arcipelago (m)	[artʃi'pelago]
bay, cove	baia (f)	['baja]
harbor	porto (m)	['porto]
lagoon	laguna (f)	[la'guna]
cape	capo (m)	['kapo]
atoll	atollo (m)	[a'tollo]

reef	scogliera (f)	[skoʎˈʎera]
coral	corallo (m)	[koˈrallo]
coral reef	barriera (f) corallina	[barˈrjera koralˈlina]

deep (adj)	profondo	[proˈfondo]
depth (deep water)	profondità (f)	[profondiˈta]
abyss	abisso (m)	[aˈbisso]
trench (e.g., Mariana ~)	fossa (f)	[ˈfossa]

| current (Ocean ~) | corrente (f) | [korˈrente] |
| to surround (bathe) | circondare (vt) | [tʃirkonˈdare] |

| shore | litorale (m) | [litoˈrale] |
| coast | costa (f) | [ˈkosta] |

flow (flood tide)	alta marea (f)	[ˈalta maˈrea]
ebb (ebb tide)	bassa marea (f)	[ˈbassa maˈrea]
shoal	banco (m) di sabbia	[ˈbanko di ˈsabbia]
bottom (~ of the sea)	fondo (m)	[ˈfondo]
wave	onda (f)	[ˈonda]
crest (~ of a wave)	cresta (f) dell'onda	[ˈkresta dell ˈonda]
spume (sea foam)	schiuma (f)	[ˈskjuma]

storm (sea storm)	tempesta (f)	[temˈpesta]
hurricane	uragano (m)	[uraˈgano]
tsunami	tsunami (m)	[tsuˈnami]
calm (dead ~)	bonaccia (f)	[boˈnatʃa]
quiet, calm (adj)	tranquillo	[tranˈkwillo]

| pole | polo (m) | [ˈpolo] |
| polar (adj) | polare | [poˈlare] |

latitude	latitudine (f)	[latiˈtudine]
longitude	longitudine (f)	[londʒiˈtudine]
parallel	parallelo (m)	[paralˈlelo]
equator	equatore (m)	[ekwaˈtore]

sky	cielo (m)	[ˈtʃelo]
horizon	orizzonte (m)	[oridˈdzonte]
air	aria (f)	[ˈaria]

lighthouse	faro (m)	[ˈfaro]
to dive (vi)	tuffarsi (vr)	[tufˈfarsi]
to sink (ab. boat)	affondare (vi)	[affonˈdare]
treasures	tesori (m)	[teˈzori]

168. Mountains

| mountain | monte (m), montagna (f) | [ˈmonte], [monˈtaɲa] |
| mountain range | catena (f) montuosa | [kaˈtena montuˈoza] |

mountain ridge	crinale (m)	[kri'nale]
summit, top	cima (f)	['tʃima]
peak	picco (m)	['pikko]
foot (~ of the mountain)	piedi (m pl)	['pjede]
slope (mountainside)	pendio (m)	[pen'dio]
volcano	vulcano (m)	[vul'kano]
active volcano	vulcano (m) attivo	[vul'kano at'tivo]
dormant volcano	vulcano (m) inattivo	[vul'kano inat'tivo]
eruption	eruzione (f)	[eru'tsjone]
crater	cratere (m)	[kra'tere]
magma	magma (m)	['magma]
lava	lava (f)	['lava]
molten (~ lava)	fuso	['fuzo]
canyon	canyon (m)	['kenjon]
gorge	gola (f)	['gola]
crevice	crepaccio (m)	[kre'patʃo]
abyss (chasm)	precipizio (m)	[pretʃi'pitsio]
pass, col	passo (m), valico (m)	['passo], ['valiko]
plateau	altopiano (m)	[alto'pjano]
cliff	falesia (f)	[fa'lezia]
hill	collina (f)	[kol'lina]
glacier	ghiacciaio (m)	[gja'tʃajo]
waterfall	cascata (f)	[kas'kata]
geyser	geyser (m)	['gejzer]
lake	lago (m)	['lago]
plain	pianura (f)	[pja'nura]
landscape	paesaggio (m)	[pae'zadʒo]
echo	eco (f)	['eko]
alpinist	alpinista (m)	[alpi'nista]
rock climber	scalatore (m)	[skala'tore]
to conquer (in climbing)	conquistare (vt)	[konkwi'stare]
climb (an easy ~)	scalata (f)	[ska'lata]

169. Rivers

river	fiume (m)	['fjume]
spring (natural source)	fonte (f)	['fonte]
riverbed (river channel)	letto (m)	['letto]
basin (river valley)	bacino (m)	[ba'tʃino]
to flow into ...	sfociare nel ...	[sfo'tʃare nel]
tributary	affluente (m)	[afflu'ente]
bank (of river)	riva (f)	['riva]

current (stream)	corrente (f)	[kor'rente]
downstream (adv)	a valle	[a 'valle]
upstream (adv)	a monte	[a 'monte]

inundation	inondazione (f)	[inonda'tsjone]
flooding	piena (f)	['pjena]
to overflow (vi)	straripare (vi)	[strari'pare]
to flood (vt)	inondare (vt)	[inon'dare]

| shallow (shoal) | secca (f) | ['sekka] |
| rapids | rapida (f) | ['rapida] |

dam	diga (f)	['diga]
canal	canale (m)	[ka'nale]
reservoir (artificial lake)	bacino (m) di riserva	[ba'tʃino di ri'zerva]
sluice, lock	chiusa (f)	['kjuza]

water body (pond, etc.)	bacino (m) idrico	[ba'tʃino 'idriko]
swamp (marshland)	palude (f)	[pa'lude]
bog, marsh	pantano (m)	[pan'tano]
whirlpool	vortice (m)	['vortitʃe]

stream (brook)	ruscello (m)	[ru'ʃello]
drinking (ab. water)	potabile	[po'tabile]
fresh (~ water)	dolce	['doltʃe]

| ice | ghiaccio (m) | ['gjatʃo] |
| to freeze over (ab. river, etc.) | ghiacciarsi (vr) | [gja'tʃarsi] |

170. Forest

| forest, wood | foresta (f) | [fo'resta] |
| forest (as adj) | forestale | [fores'tale] |

thick forest	foresta (f) fitta	[fo'resta 'fitta]
grove	boschetto (m)	[bos'ketto]
forest clearing	radura (f)	[ra'dura]

| thicket | roveto (m) | [ro'veto] |
| scrubland | boscaglia (f) | [bos'kaʎʎa] |

| footpath (troddenpath) | sentiero (m) | [sen'tjero] |
| gully | calanco (m) | [ka'lanko] |

tree	albero (m)	['albero]
leaf	foglia (f)	['foʎʎa]
leaves (foliage)	fogliame (m)	[foʎ'ʎame]
fall of leaves	caduta (f) delle foglie	[ka'duta 'delle 'foʎʎe]
to fall (ab. leaves)	cadere (vi)	[ka'dere]

top (of the tree)	**cima** (f)	['tʃima]
branch	**ramo** (m), **ramoscello** (m)	['ramo], [ramo'ʃello]
bough	**ramo** (m)	['ramo]
bud (on shrub, tree)	**gemma** (f)	['dʒemma]
needle (of pine tree)	**ago** (m)	['ago]
pine cone	**pigna** (f)	['piɲa]
tree hollow	**cavità** (f)	[kavi'ta]
nest	**nido** (m)	['nido]
burrow (animal hole)	**tana** (f)	['tana]
trunk	**tronco** (m)	['tronko]
root	**radice** (f)	[ra'ditʃe]
bark	**corteccia** (f)	[kor'tetʃa]
moss	**musco** (m)	['musko]
to uproot (remove trees or tree stumps)	**sradicare** (vt)	[zradi'kare]
to chop down	**abbattere** (vt)	[ab'battere]
to deforest (vt)	**disboscare** (vt)	[dizbo'skare]
tree stump	**ceppo** (m)	['tʃeppo]
campfire	**falò** (m)	[fa'lo]
forest fire	**incendio** (m) **boschivo**	[in'tʃendio bos'kivo]
to extinguish (vt)	**spegnere** (vt)	['speɲere]
forest ranger	**guardia** (f) **forestale**	['gwardia fores'tale]
protection	**protezione** (f)	[prote'tsjone]
to protect (~ nature)	**proteggere** (vt)	[pro'tedʒere]
poacher	**bracconiere** (m)	[brakko'njere]
steel trap	**tagliola** (f)	[taʎ'ʎoʎa]
to gather, to pick (vt)	**raccogliere** (vt)	[rak'koʎʎere]
to lose one's way	**perdersi** (vr)	['perdersi]

171. Natural resources

natural resources	**risorse** (f pl) **naturali**	[ri'sorse natu'rali]
minerals	**minerali** (m pl)	[mine'rali]
deposits	**deposito** (m)	[de'pozito]
field (e.g., oilfield)	**giacimento** (m)	[dʒatʃi'mento]
to mine (extract)	**estrarre** (vt)	[e'strarre]
mining (extraction)	**estrazione** (f)	[estra'tsjone]
ore	**minerale** (m) **grezzo**	[mine'rale 'greddzo]
mine (e.g., for coal)	**miniera** (f)	[mi'njera]
shaft (mine ~)	**pozzo** (m) **di miniera**	['pottso di mi'njera]
miner	**minatore** (m)	[mina'tore]
gas (natural ~)	**gas** (m)	[gas]
gas pipeline	**gasdotto** (m)	[gas'dotto]

oil (petroleum)	**petrolio** (m)	[pe'trolio]
oil pipeline	**oleodotto** (m)	[oleo'dotto]
oil well	**torre** (f) **di estrazione**	['torre di estra'tsjone]
derrick (tower)	**torre** (f) **di trivellazione**	['torre di trivella'tsjone]
tanker	**petroliera** (f)	[petro'ljera]
sand	**sabbia** (f)	['sabbia]
limestone	**calcare** (m)	[kal'kare]
gravel	**ghiaia** (f)	['gjaja]
peat	**torba** (f)	['torba]
clay	**argilla** (f)	[ar'dʒilla]
coal	**carbone** (m)	[kar'bone]
iron (ore)	**ferro** (m)	['ferro]
gold	**oro** (m)	['oro]
silver	**argento** (m)	[ar'dʒento]
nickel	**nichel** (m)	['nikel]
copper	**rame** (m)	['rame]
zinc	**zinco** (m)	['dzinko]
manganese	**manganese** (m)	[manga'neze]
mercury	**mercurio** (m)	[mer'kurio]
lead	**piombo** (m)	['pjombo]
mineral	**minerale** (m)	[mine'rale]
crystal	**cristallo** (m)	[kris'tallo]
marble	**marmo** (m)	['marmo]
uranium	**uranio** (m)	[u'ranio]

The Earth. Part 2

172. Weather

weather	tempo (m)	['tempo]
weather forecast	previsione (f) del tempo	[previ'zjone del 'tempo]
temperature	temperatura (f)	[tempera'tura]
thermometer	termometro (m)	[ter'mometro]
barometer	barometro (m)	[ba'rometro]
humid (adj)	umido	['umido]
humidity	umidità (f)	[umidi'ta]
heat (extreme ~)	caldo (m), afa (f)	['kaldo], ['afa]
hot (torrid)	molto caldo	['molto 'kaldo]
it's hot	fa molto caldo	[fa 'molto 'kaldo]
it's warm	fa caldo	[fa 'kaldo]
warm (moderately hot)	caldo	['kaldo]
it's cold	fa freddo	[fa 'freddo]
cold (adj)	freddo	['freddo]
sun	sole (m)	['sole]
to shine (vi)	splendere (vi)	['splendere]
sunny (day)	di sole	[di 'sole]
to come up (vi)	levarsi (vr)	[le'varsi]
to set (vi)	tramontare (vi)	[tramon'tare]
cloud	nuvola (f)	['nuvola]
cloudy (adj)	nuvoloso	[nuvo'lozo]
rain cloud	nube (f) di pioggia	['nube di 'pjoʤa]
somber (gloomy)	nuvoloso	[nuvo'lozo]
rain	pioggia (f)	['pjoʤa]
it's raining	piove	['pjove]
rainy (~ day, weather)	piovoso	[pjo'vozo]
to drizzle (vi)	piovigginare (vi)	[pjoviʤi'nare]
pouring rain	pioggia (f) torrenziale	['pjoʤa torren'tsjale]
downpour	acquazzone (m)	[akwat'tsone]
heavy (e.g., ~ rain)	forte	['forte]
puddle	pozzanghera (f)	[pot'tsangera]
to get wet (in rain)	bagnarsi (vr)	[ba'narsi]
fog (mist)	foschia (f), nebbia (f)	[fos'kia], ['nebbia]
foggy	nebbioso	[neb'bjozo]

| snow | neve (f) | ['neve] |
| it's snowing | nevica | ['nevika] |

173. Severe weather. Natural disasters

thunderstorm	temporale (m)	[tempo'rale]
lightning (~ strike)	fulmine (f)	['fulmine]
to flash (vi)	lampeggiare (vi)	[lampe'dʒare]

thunder	tuono (m)	[tu'ono]
to thunder (vi)	tuonare (vi)	[tuo'nare]
it's thundering	tuona	[tu'ona]

| hail | grandine (f) | ['grandine] |
| it's hailing | grandina | ['grandina] |

| to flood (vt) | inondare (vt) | [inon'dare] |
| flood, inundation | inondazione (f) | [inonda'tsjone] |

earthquake	terremoto (m)	[terre'moto]
tremor, shoke	scossa (f)	['skossa]
epicenter	epicentro (m)	[epi'tʃentro]

| eruption | eruzione (f) | [eru'tsjone] |
| lava | lava (f) | ['lava] |

twister	tromba (f) d'aria	['tromba 'daria]
tornado	tornado (m)	[tor'nado]
typhoon	tifone (m)	[ti'fone]

hurricane	uragano (m)	[ura'gano]
storm	tempesta (f)	[tem'pesta]
tsunami	tsunami (m)	[tsu'nami]

cyclone	ciclone (m)	[tʃi'klone]
bad weather	maltempo (m)	[mal'tempo]
fire (accident)	incendio (m)	[in'tʃendio]
disaster	disastro (m)	[di'zastro]
meteorite	meteorite (m)	[meteo'rite]

avalanche	valanga (f)	[va'langa]
snowslide	slavina (f)	[zla'vina]
blizzard	tempesta (f) di neve	[tem'pesta di 'neve]
snowstorm	bufera (f) di neve	['bufera di 'neve]

Fauna

174. Mammals. Predators

predator	**predatore** (m)	[preda'tore]
tiger	**tigre** (f)	['tigre]
lion	**leone** (m)	[le'one]
wolf	**lupo** (m)	['lupo]
fox	**volpe** (m)	['volpe]
jaguar	**giaguaro** (m)	[dʒa'gwaro]
leopard	**leopardo** (m)	[leo'pardo]
cheetah	**ghepardo** (m)	[ge'pardo]
black panther	**pantera** (f)	[pan'tera]
puma	**puma** (f)	['puma]
snow leopard	**leopardo** (m) **delle nevi**	[leo'pardo 'delle 'nevi]
lynx	**lince** (f)	['lintʃe]
coyote	**coyote** (m)	[ko'jote]
jackal	**sciacallo** (m)	[ʃa'kallo]
hyena	**iena** (f)	['jena]

175. Wild animals

animal	**animale** (m)	[ani'male]
beast (animal)	**bestia** (f)	['bestia]
squirrel	**scoiattolo** (m)	[sko'jattolo]
hedgehog	**riccio** (m)	['ritʃo]
hare	**lepre** (f)	['lepre]
rabbit	**coniglio** (m)	[ko'niʎʎo]
badger	**tasso** (m)	['tasso]
raccoon	**procione** (f)	[pro'tʃone]
hamster	**criceto** (m)	[kri'tʃeto]
marmot	**marmotta** (f)	[mar'motta]
mole	**talpa** (f)	['talpa]
mouse	**topo** (m)	['topo]
rat	**ratto** (m)	['ratto]
bat	**pipistrello** (m)	[pipi'strello]
ermine	**ermellino** (m)	[ermel'lino]
sable	**zibellino** (m)	[dzibel'lino]

marten	martora (f)	['martora]
weasel	donnola (f)	['donnola]
mink	visone (m)	[vi'zone]

| beaver | castoro (m) | [kas'toro] |
| otter | lontra (f) | ['lontra] |

horse	cavallo (m)	[ka'vallo]
moose	alce (m)	['altʃe]
deer	cervo (m)	['tʃervo]
camel	cammello (m)	[kam'mello]

bison	bisonte (m) americano	[bi'zonte ameri'kano]
wisent	bisonte (m) europeo	[bi'zonte euro'peo]
buffalo	bufalo (m)	['bufalo]

zebra	zebra (f)	['dzebra]
antelope	antilope (f)	[an'tilope]
roe deer	capriolo (m)	[kapri'olo]
fallow deer	daino (m)	['daino]
chamois	camoscio (m)	[ka'moʃo]
wild boar	cinghiale (m)	[tʃin'gjale]

whale	balena (f)	[ba'lena]
seal	foca (f)	['foka]
walrus	tricheco (m)	[tri'keko]
fur seal	otaria (f)	[o'taria]
dolphin	delfino (m)	[del'fino]

bear	orso (m)	['orso]
polar bear	orso (m) bianco	['orso 'bjanko]
panda	panda (m)	['panda]

monkey	scimmia (f)	['ʃimmia]
chimpanzee	scimpanzè (m)	[ʃimpan'dze]
orangutan	orango (m)	[o'rango]
gorilla	gorilla (m)	[go'rilla]
macaque	macaco (m)	[ma'kako]
gibbon	gibbone (m)	[dʒib'bone]

elephant	elefante (m)	[ele'fante]
rhinoceros	rinoceronte (m)	[rinotʃe'ronte]
giraffe	giraffa (f)	[dʒi'raffa]
hippopotamus	ippopotamo (m)	[ippo'potamo]

| kangaroo | canguro (m) | [kan'guro] |
| koala (bear) | koala (m) | [ko'ala] |

mongoose	mangusta (f)	[man'gusta]
chinchilla	cincillà (f)	[tʃintʃil'la]
skunk	moffetta (f)	[mof'fetta]
porcupine	istrice (m)	['istritʃe]

176. Domestic animals

cat	**gatta** (f)	['gatta]
tomcat	**gatto** (m)	['gatto]
dog	**cane** (m)	['kane]
horse	**cavallo** (m)	[ka'vallo]
stallion (male horse)	**stallone** (m)	[stal'lone]
mare	**giumenta** (f)	[dʒu'menta]
cow	**mucca** (f)	['mukka]
bull	**toro** (m)	['toro]
ox	**bue** (m)	['bue]
sheep (ewe)	**pecora** (f)	['pekora]
ram	**montone** (m)	[mon'tone]
goat	**capra** (f)	['kapra]
billy goat, he-goat	**caprone** (m)	[kap'rone]
donkey	**asino** (m)	['azino]
mule	**mulo** (m)	['mulo]
pig, hog	**porco** (m)	['porko]
piglet	**porcellino** (m)	[portʃel'lino]
rabbit	**coniglio** (m)	[ko'niʎʎo]
hen (chicken)	**gallina** (f)	[gal'lina]
rooster	**gallo** (m)	['gallo]
duck	**anatra** (f)	['anatra]
drake	**maschio** (m) **dell'anatra**	['maskio dell 'anatra]
goose	**oca** (f)	['oka]
tom turkey, gobbler	**tacchino** (m)	[tak'kino]
turkey (hen)	**tacchina** (f)	[tak'kina]
domestic animals	**animali** (m pl) **domestici**	[ani'mali do'mestitʃi]
tame (e.g., ~ hamster)	**addomesticato**	[addomesti'kato]
to tame (vt)	**addomesticare** (vt)	[addomesti'kare]
to breed (vt)	**allevare** (vt)	[alle'vare]
farm	**fattoria** (f)	[fatto'ria]
poultry	**pollame** (m)	[pol'lame]
cattle	**bestiame** (m)	[bes'tjame]
herd (cattle)	**branco** (m), **mandria** (f)	['branko], ['mandria]
stable	**scuderia** (f)	[skude'ria]
pigpen	**porcile** (m)	[por'tʃile]
cowshed	**stalla** (f)	['stalla]
rabbit hutch	**conigliera** (f)	[koniʎ'ʎera]
hen house	**pollaio** (m)	[pol'lajo]

177. Dogs. Dog breeds

dog	cane (m)	['kane]
sheepdog	cane (m) da pastore	['kane da pas'tore]
German shepherd	battaglia (f)	[bat'taʎʎa]
poodle	barbone (m)	[bar'bone]
dachshund	bassotto (m)	[bas'sotto]
bulldog	bulldog (m)	[bull'dog]
boxer	boxer (m)	['bokser]
mastiff	mastino (m)	[ma'stino]
Rottweiler	rottweiler (m)	[rot'vajler]
Doberman	dobermann (m)	[dober'mann]
basset	bassotto (m)	[bas'sotto]
bobtail	bobtail (m)	['bobtejl]
Dalmatian	dalmata (m)	['dalmata]
cocker spaniel	cocker (m)	['kokker]
Newfoundland	terranova (m)	[terra'nova]
Saint Bernard	sanbernardo (m)	[sanber'nardo]
husky	husky (m)	['aski]
Chow Chow	chow chow (m)	['tʃau 'tʃau]
spitz	volpino (m)	[vol'pino]
pug	carlino (m)	[kar'lino]

178. Sounds made by animals

barking (n)	abbaiamento (m)	[abaja'mento]
to bark (vi)	abbaiare (vi)	[abba'jare]
to meow (vi)	miagolare (vi)	[mjago'lare]
to purr (vi)	fare le fusa	['fare le 'fuza]
to moo (vi)	muggire (vi)	[mu'dʒire]
to bellow (bull)	muggire (vi)	[mu'dʒire]
to growl (vi)	ringhiare (vi)	[rin'gjare]
howl (n)	ululato (m)	[ulu'lato]
to howl (vi)	ululare (vi)	[ulu'lare]
to whine (vi)	guaire (vi)	[gwa'ire]
to bleat (sheep)	belare (vi)	[be'lare]
to oink, to grunt (pig)	grugnire (vi)	[gru'ɲire]
to squeal (vi)	squittire (vi)	[skwit'tire]
to croak (vi)	gracidare (vi)	[gratʃi'dare]
to buzz (insect)	ronzare (vi)	[ron'dzare]
to chirp (crickets, grasshopper)	frinire (vi)	[fri'nire]

179. Birds

bird	uccello (m)	[u'tʃello]
pigeon	colombo (m),	[kolombo],
	piccione (m)	[pi'tʃone]
sparrow	passero (m)	['passero]
tit (great tit)	cincia (f)	['tʃintʃa]
magpie	gazza (f)	['gattsa]
raven	corvo (m)	['korvo]
crow	cornacchia (f)	[kor'nakkia]
jackdaw	taccola (f)	['takkola]
rook	corvo (m) nero	['korvo 'nero]
duck	anatra (f)	['anatra]
goose	oca (f)	['oka]
pheasant	fagiano (m)	[fa'dʒano]
eagle	aquila (f)	['akwila]
hawk	astore (m)	[a'store]
falcon	falco (m)	['falko]
vulture	grifone (m)	[gri'fone]
condor (Andean ~)	condor (m)	['kondor]
swan	cigno (m)	['tʃiɲo]
crane	gru (f)	[gru]
stork	cicogna (f)	[tʃi'koɲa]
parrot	pappagallo (m)	[pappa'gallo]
hummingbird	colibrì (m)	[koli'bri]
peacock	pavone (m)	[pa'vone]
ostrich	struzzo (m)	['struttso]
heron	airone (m)	[ai'rone]
flamingo	fenicottero (m)	[feni'kottero]
pelican	pellicano (m)	[pelli'kano]
nightingale	usignolo (m)	[uzi'ɲolo]
swallow	rondine (f)	['rondine]
thrush	tordo (m)	['tordo]
song thrush	tordo (m) sasello	['tordo sa'zello]
blackbird	merlo (m)	['merlo]
swift	rondone (m)	[ron'done]
lark	allodola (f)	[al'lodola]
quail	quaglia (f)	['kwaʎʎa]
woodpecker	picchio (m)	['pikkio]
cuckoo	cuculo (m)	['kukulo]
owl	civetta (f)	[tʃi'vetta]

eagle owl	gufo (m) reale	['gufo re'ale]
wood grouse	urogallo (m)	[uro'gallo]
black grouse	fagiano (m) di monte	[fa'dʒano di 'monte]
partridge	pernice (f)	[per'nitʃe]
starling	storno (m)	['storno]
canary	canarino (m)	[kana'rino]
hazel grouse	francolino (m) di monte	[franko'lino di 'monte]
chaffinch	fringuello (m)	[frin'gwello]
bullfinch	ciuffolotto (m)	[tʃuffo'lotto]
seagull	gabbiano (m)	[gab'bjano]
albatross	albatro (m)	['albatro]
penguin	pinguino (m)	[pin'gwino]

180. Birds. Singing and sounds

to sing (vi)	cantare (vi)	[kan'tare]
to call (animal, bird)	gridare (vi)	[gri'dare]
to crow (rooster)	cantare, chicchiriare	[kan'tare], [kikki'rjare]
cock-a-doodle-doo	chicchirichì (m)	[kikkiri'ki]
to cluck (hen)	chiocciare (vi)	[kio'tʃare]
to caw (crow call)	gracchiare (vi)	[grak'kjare]
to quack (duck call)	fare qua qua	['fare kwa kwa]
to cheep (vi)	pigolare (vi)	[pigo'lare]
to chirp, to twitter	cinguettare (vi)	[tʃingwet'tare]

181. Fish. Marine animals

bream	abramide (f)	[a'bramide]
carp	carpa (f)	['karpa]
perch	perca (f)	['perka]
catfish	pesce (m) gatto	['peʃe 'gatto]
pike	luccio (m)	['lutʃo]
salmon	salmone (m)	[sal'mone]
sturgeon	storione (m)	[sto'rjone]
herring	aringa (f)	[a'ringa]
Atlantic salmon	salmone (m)	[sal'mone]
mackerel	scombro (m)	['skombro]
flatfish	sogliola (f)	['soʎʎoʎa]
zander, pike perch	lucioperca (f)	[lutʃo'perka]
cod	merluzzo (m)	[mer'luttso]
tuna	tonno (m)	['tonno]
trout	trota (f)	['trota]

eel	anguilla (f)	[an'gwilla]
electric ray	torpedine (f)	[tor'pedine]
moray eel	murena (f)	[mu'rena]
piranha	piranha, piragna (f)	[pi'rania]

shark	squalo (m)	['skwalo]
dolphin	delfino (m)	[del'fino]
whale	balena (f)	[ba'lena]

crab	granchio (m)	['grankio]
jellyfish	medusa (f)	[me'duza]
octopus	polpo (m)	['polpo]

starfish	stella (f) marina	['stella ma'rina]
sea urchin	riccio (m) di mare	['ritʃo di 'mare]
seahorse	cavalluccio (m) marino	[kaval'lutʃo ma'rino]

oyster	ostrica (f)	['ostrika]
shrimp	gamberetto (m)	[gambe'retto]
lobster	astice (m)	['astitʃe]
spiny lobster	aragosta (f)	[ara'gosta]

182. Amphibians. Reptiles

| snake | serpente (m) | [ser'pente] |
| venomous (snake) | velenoso | [vele'nozo] |

| viper | vipera (f) | ['vipera] |
| cobra | cobra (m) | ['kobra] |

| python | pitone (m) | [pi'tone] |
| boa | boa (m) | ['boa] |

grass snake	biscia (f)	['biʃa]
rattle snake	serpente (m) a sonagli	[ser'pente a so'naʎʎi]
anaconda	anaconda (f)	[ana'konda]

lizard	lucertola (f)	[lu'tʃertola]
iguana	iguana (f)	[i'gwana]
monitor lizard	varano (m)	[va'rano]
salamander	salamandra (f)	[sala'mandra]

| chameleon | camaleonte (m) | [kamale'onte] |
| scorpion | scorpione (m) | [skor'pjone] |

| turtle | tartaruga (f) | [tarta'ruga] |
| frog | rana (f) | ['rana] |

| toad | rospo (m) | ['rospo] |
| crocodile | coccodrillo (m) | [kokko'drillo] |

183. Insects

insect, bug	**insetto** (m)	[in'setto]
butterfly	**farfalla** (f)	[far'falla]
ant	**formica** (f)	[for'mika]
fly	**mosca** (f)	['moska]
mosquito	**zanzara** (f)	[dzan'dzara]
beetle	**scarabeo** (m)	[skara'beo]
wasp	**vespa** (f)	['vespa]
bee	**ape** (f)	['ape]
bumblebee	**bombo** (m)	['bombo]
gadfly (botfly)	**tafano** (m)	[ta'fano]
spider	**ragno** (m)	['raɲo]
spiderweb	**ragnatela** (f)	[raɲa'tela]
dragonfly	**libellula** (f)	[li'bellula]
grasshopper	**cavalletta** (f)	[kaval'letta]
moth (night butterfly)	**farfalla** (f) **notturna**	[far'falla not'turna]
cockroach	**scarafaggio** (m)	[skara'fadʒo]
tick	**zecca** (f)	['tsekka]
flea	**pulce** (f)	['pultʃe]
midge	**moscerino** (m)	[moʃe'rino]
locust	**locusta** (f)	[lo'kusta]
snail	**lumaca** (f)	[lu'maka]
cricket	**grillo** (m)	['grillo]
lightning bug	**lucciola** (f)	['lutʃola]
ladybug	**coccinella** (f)	[kotʃi'nella]
cockchafer	**maggiolino** (m)	[madʒo'lino]
leech	**sanguisuga** (f)	[sangwi'zuga]
caterpillar	**bruco** (m)	['bruko]
earthworm	**verme** (m)	['verme]
larva	**larva** (m)	['larva]

184. Animals. Body parts

beak	**becco** (m)	['bekko]
wings	**ali** (f pl)	['ali]
foot (of bird)	**zampa** (f)	['dzampa]
feathers (plumage)	**piumaggio** (m)	[pju'madʒo]
feather	**penna** (f), **piuma** (f)	['penna], ['pjuma]
crest	**cresta** (f)	['kresta]
gills	**branchia** (f)	['brankia]
spawn	**uova** (f pl)	[u'ova]

larva	**larva** (f)	['larva]
fin	**pinna** (f)	['pinna]
scales (of fish, reptile)	**squama** (f)	['skwama]
fang (canine)	**zanna** (f)	['tzanna]
paw (e.g., cat's ~)	**zampa** (f)	['dzampa]
muzzle (snout)	**muso** (m)	['muzo]
maw (mouth)	**bocca** (f)	['bokka]
tail	**coda** (f)	['koda]
whiskers	**baffi** (m pl)	['baffi]
hoof	**zoccolo** (m)	['dzokkolo]
horn	**corno** (m)	['korno]
carapace	**carapace** (f)	[kara'patʃe]
shell (of mollusk)	**conchiglia** (f)	[kon'kiʎʎa]
eggshell	**guscio** (m) **dell'uovo**	['guʃo dell u'ovo]
animal's hair (pelage)	**pelo** (m)	['pelo]
pelt (hide)	**pelle** (f)	['pelle]

185. Animals. Habitats

habitat	**ambiente** (m) **naturale**	[am'bjente natu'rale]
migration	**migrazione** (f)	[migra'tsjone]
mountain	**monte** (m), **montagna** (f)	['monte], [mon'taɲa]
reef	**scogliera** (f)	[skoʎ'ʎera]
cliff	**falesia** (f)	[fa'lezia]
forest	**foresta** (f)	[fo'resta]
jungle	**giungla** (f)	['dʒungla]
savanna	**savana** (f)	[sa'vana]
tundra	**tundra** (f)	['tundra]
steppe	**steppa** (f)	['steppa]
desert	**deserto** (m)	[de'zerto]
oasis	**oasi** (f)	['oazi]
sea	**mare** (m)	['mare]
lake	**lago** (m)	['lago]
ocean	**oceano** (m)	[o'tʃeano]
swamp (marshland)	**palude** (f)	[pa'lude]
freshwater (adj)	**di acqua dolce**	[di 'akwa 'doltʃe]
pond	**stagno** (m)	['staɲo]
river	**fiume** (m)	['fjume]
den (bear's ~)	**tana** (f)	['tana]
nest	**nido** (m)	['nido]

tree hollow	**cavità** (f)	[kavi'ta]
burrow (animal hole)	**tana** (f)	['tana]
anthill	**formicaio** (m)	[formi'kajo]

Flora

186. Trees

tree	**albero** (m)	['albero]
deciduous (adj)	**deciduo**	[de'tʃiduo]
coniferous (adj)	**conifero**	[ko'nifero]
evergreen (adj)	**sempreverde**	[sempre'verde]
apple tree	**melo** (m)	['melo]
pear tree	**pero** (m)	['pero]
sweet cherry tree	**ciliegio** (m)	[tʃi'ljedʒo]
sour cherry tree	**amareno** (m)	[ama'reno]
plum tree	**prugno** (m)	['pruɲo]
birch	**betulla** (f)	[be'tulla]
oak	**quercia** (f)	['kwertʃa]
linden tree	**tiglio** (m)	['tiʎʎo]
aspen	**pioppo** (m) **tremolo**	['pjoppo 'tremolo]
maple	**acero** (m)	['atʃero]
spruce	**abete** (m)	[a'bete]
pine	**pino** (m)	['pino]
larch	**larice** (m)	['laritʃe]
fir tree	**abete** (m) **bianco**	[a'bete 'bjanko]
cedar	**cedro** (m)	['tʃedro]
poplar	**pioppo** (m)	['pjoppo]
rowan	**sorbo** (m)	['sorbo]
willow	**salice** (m)	['salitʃe]
alder	**alno** (m)	['alno]
beech	**faggio** (m)	['fadʒo]
elm	**olmo** (m)	['olmo]
ash (tree)	**frassino** (m)	['frassino]
chestnut	**castagno** (m)	[ka'staɲo]
magnolia	**magnolia** (f)	[ma'ɲolia]
palm tree	**palma** (f)	['palma]
cypress	**cipresso** (m)	[tʃi'presso]
mangrove	**mangrovia** (f)	[man'growia]
baobab	**baobab** (m)	[bao'bab]
eucalyptus	**eucalipto** (m)	[ewka'lipto]
sequoia	**sequoia** (f)	[se'kwoja]

187. Shrubs

bush	cespuglio (m)	[tʃes'puʎʎo]
shrub	arbusto (m)	[ar'busto]
grapevine	vite (f)	['vite]
vineyard	vigneto (m)	[vi'ɲeto]
raspberry bush	lampone (m)	[lam'pone]
redcurrant bush	ribes (m) rosso	['ribes 'rosso]
gooseberry bush	uva (f) spina	['uva 'spina]
acacia	acacia (f)	[a'katʃa]
barberry	crespino (m)	[kres'pino]
jasmine	gelsomino (m)	[dʒelso'mino]
juniper	ginepro (m)	[dʒi'nepro]
rosebush	roseto (m)	[ro'zeto]
dog rose	rosa (f) canina	['roza ka'nina]

188. Mushrooms

mushroom	fungo (m)	['fungo]
edible mushroom	fungo (m) commestibile	['fungo komme'stibile]
poisonous mushroom	fungo (m) velenoso	['fungo vele'nozo]
cap (of mushroom)	cappello (m)	[kap'pello]
stipe (of mushroom)	gambo (m)	['gambo]
cep (Boletus edulis)	porcino (m)	[por'tʃino]
orange-cap boletus	boleto (m) rufo	[bo'leto 'rufo]
birch bolete	porcinello (m)	[portʃi'nello]
chanterelle	gallinaccio (m)	[galli'natʃo]
russula	rossola (f)	['rossola]
morel	spugnola (f)	['spuɲola]
fly agaric	ovolaccio (m)	[ovo'latʃo]
death cap	fungo (m) moscario	['fungo mos'kario]

189. Fruits. Berries

fruit	frutto (m)	['frutto]
fruits	frutti (m pl)	['frutti]
apple	mela (f)	['mela]
pear	pera (f)	['pera]
plum	prugna (f)	['pruɲa]
strawberry (garden ~)	fragola (f)	['fragola]
sour cherry	amarena (f)	[ama'rena]

sweet cherry	**ciliegia** (f)	[tʃiˈljedʒa]
grape	**uva** (f)	[ˈuva]
raspberry	**lampone** (m)	[lamˈpone]
blackcurrant	**ribes** (m) **nero**	[ˈribes ˈnero]
redcurrant	**ribes** (m) **rosso**	[ˈribes ˈrosso]
gooseberry	**uva** (f) **spina**	[ˈuva ˈspina]
cranberry	**mirtillo** (m) **di palude**	[mirˈtillo di paˈlude]
orange	**arancia** (f)	[aˈrantʃa]
mandarin	**mandarino** (m)	[mandaˈrino]
pineapple	**ananas** (m)	[anaˈnas]
banana	**banana** (f)	[baˈnana]
date	**dattero** (m)	[ˈdattero]
lemon	**limone** (m)	[liˈmone]
apricot	**albicocca** (f)	[albiˈkokka]
peach	**pesca** (f)	[ˈpeska]
kiwi	**kiwi** (m)	[ˈkiwi]
grapefruit	**pompelmo** (m)	[pomˈpelmo]
berry	**bacca** (f)	[ˈbakka]
berries	**bacche** (f pl)	[ˈbakke]
cowberry	**mirtillo** (m) **rosso**	[mirˈtillo ˈrosso]
wild strawberry	**fragola** (f) **di bosco**	[ˈfragola di ˈbosko]
bilberry	**mirtillo** (m)	[mirˈtillo]

190. Flowers. Plants

flower	**fiore** (m)	[ˈfjore]
bouquet (of flowers)	**mazzo** (m) **di fiori**	[ˈmattso di ˈfjori]
rose (flower)	**rosa** (f)	[ˈroza]
tulip	**tulipano** (m)	[tuliˈpano]
carnation	**garofano** (m)	[gaˈrofano]
gladiolus	**gladiolo** (m)	[glaˈdjolo]
cornflower	**fiordaliso** (m)	[fjordaˈlizo]
harebell	**campanella** (f)	[kampaˈnella]
dandelion	**soffione** (m)	[sofˈfjone]
camomile	**camomilla** (f)	[kamoˈmilla]
aloe	**aloe** (m)	[ˈaloe]
cactus	**cactus** (m)	[ˈkaktus]
rubber plant, ficus	**ficus** (m)	[ˈfikus]
lily	**giglio** (m)	[ˈdʒiʎʎo]
geranium	**geranio** (m)	[dʒeˈranio]
hyacinth	**giacinto** (m)	[dʒaˈtʃinto]
mimosa	**mimosa** (f)	[miˈmoza]

| narcissus | narciso (m) | [nar'tʃizo] |
| nasturtium | nasturzio (m) | [na'sturtsio] |

orchid	orchidea (f)	[orki'dea]
peony	peonia (f)	[pe'onia]
violet	viola (f)	[vi'ola]

pansy	viola (f) del pensiero	[vi'ola del pen'sjero]
forget-me-not	nontiscordardimè (m)	[non·ti·skordar·di'me]
daisy	margherita (f)	[marge'rita]

poppy	papavero (m)	[pa'pavero]
hemp	canapa (f)	['kanapa]
mint	menta (f)	['menta]

| lily of the valley | mughetto (m) | [mu'getto] |
| snowdrop | bucaneve (m) | [buka'neve] |

nettle	ortica (f)	[or'tika]
sorrel	acetosa (f)	[atʃe'toza]
water lily	ninfea (f)	[nin'fea]
fern	felce (f)	['feltʃe]
lichen	lichene (m)	[li'kene]

conservatory (greenhouse)	serra (f)	['serra]
lawn	prato (m) erboso	['prato er'bozo]
flowerbed	aiuola (f)	[aju'ola]

plant	pianta (f)	['pjanta]
grass	erba (f)	['erba]
blade of grass	filo (m) d'erba	['filo 'derba]

leaf	foglia (f)	['foʎʎa]
petal	petalo (m)	['petalo]
stem	stelo (m)	['stelo]
tuber	tubero (m)	['tubero]

| young plant (shoot) | germoglio (m) | [dʒer'moʎʎo] |
| thorn | spina (f) | ['spina] |

to blossom (vi)	fiorire (vi)	[fjo'rire]
to fade, to wither	appassire (vi)	[appas'sire]
smell (odor)	odore (m), profumo (m)	[o'dore], [pro'fumo]
to cut (flowers)	tagliare (vt)	[taʎ'ʎare]
to pick (a flower)	cogliere (vt)	['koʎʎere]

191. Cereals, grains

| grain | grano (m) | ['grano] |
| cereal crops | cereali (m pl) | [tʃere'ali] |

ear (of barley, etc.)	**spiga** (f)	['spiga]
wheat	**frumento** (m)	[fru'mento]
rye	**segale** (f)	['segale]
oats	**avena** (f)	[a'vena]
millet	**miglio** (m)	['miʎʎo]
barley	**orzo** (m)	['ortso]
corn	**mais** (m)	['mais]
rice	**riso** (m)	['rizo]
buckwheat	**grano** (m) **saraceno**	['grano sara'tʃeno]
pea plant	**pisello** (m)	[pi'zello]
kidney bean	**fagiolo** (m)	[fa'dʒolo]
soy	**soia** (f)	['soja]
lentil	**lenticchie** (f pl)	[len'tikkje]
beans (pulse crops)	**fave** (f pl)	['fave]

REGIONAL GEOGRAPHY

Countries. Nationalities

192. Politics. Government. Part 1

politics	**politica** (f)	[po'litika]
political (adj)	**politico** (agg)	[po'litiko]
politician	**politico** (m)	[po'litiko]
state (country)	**stato** (m)	['stato]
citizen	**cittadino** (m)	[tʃitta'dino]
citizenship	**cittadinanza** (f)	[tʃittadi'nantsa]
national emblem	**emblema** (m) **nazionale**	[em'blema natsjo'nale]
national anthem	**inno** (m) **nazionale**	['inno natsjo'nale]
government	**governo** (m)	[go'verno]
head of state	**capo** (m) **di Stato**	['kapo di 'stato]
parliament	**parlamento** (m)	[parla'mento]
party	**partito** (m)	[par'tito]
capitalism	**capitalismo** (m)	[kapita'lizmo]
capitalist (adj)	**capitalistico**	[kapita'listiko]
socialism	**socialismo** (m)	[sotʃia'lizmo]
socialist (adj)	**socialista**	[sotʃia'lista]
communism	**comunismo** (m)	[komu'nizmo]
communist (adj)	**comunista**	[komu'nista]
communist (n)	**comunista** (m)	[komu'nista]
democracy	**democrazia** (f)	[demokra'tsia]
democrat	**democratico** (m)	[demo'kratiko]
democratic (adj)	**democratico**	[demo'kratiko]
Democratic party	**partito** (m) **democratico**	[par'tito demo'kratiko]
liberal (n)	**liberale** (m)	[libe'rale]
liberal (adj)	**liberale** (agg)	[libe'rale]
conservative (n)	**conservatore** (m)	[konserva'tore]
conservative (adj)	**conservatore** (agg)	[konserva'tore]
republic (n)	**repubblica** (f)	[re'pubblika]
republican (n)	**repubblicano** (m)	[repubbli'kano]

Republican party	partito (m) repubblicano	[par'tito repubbli'kano]
elections	elezioni (f pl)	[ele'tsjoni]
to elect (vt)	eleggere (vt)	[e'ledʒere]
elector, voter	elettore (m)	[elet'tore]
election campaign	campagna (f) elettorale	[kam'paɲa eletto'rale]

voting (n)	votazione (f)	[vota'tsjone]
to vote (vi)	votare (vi)	[vo'tare]
suffrage, right to vote	diritto (m) di voto	[di'ritto di 'voto]

candidate	candidato (m)	[kandi'dato]
to be a candidate	candidarsi (vr)	[kandi'darsi]
campaign	campagna (f)	[kam'paɲa]

| opposition (as adj) | d'opposizione | [doppozi'tsjone] |
| opposition (n) | opposizione (f) | [oppozi'tsjone] |

visit	visita (f)	['vizita]
official visit	visita (f) ufficiale	['vizita uffi'tʃale]
international (adj)	internazionale	[internatsjo'nale]

| negotiations | trattative (f pl) | [tratta'tive] |
| to negotiate (vi) | negoziare (vi) | [nego'tsjare] |

193. Politics. Government. Part 2

society	società (f)	[soˈtʃeta]
constitution	costituzione (f)	[kostitu'tsjone]
power (political control)	potere (m)	[po'tere]
corruption	corruzione (f)	[korru'tsjone]

| law (justice) | legge (f) | ['ledʒe] |
| legal (legitimate) | legittimo | [le'dʒittimo] |

| justice (fairness) | giustizia (f) | [dʒu'stitsia] |
| just (fair) | giusto | ['dʒusto] |

committee	comitato (m)	[komi'tato]
bill (draft law)	disegno (m) di legge	[di'zeɲo di 'ledʒe]
budget	bilancio (m)	[bi'lantʃo]
policy	politica (f)	[po'litika]
reform	riforma (f)	[ri'forma]
radical (adj)	radicale	[radi'kale]

power (strength, force)	forza (f), potenza (f)	['fortsa], [po'tentsa]
powerful (adj)	potente	[po'tente]
supporter	sostenitore (m)	[sosteni'tore]
influence	influenza (f)	[influ'entsa]
regime (e.g., military ~)	regime (m)	[re'dʒime]
conflict	conflitto (m)	[kon'flitto]

conspiracy (plot)	**complotto** (m)	[kom'plotto]
provocation	**provocazione** (f)	[provoka'tsjone]
to overthrow (regime, etc.)	**rovesciare** (vt)	[rove'ʃare]
overthrow (of government)	**rovesciamento** (m)	[roveʃa'mento]
revolution	**rivoluzione** (f)	[rivolu'tsjone]
coup d'état	**colpo** (m) **di Stato**	['kolpo di 'stato]
military coup	**golpe** (m) **militare**	['golpe mili'tare]
crisis	**crisi** (f)	['krizi]
economic recession	**recessione** (f) **economica**	[retʃes'sjone eko'nomika]
demonstrator (protester)	**manifestante** (m)	[manife'stante]
demonstration	**manifestazione** (f)	[manifesta'tsjone]
martial law	**legge** (f) **marziale**	['ledʒe mar'tsjale]
military base	**base** (f) **militare**	['baze mili'tare]
stability	**stabilità** (f)	[stabili'ta]
stable (adj)	**stabile**	['stabile]
exploitation	**sfruttamento** (m)	[sfrutta'mento]
to exploit (workers)	**sfruttare** (vt)	[sfrut'tare]
racism	**razzismo** (m)	[rat'tsizmo]
racist	**razzista** (m)	[rat'tsista]
fascism	**fascismo** (m)	[fa'ʃizmo]
fascist	**fascista** (m)	[fa'ʃista]

194. Countries. Miscellaneous

foreigner	**straniero** (m)	[stra'njero]
foreign (adj)	**straniero** (agg)	[stra'njero]
abroad (in a foreign country)	**all'estero**	[all 'estero]
emigrant	**emigrato** (m)	[emi'grato]
emigration	**emigrazione** (f)	[emigra'tsjone]
to emigrate (vi)	**emigrare** (vi)	[emi'grare]
the West	**Ovest** (m)	['ovest]
the East	**Est** (m)	[est]
the Far East	**Estremo Oriente** (m)	[e'stremo o'rjente]
civilization	**civiltà** (f)	[tʃivil'ta]
humanity (mankind)	**umanità** (f)	[umani'ta]
the world (earth)	**mondo** (m)	['mondo]
peace	**pace** (f)	['patʃe]
worldwide (adj)	**mondiale**	[mon'djale]
homeland	**patria** (f)	['patria]
people (population)	**popolo** (m)	['popolo]

population	popolazione (f)	[popola'tsjone]
people (a lot of ~)	gente (f)	['dʒente]
nation (people)	nazione (f)	[na'tsjone]
generation	generazione (f)	[dʒenera'tsjone]

territory (area)	territorio (m)	[terri'torio]
region	regione (f)	[re'dʒone]
state (part of a country)	stato (m)	['stato]

tradition	tradizione (f)	[tradi'tsjone]
custom (tradition)	costume (m)	[ko'stume]
ecology	ecologia (f)	[ekolo'dʒia]

Indian (Native American)	indiano (m)	[indi'ano]
Gypsy (masc.)	zingaro (m)	['tsingaro]
Gypsy (fem.)	zingara (f)	['tsingara]
Gypsy (adj)	di zingaro	[di 'tsingaro]

empire	impero (m)	[im'pero]
colony	colonia (f)	[ko'lonia]
slavery	schiavitù (f)	[skjavi'tu]
invasion	invasione (f)	[inva'zjone]
famine	carestia (f)	[kare'stia]

195. Major religious groups. Confessions

| religion | religione (f) | [reli'dʒone] |
| religious (adj) | religioso | [reli'dʒozo] |

faith, belief	fede (f)	['fede]
to believe (in God)	credere (vi)	['kredere]
believer	credente (m)	[kre'dente]

| atheism | ateismo (m) | [ate'izmo] |
| atheist | ateo (m) | ['ateo] |

Christianity	cristianesimo (m)	[kristja'nezimo]
Christian (n)	cristiano (m)	[kri'stjano]
Christian (adj)	cristiano (agg)	[kri'stjano]

Catholicism	Cattolicesimo (m)	[kattoli'tʃezimo]
Catholic (n)	cattolico (m)	[kat'toliko]
Catholic (adj)	cattolico (agg)	[kat'toliko]

Protestantism	Protestantesimo (m)	[protestan'tesimo]
Protestant Church	Chiesa (f) protestante	['kjeza protes'tante]
Protestant (n)	protestante (m)	[prote'stante]

| Orthodoxy | Ortodossia (f) | [ortodos'sia] |
| Orthodox Church | Chiesa (f) ortodossa | ['kjeza orto'dossa] |

Orthodox (n)	**ortodosso** (m)	[orto'dosso]
Presbyterianism	**Presbiterianesimo** (m)	[presbiterja'nezimo]
Presbyterian Church	**Chiesa** (f) **presbiteriana**	['kjeza presbite'rjana]
Presbyterian (n)	**presbiteriano** (m)	[presbite'rjano]
Lutheranism	**Luteranesimo** (m)	[lutera'nezimo]
Lutheran (n)	**luterano** (m)	[lute'rano]
Baptist Church	**confessione** (f) **battista**	[konfes'sjone bat'tista]
Baptist (n)	**battista** (m)	[bat'tista]
Anglican Church	**Chiesa** (f) **anglicana**	['kjeza angli'kana]
Anglican (n)	**anglicano** (m)	[angli'kano]
Mormonism	**Mormonismo** (m)	[mormo'nizmo]
Mormon (n)	**mormone** (m)	[mor'mone]
Judaism	**giudaismo** (m)	[dʒuda'izmo]
Jew (n)	**ebreo** (m)	[e'breo]
Buddhism	**buddismo** (m)	[bud'dizmo]
Buddhist (n)	**buddista** (m)	[bud'dista]
Hinduism	**Induismo** (m)	[indu'izmo]
Hindu (n)	**induista** (m)	[indu'ista]
Islam	**Islam** (m)	['izlam]
Muslim (n)	**musulmano** (m)	[musul'mano]
Muslim (adj)	**musulmano**	[musul'mano]
Shiah Islam	**sciismo** (m)	[ʃi'izmo]
Shiite (n)	**sciita** (m)	[ʃi'ita]
Sunni Islam	**sunnismo** (m)	[sun'nizmo]
Sunnite (n)	**sunnita** (m)	[sun'nita]

196. Religions. Priests

priest	**prete** (m)	['prete]
the Pope	**Papa** (m)	['papa]
monk, friar	**monaco** (m)	['monako]
nun	**monaca** (f)	['monaka]
pastor	**pastore** (m)	[pa'store]
abbot	**abate** (m)	[a'bate]
vicar (parish priest)	**vicario** (m)	[vi'kario]
bishop	**vescovo** (m)	['veskovo]
cardinal	**cardinale** (m)	[kardi'nale]
preacher	**predicatore** (m)	[predika'tore]

| preaching | **predica** (f) | ['predika] |
| parishioners | **parrocchiani** (m) | [parrok'kjani] |

| believer | **credente** (m) | [kre'dente] |
| atheist | **ateo** (m) | ['ateo] |

197. Faith. Christianity. Islam

| Adam | **Adamo** | [a'damo] |
| Eve | **Eva** | ['eva] |

God	**Dio** (m)	['dio]
the Lord	**Signore** (m)	[si'ɲore]
the Almighty	**Onnipotente** (m)	[onnipo'tente]

sin	**peccato** (m)	[pek'kato]
to sin (vi)	**peccare** (vi)	[pek'kare]
sinner (masc.)	**peccatore** (m)	[pekka'tore]
sinner (fem.)	**peccatrice** (f)	[pekka'tritʃe]

| hell | **inferno** (m) | [in'ferno] |
| paradise | **paradiso** (m) | [para'dizo] |

| Jesus | **Gesù** | [dʒe'su] |
| Jesus Christ | **Gesù Cristo** | [dʒe'su 'kristo] |

the Holy Spirit	**Spirito** (m) **Santo**	['spirito 'santo]
the Savior	**Salvatore** (m)	[salva'tore]
the Virgin Mary	**Madonna**	[ma'donna]

the Devil	**Diavolo** (m)	['djavolo]
devil's (adj)	**del diavolo**	[del 'djavolo]
Satan	**Satana** (m)	['satana]
satanic (adj)	**satanico**	[sa'taniko]

angel	**angelo** (m)	['andʒelo]
guardian angel	**angelo** (m) **custode**	['andʒelo kus'tode]
angelic (adj)	**angelico**	[an'dʒeliko]

apostle	**apostolo** (m)	[a'postolo]
archangel	**arcangelo** (m)	[ar'kandʒelo]
the Antichrist	**Anticristo** (m)	[anti'kristo]

Church	**Chiesa** (f)	['kjeza]
Bible	**Bibbia** (f)	['bibbia]
biblical (adj)	**biblico**	['bibliko]

Old Testament	**Vecchio Testamento** (m)	['vekkio testa'mento]
New Testament	**Nuovo Testamento** (m)	[nu'ovo testa'mento]
Gospel	**Vangelo** (m)	[van'dʒelo]

Holy Scripture	Sacra Scrittura (f)	['sakra skrit'tura]
Heaven	Il Regno dei Cieli	[il 'reɲo dei 'ʧeli]
Commandment	comandamento (m)	[komanda'mento]
prophet	profeta (m)	[pro'feta]
prophecy	profezia (f)	[profe'tsia]
Allah	Allah	[al'la]
Mohammed	Maometto	[mao'meto]
the Koran	Corano (m)	[ko'rano]
mosque	moschea (f)	[mos'kea]
mullah	mullah (m)	[mul'la]
prayer	preghiera (f)	[pre'gjera]
to pray (vi, vt)	pregare (vi, vt)	[pre'gare]
pilgrimage	pellegrinaggio (m)	[pellegri'nadʒo]
pilgrim	pellegrino (m)	[pelle'grino]
Mecca	La Mecca (f)	[la 'mekka]
church	chiesa (f)	['kjeza]
temple	tempio (m)	['tempjo]
cathedral	cattedrale (f)	[katte'drale]
Gothic (adj)	gotico	['gotiko]
synagogue	sinagoga (f)	[sina'goga]
mosque	moschea (f)	[mos'kea]
chapel	cappella (f)	[kap'pella]
abbey	abbazia (f)	[abba'tsia]
convent	convento (m) di suore	[kon'vento di su'ore]
monastery	monastero (m)	[mona'stero]
bell (church ~s)	campana (f)	[kam'pana]
bell tower	campanile (m)	[kampa'nile]
to ring (ab. bells)	suonare (vi)	[suo'nare]
cross	croce (f)	['krotʃe]
cupola (roof)	cupola (f)	['kupola]
icon	icona (f)	[i'kona]
soul	anima (f)	['anima]
fate (destiny)	destino (m), sorte (f)	[de'stino], ['sorte]
evil (n)	male (m)	['male]
good (n)	bene (m)	['bene]
vampire	vampiro (m)	[vam'piro]
witch (evil ~)	strega (f)	['strega]
demon	demone (m)	['demone]
spirit	spirito (m)	['spirito]
redemption (giving us ~)	redenzione (f)	[reden'tsjone]
to redeem (vt)	redimere (vt)	[re'dimere]

church service, mass	**messa** (f)	['messa]
to say mass	**dire la messa**	['dire la 'messa]
confession	**confessione** (f)	[konfes'sjone]
to confess (vi)	**confessarsi** (vr)	[konfes'sarsi]
saint (n)	**santo** (m)	['santo]
sacred (holy)	**sacro**	['sakro]
holy water	**acqua** (f) **santa**	['akwa 'santa]
ritual (n)	**rito** (m)	['rito]
ritual (adj)	**rituale**	[ritu'ale]
sacrifice	**sacrificio** (m)	[sakri'fitʃo]
superstition	**superstizione** (f)	[supersti'tsjone]
superstitious (adj)	**superstizioso**	[supersti'tsjozo]
afterlife	**vita** (f) **dell'oltretomba**	['vita dell oltre'tomba]
eternal life	**vita** (f) **eterna**	['vita e'terna]

MISCELLANEOUS

198. Various useful words

background (green ~)	**sfondo** (m)	['sfondo]
balance (of situation)	**bilancio** (m)	[bi'lantʃo]
barrier (obstacle)	**barriera** (f)	[bar'rjera]
base (basis)	**base** (f)	['baze]
beginning	**inizio** (m)	[i'nitsio]
category	**categoria** (f)	[katego'ria]
cause (reason)	**causa** (f)	['kauza]
choice	**scelta** (f)	['ʃelta]
coincidence	**coincidenza** (f)	[kojntʃi'dentsa]
comfortable (~ chair)	**comodo**	['komodo]
comparison	**confronto** (m)	[kon'fronto]
compensation	**compenso** (m)	[kom'penso]
degree (extent, amount)	**grado** (m)	['grado]
development	**sviluppo** (m)	[zvi'luppo]
difference	**differenza** (f)	[diffe'rentsa]
effect (e.g., of drugs)	**effetto** (m)	[ef'fetto]
effort (exertion)	**sforzo** (m)	['sfortso]
element	**elemento** (m)	[ele'mento]
end (finish)	**termine** (m)	['termine]
example (illustration)	**esempio** (m)	[e'zempjo]
fact	**fatto** (m)	['fatto]
frequent (adj)	**frequente**	[fre'kwente]
growth (development)	**crescita** (f)	['kreʃita]
help	**aiuto** (m)	[a'juto]
ideal	**ideale** (m)	[ide'ale]
kind (sort, type)	**genere** (m)	['dʒenere]
labyrinth	**labirinto** (m)	[labi'rinto]
mistake, error	**errore** (m)	[er'rore]
moment	**momento** (m)	[mo'mento]
object (thing)	**oggetto** (m)	[o'dʒetto]
obstacle	**ostacolo** (m)	[os'takolo]
original (original copy)	**originale** (m)	[oridʒi'nale]
part (~ of sth)	**parte** (f)	['parte]
particle, small part	**particella** (f)	[parti'tʃella]
pause (break)	**pausa** (f)	['pauza]

position	**posizione** (f)	[pozi'tsjone]
principle	**principio** (m)	[prin'tʃipjo]
problem	**problema** (m)	[pro'blema]
process	**processo** (m)	[pro'tʃesso]
progress	**progresso** (m)	[pro'gresso]
property (quality)	**proprietà** (f)	[proprie'ta]
reaction	**reazione** (f)	[rea'tsjone]
risk	**rischio** (m)	['riskio]
secret	**segreto** (m)	[se'greto]
series	**serie** (f)	['serie]
shape (outer form)	**forma** (f)	['forma]
situation	**situazione** (f)	[situa'tsjone]
solution	**soluzione** (f)	[solu'tsjone]
standard (adj)	**standard**	['standar]
standard (level of quality)	**standard** (m)	['standar]
stop (pause)	**pausa** (f)	['pauza]
style	**stile** (m)	['stile]
system	**sistema** (m)	[si'stema]
table (chart)	**tabella** (f)	[ta'bella]
tempo, rate	**ritmo** (m)	['ritmo]
term (word, expression)	**termine** (m)	['termine]
thing (object, item)	**cosa** (f)	['koza]
truth (e.g., moment of ~)	**verità** (f)	[veri'ta]
turn (please wait your ~)	**turno** (m)	['turno]
type (sort, kind)	**tipo** (m)	['tipo]
urgent (adj)	**urgente**	[ur'dʒente]
urgently (adv)	**urgentemente**	[urdʒente'mente]
utility (usefulness)	**utilità** (f)	[utili'ta]
variant (alternative)	**variante** (f)	[vari'ante]
way (means, method)	**modo** (m)	['modo]
zone	**zona** (f)	['dzona]

Made in United States
North Haven, CT
27 April 2022

18642982R00115